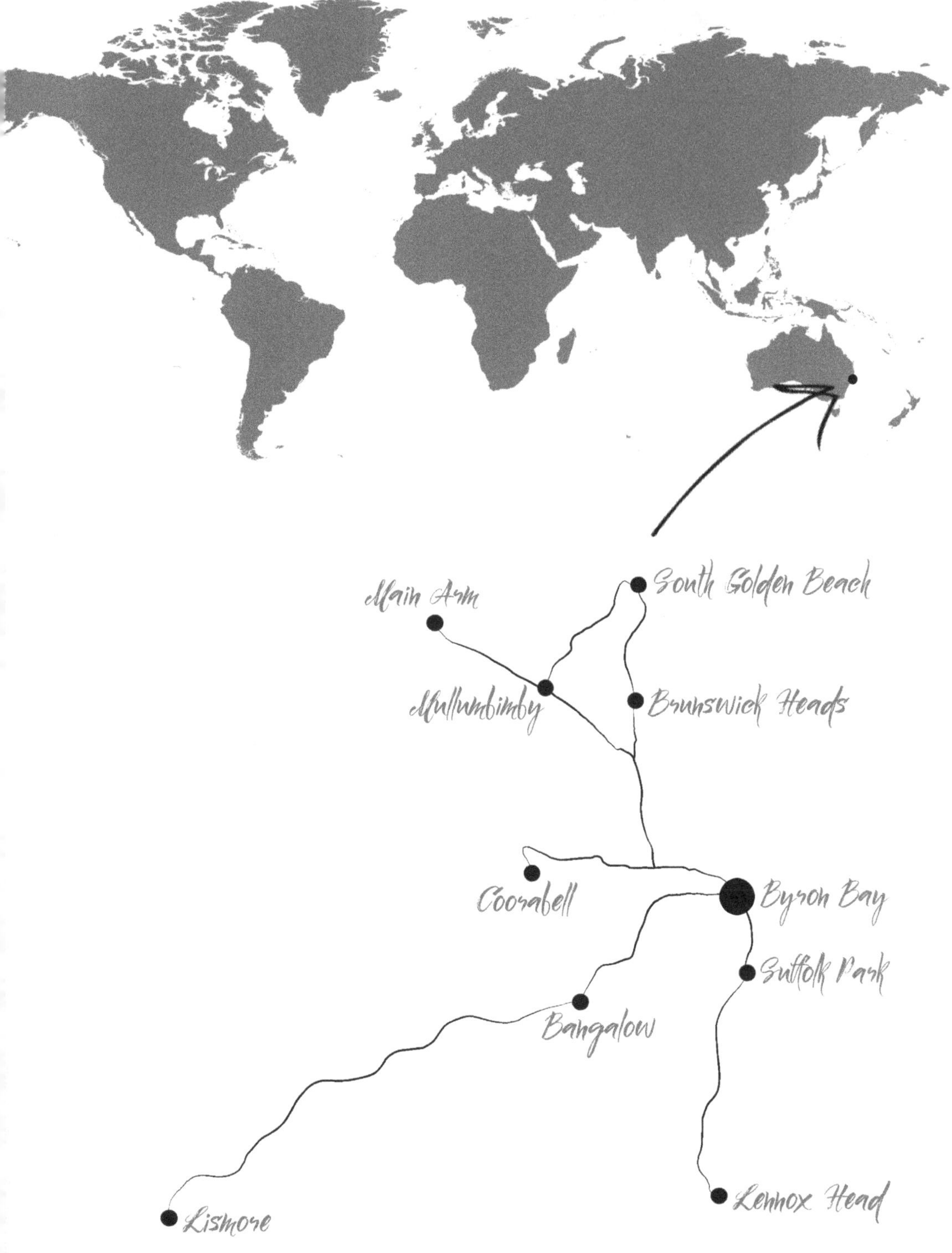

Main Arm
South Golden Beach
Mullumbimby
Brunswick Heads
Coorabell
Byron Bay
Suffolk Park
Bangalow
Lennox Head
Lismore

For Harry and Cheree, who made this pocket feel like home.
- AD



National Library of Australia Cataloguing-in-Publication entry

Author: Mitchell, Lauren

Photographer: Doak, Amy

Title: Artist Spaces Of The Northern Rivers

ISBN:9780995442504

Subject: Interior Decoration, Decoration Of Specific Rooms In Residential Buildings, Art

Dewey Number: 747.7

Published by:
Of The World Publishing
PO Box 8070
BENDIGO SOUTH LPO VIC 3550

www.oftheworldbooks.com

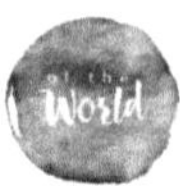

# Artist Spaces
## of the Northern Rivers

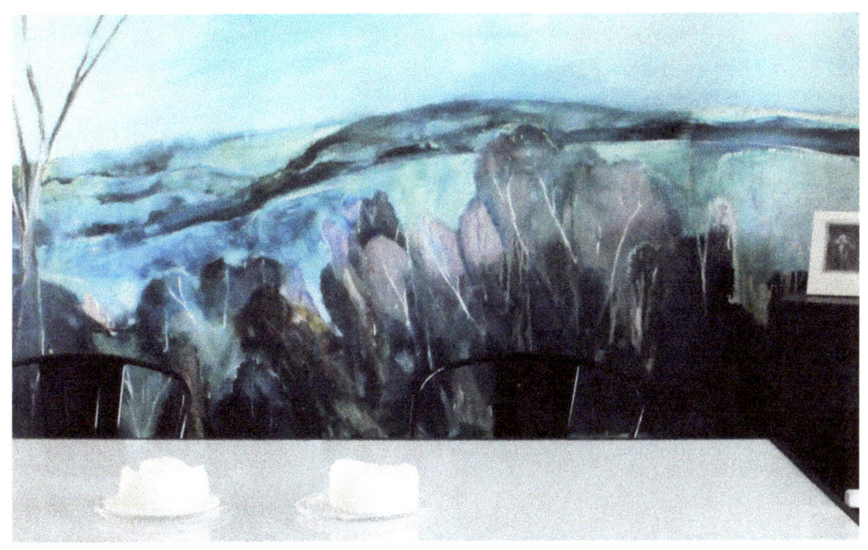

Words by Lauren Mitchell
Images by Amy Doak

# Contents

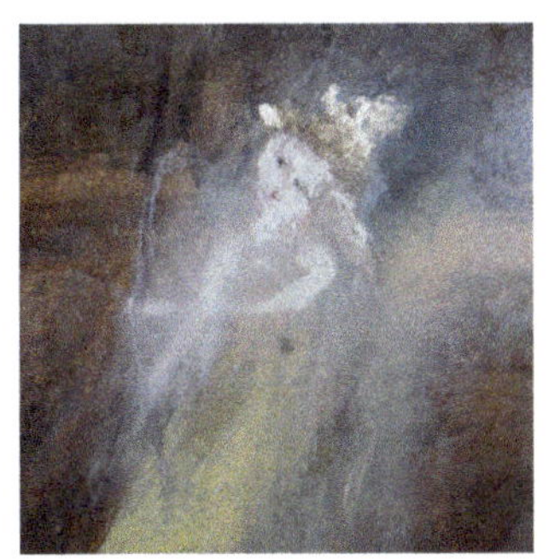

8
Hilary Herrmann
Bangalow

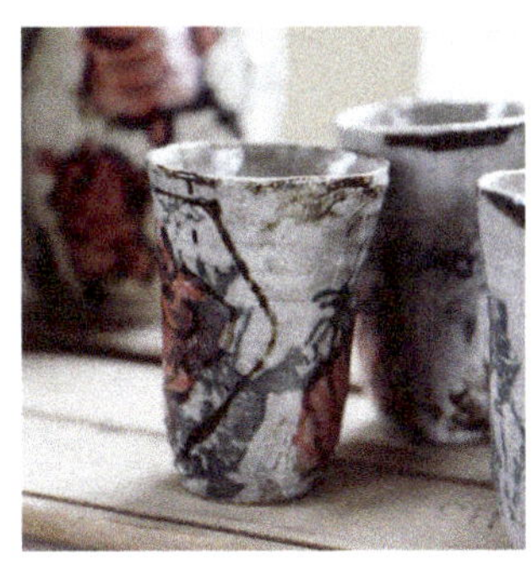

20
Rebecca Ross
Bangalow

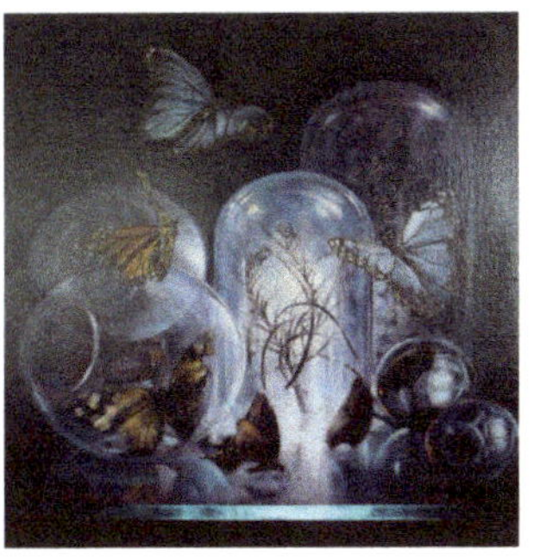

58
Gatya Kelly
Mullumbimby

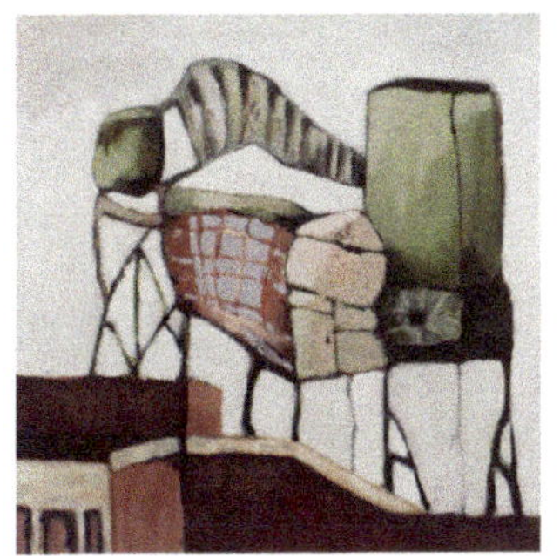

68
Leora Sibony
Mullumbimby

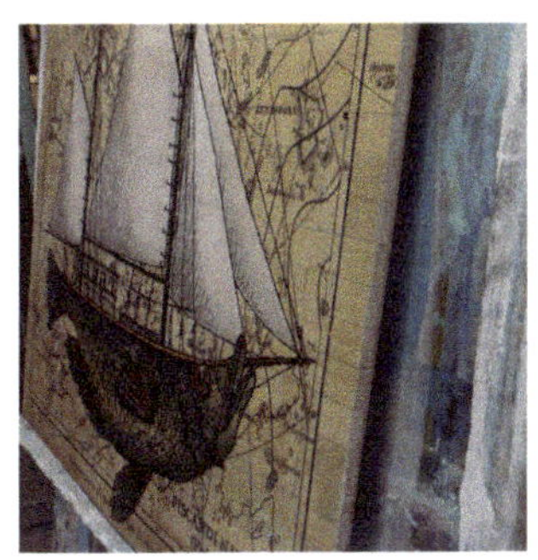

76
Potts
Mullumbimby

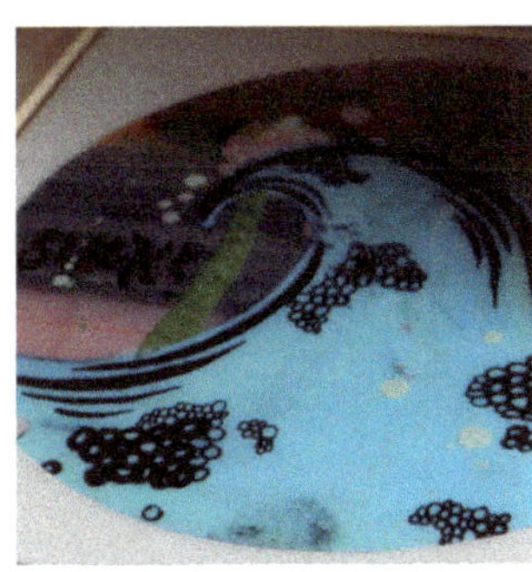

110
James McMillan
Byron Bay

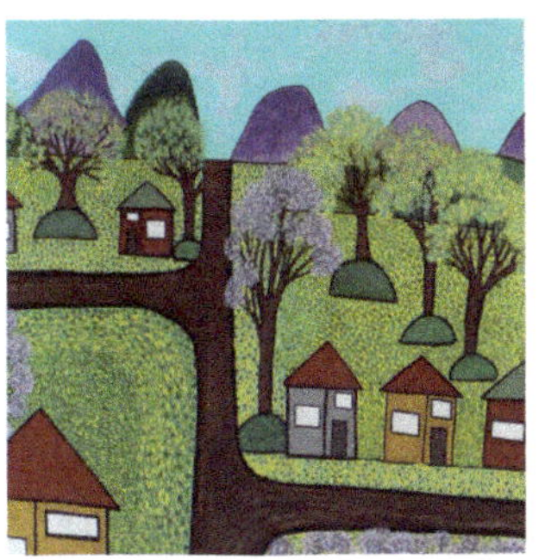

118
Timothy Ives
Suffolk Park

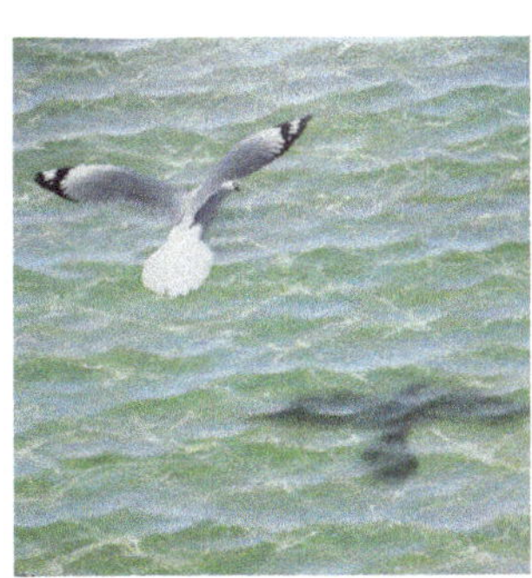

126
Mark Waller
Lennox Head

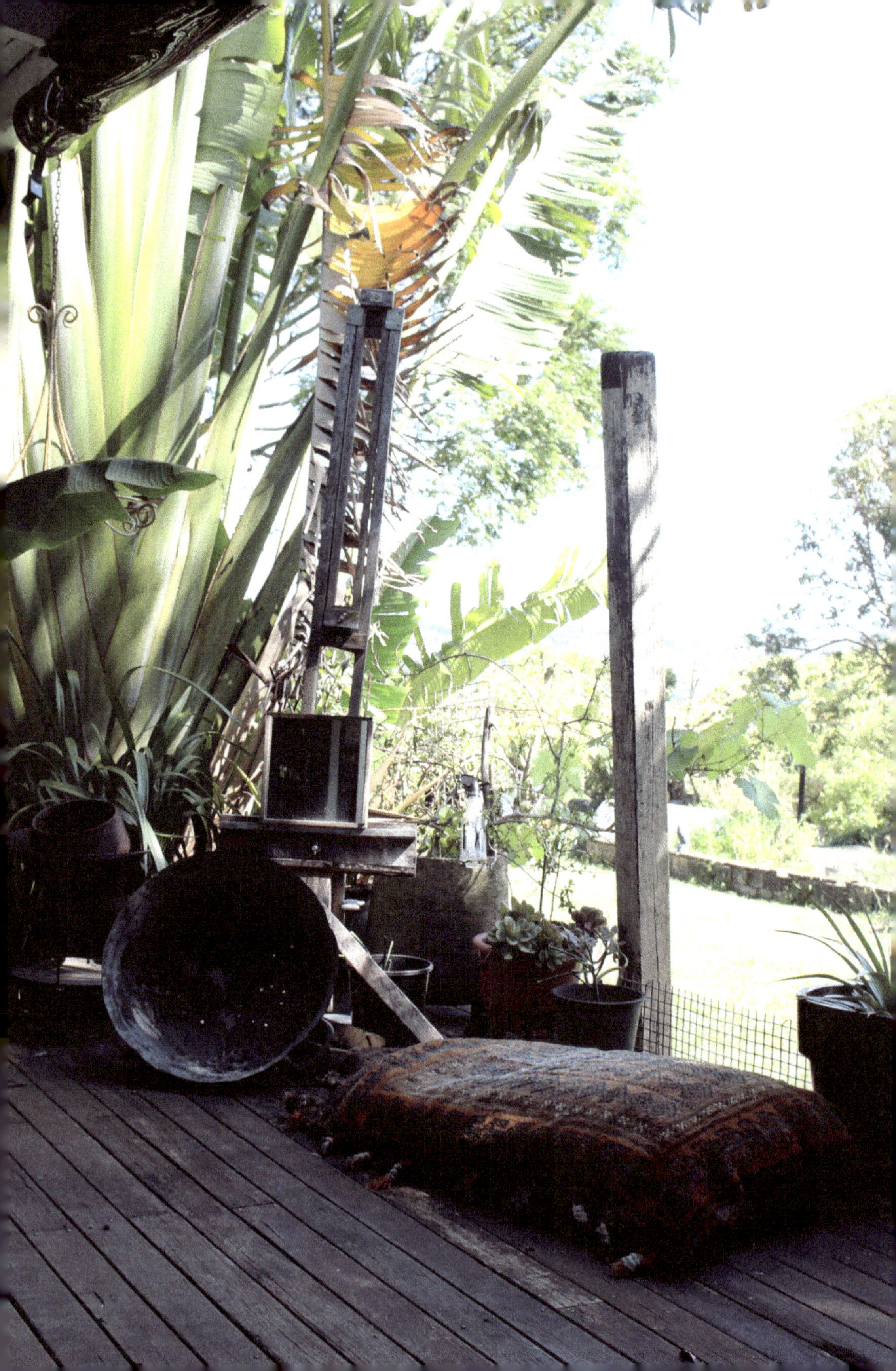

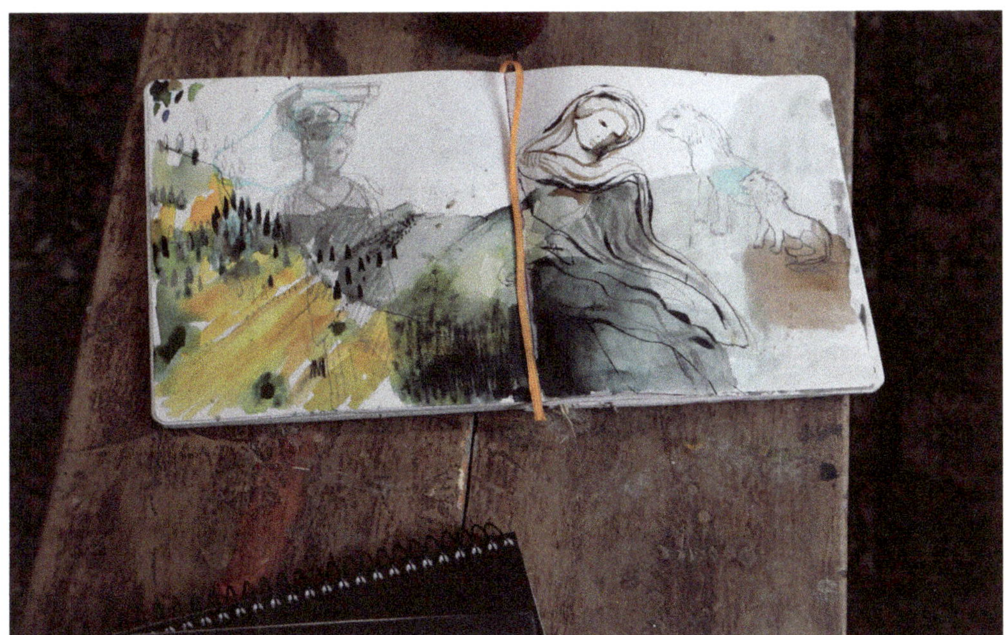

*Dear reader,*

This journey into the creative communities of the New South Wales Northern Rivers reveals a laid-back group of artists heavily influenced by warmth and nature. Life here largely runs in line with the tide. Brushes are put down as days heat up and studios ditched for the cool relief of Australia's most easterly coastline.

In this book you'll find much more than the four walls in which these people paint, create and potter. These stories tell of the artists' head spaces. The spaces they've moved from and through to settle in this iconic pocket of Australia, where tiny towns cling to mirrored rivers and breathtaking beaches.

We take you into the spaces of surfers with studio views to the shoreline, potters in historic timber halls, an artist living off-grid in steep timbered hinterland, and others finding solitude in sheds, garages and the cool underbelly of homes on stilts.

Many tell a tale of increasing gentrification of their once-country towns, as tourists turn locals, and bring an insatiable appetite for shopping, dining and nightlife. "Still, it's all been good," says potter Rebecca Ross of the area's many incarnations.

At the heart of the Northern Rivers, Byron Bay continues to draw the masses, but as Indigenous artist Timothy Ives says, this has always been so. Even before white settlement, this place beckoned people for celebration and trade.

For many of the artists here, inspiration is drawn from the landscape of rivers, sea and hinterland. Driving through maple-scented cane fields, mint-fresh forests and stopping to watch mother whales and their babies breach amongst white-foamed waves, it's easy to feel inspired too. And so we made this book to share among fellow inquisitive folk who like to spend a little time in another person's world; in this case, a selection of artists, brave, dedicated and welcoming.

*Lauren Mitchell*

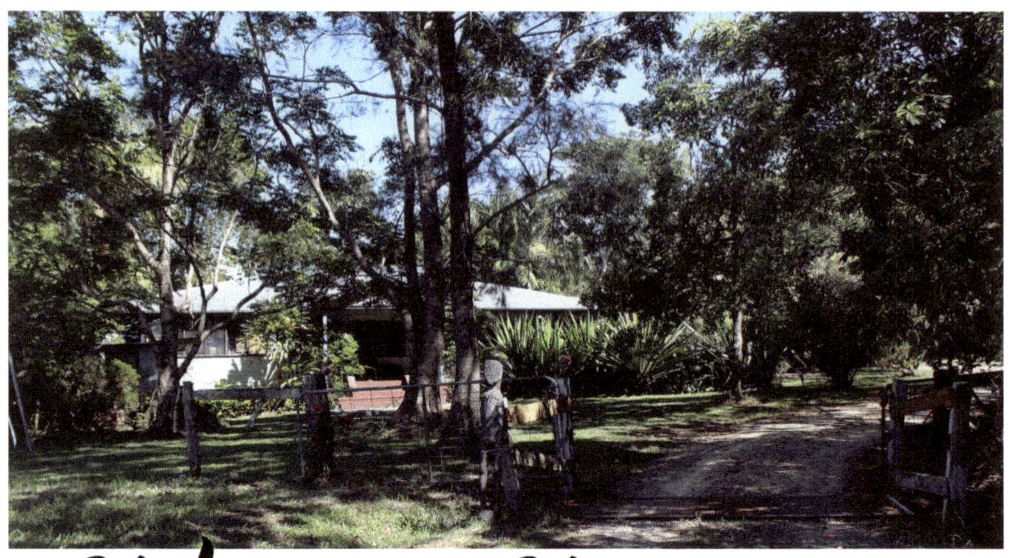

# Hilary Herrmann

## Long python days

Hilary Herrmann's place feels like a secret. Appropriately, it's the stuff of books. Fairy tales. Folklore. The sort of house children would be secreted to, to buffer them from harsh times. The boundary of Hilary's place is a buffer. Between a seemingly-perfect world and the real one. Which side of the fence is which, is for you to decide.

The property is just a short drive from the Bangalow township, through the winding warren of a new housing subdivision. Down a skinny drive between polished properties and over a cattle grate lies Hilary's place; a wide strip of wild paddock fronts an artery of rainforest trees, and beyond that a lush garden with a sprawling Queenslander home at its heart. Hidden.

A native frangipani tree is in full fragrant bloom, and French doors are thrown open to the breeze and a wide verandah. As far as welcomes go, it's a bloody beauty.

"There's a sense of contentment around me and a lot of space this year," our artist says. It's hard to imagine this not being the case at all times. But we've caught Hilary at one of life's crossroads. She's found herself thankful for a pause. For time to read in a red velvet armchair on the verandah, and hang out with the python in an elk fern beside.

"It's been a strange time for me," Hilary says. "I've been through some really big changes. I looked after someone here who was very unwell for ten years and he died. And Frieda left, which is a good thing. She needs to make her own way in the world."

Frieda is Hilary's 19-year-old daughter, who has left to study creative

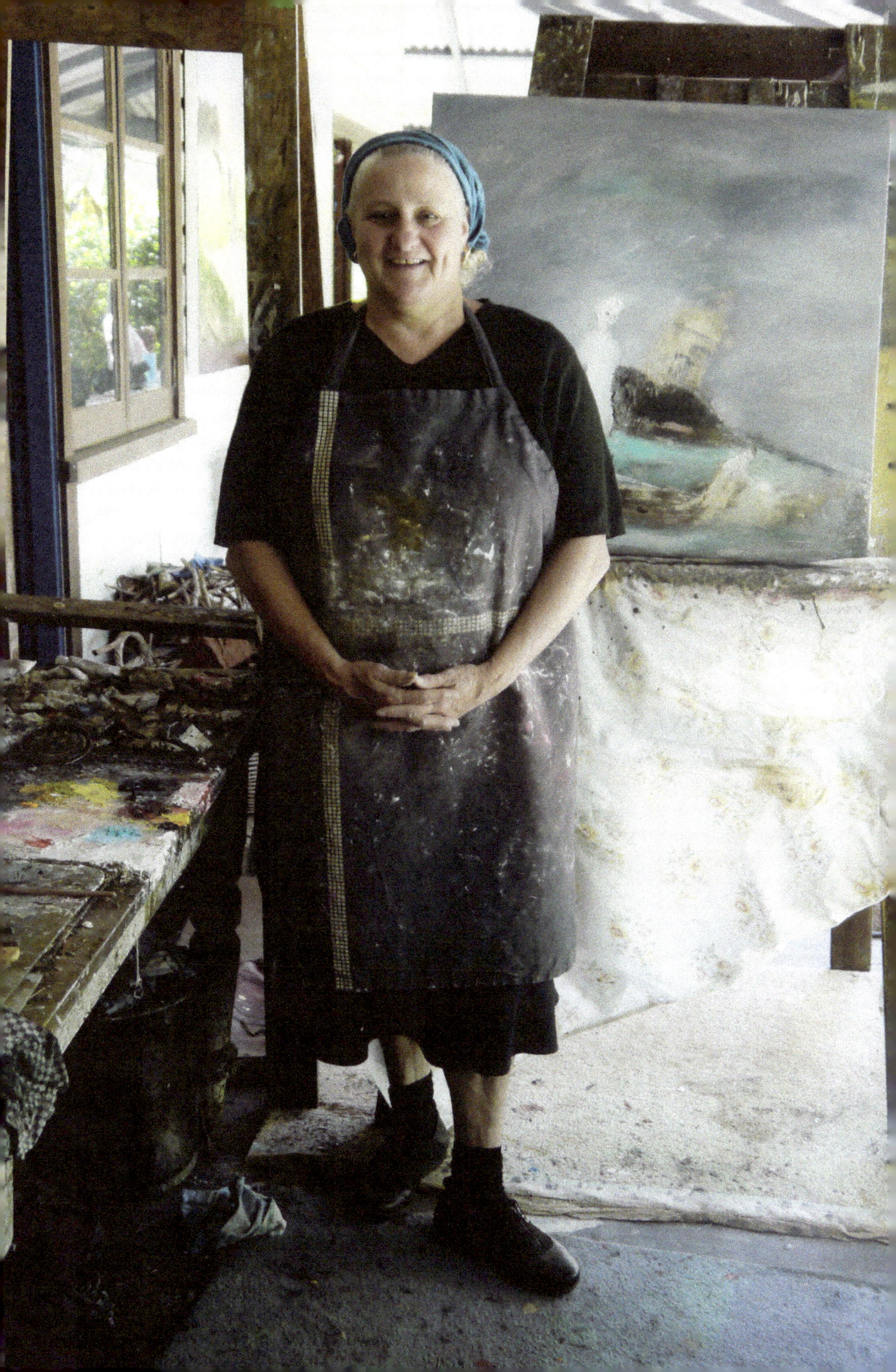

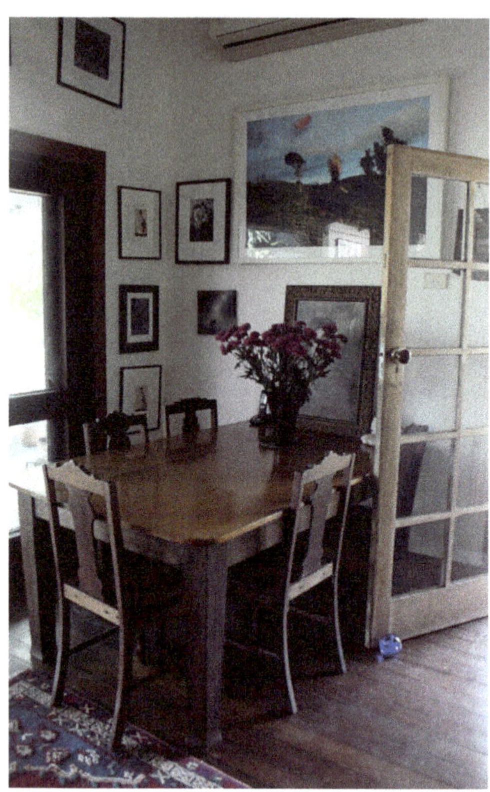

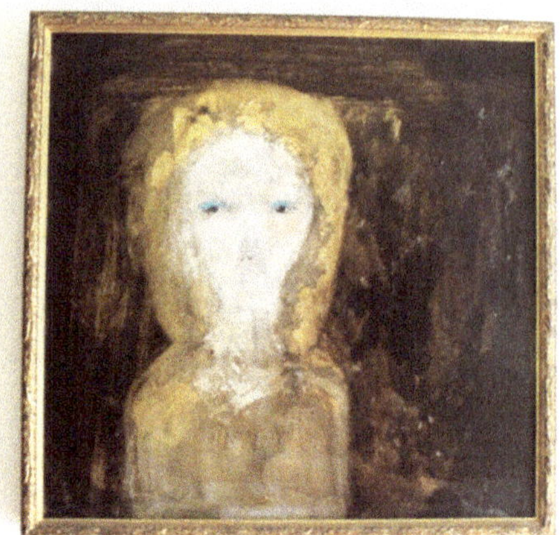

writing in Melbourne. Frieda grew up in this house, so it's the first time Hilary has been alone here. Not that that's totally true. She has old dog Bindi, plus a handful of fellow artists and creative souls who visit the property. "That just happened organically over the years," Hilary says. "One person I knew needed a studio, so a shed got restored for them and then one thing led to another... there's five rustic little studios down there."

This place has had a grounding effect on Hilary, and her art. Before settling at this family property 20 years ago, she lived her life in a moving-on fashion. "I didn't organise my life. I stumbled into it," she says.

"I came to Bangalow with my family as a tiny child. My parents were Jewish refugees, first from Germany and then from Kenya, where my brother and I were born. We arrived in Australia and my parents settled in Bangalow in 1961 when I was two. I grew up on the other side of town. This property was my aunt's and when she decided to sell it my father bought it. Then I inherited it and came to live here 20 years ago. The house was falling apart. It feels like a place we saved."

Sandwiched between Hilary's Bangalow years was a good dose of travelling, sex, drugs, rock 'n' roll; the stuff of life. "I left home at 18 and did a teaching degree, than I travelled around the world. It was exciting. I was pretty wild for a while there."

When Hilary came back to Australia she taught Vietnamese refugees in Cabramatta, then Indigenous kids in Arnhem Land. "Teaching in Cabramatta

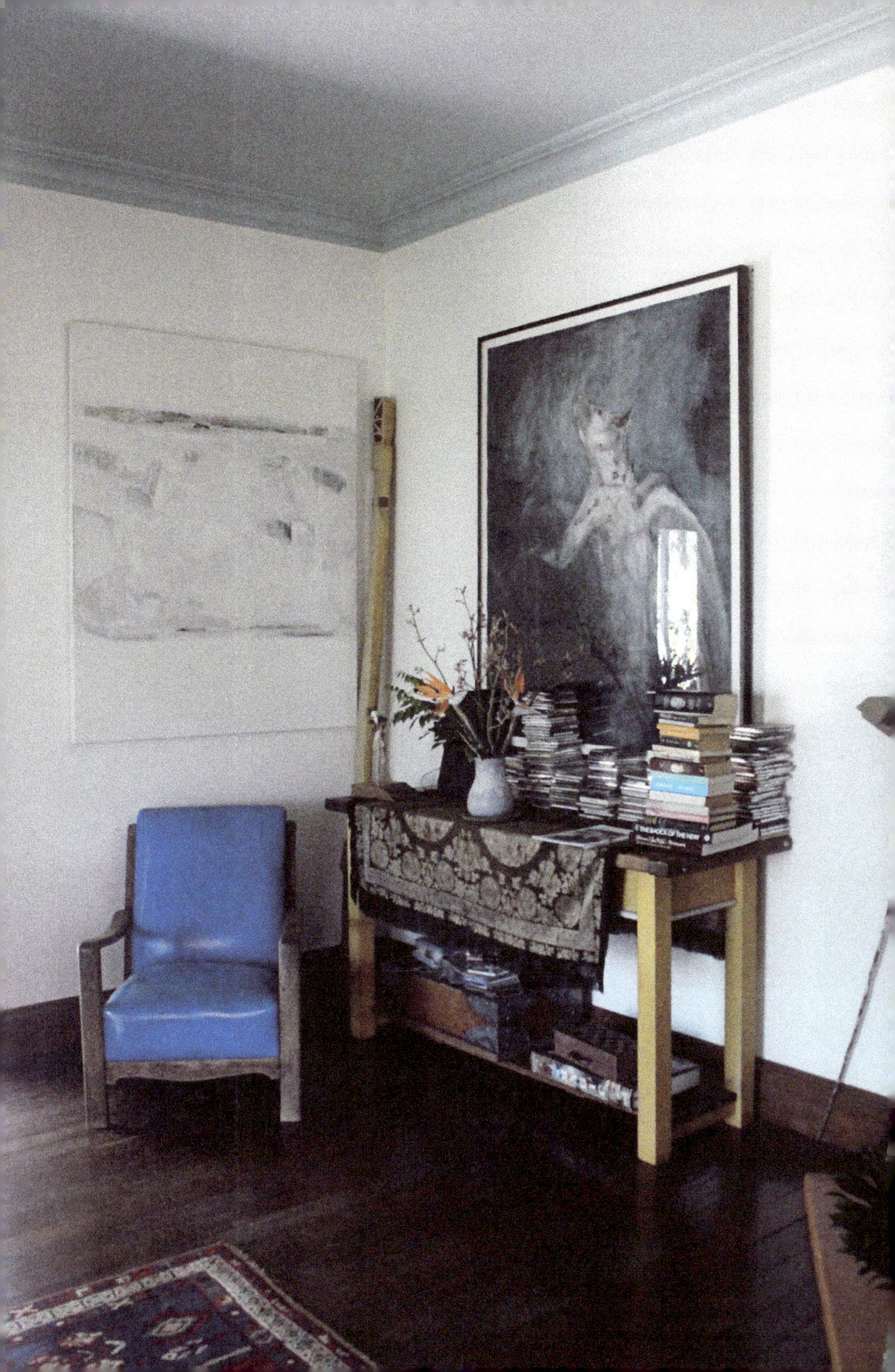

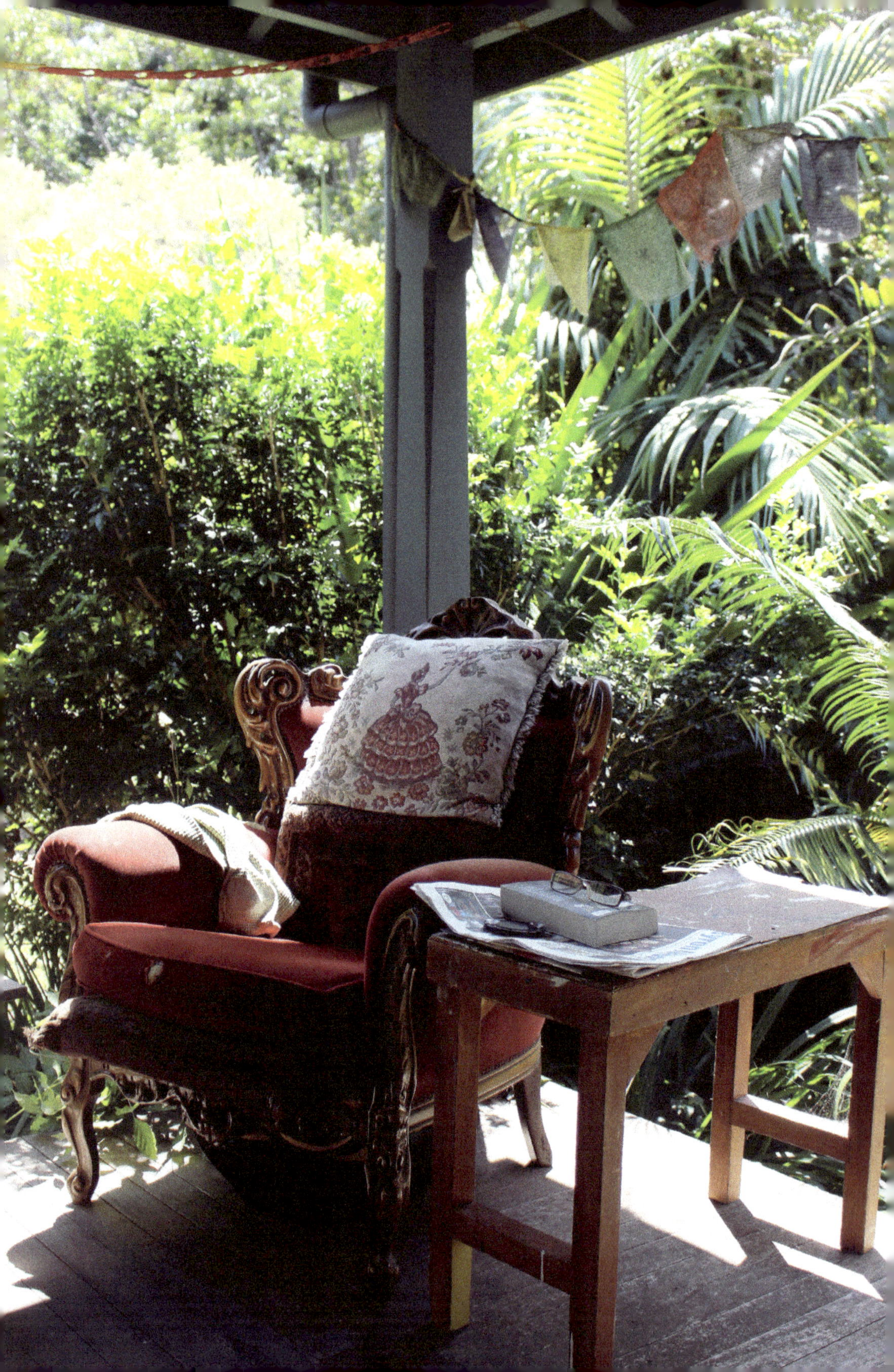

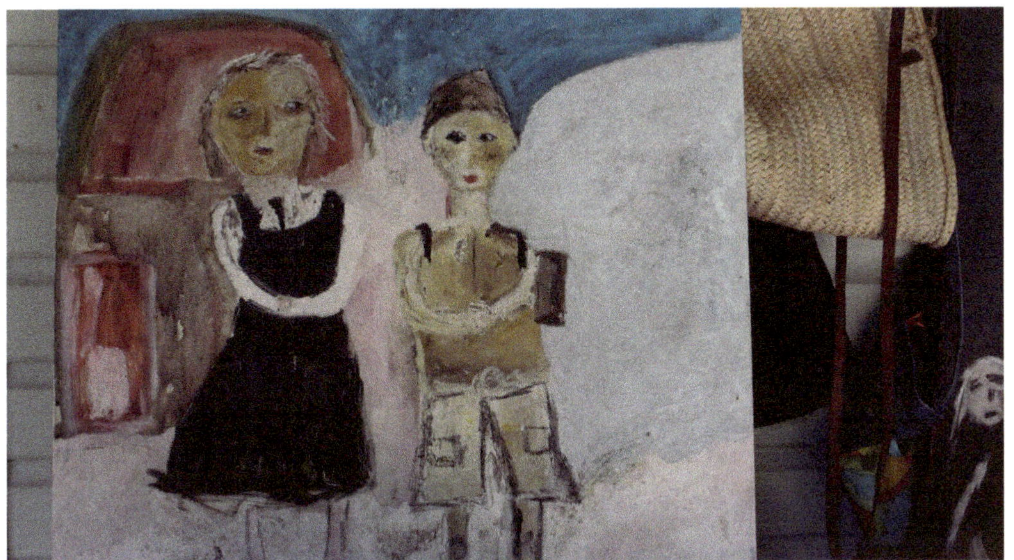

was a beautiful, transformative experience," she says. "I was teaching kids who'd lived in camps for ten years." She learnt a lot about how it must have been for her own parents as refugees. "It taught me the importance of coming into a country where people were kind to you. There was kindness in this community when my family came here. They were probably the first German Jews to arrive in Bangalow. When they came, an Anglican minister arrived at their place with a casserole. My father said, 'we're not of your conversion' and the minister said, 'we all have to eat'."

Hilary later landed a gig as a paper conservator with Sydney's Mitchell Library. "Now you have to have a five-year qualification to get a job like that, but back then there was a five-week opening for a manuscript restorer and I was mentored to do the job."

Throughout it all, however, was a nagging ambition for a 'dabbling' in paint to be so much more.

"When my daughter turned five and I was in my early 40s I realised if I wanted to be an artist, I just had to do it, to put in the time and commitment to make it work. It was an age thing really and I just wanted to see where it took me."

As she speaks Hilary is working on her latest collection of oil paintings titled *The Voyage Home*. She started them just as her daughter was leaving. "The first two were very dark and brooding and as I continued painting the work became more whimsical and ethereal," she says. "I think a lot of my paintings are about hope. They're about storytelling and the underlying theme is hope. In a way my paintings are like life. You take a step, you make a brush stroke, and you see where it takes you..."

Right now, they've taken her to a quiet place. A good place. "The world is difficult and to find yourself content in it despite that, is precious. But I think there is still great kindness in the world." Hilary says Bangalow is a great example of that, but increasingly, she needs to look harder to find the authentic goodness, as it quickly morphs from small country town to tourist hot spot.

"In the gentrification of Bangalow things are in danger of becoming soulless," she says. "It's a fantasy. By making a place neat and tidy you can lose its essence. There's so much 'trying' out there, we lose who we are. Sometimes I feel disheartened by what's happened to the township. By seeing people walking around with the 'right' sort of shoes and sunglasses and hair. But I also feel a sense of community. There are great people here."

There are great artists, too. Hilary's beautiful home is full of locals' work. Many of the pieces have been swapped for her own. "These are all local artists, and many are my friends," she says. "I can't have something in the house if I knowingly don't like the person who made it. I have to have an affection for that person, or a respect."

The walls also show Hilary's progression as an artist. "These are really old," she says of the paintings in the hallway. "But I quite like having a reminder of how my work has changed." One consistent theme that's developed over the years are the delicate metallic crowns atop those ethereal figures. As though each one is a fairy queen from an earthy kingdom. As she chats, Hilary unfurls her turquoise headband to prepare for a photograph, revealing her own halo of silver curls, as though she's just stepped out from the canvas. ■

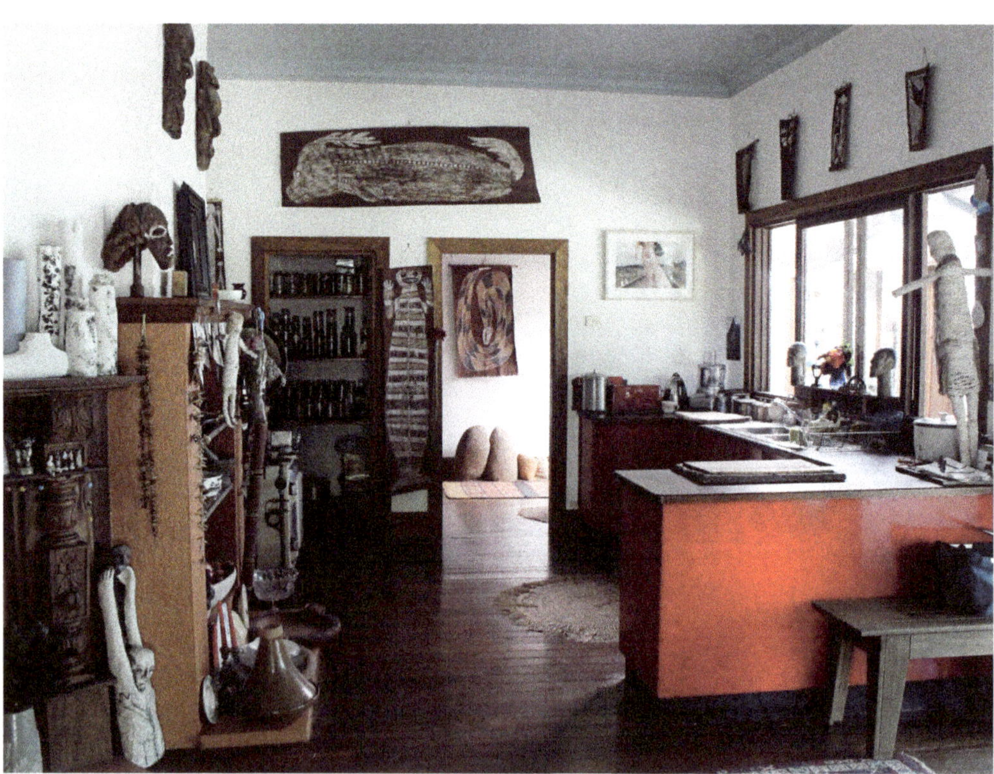

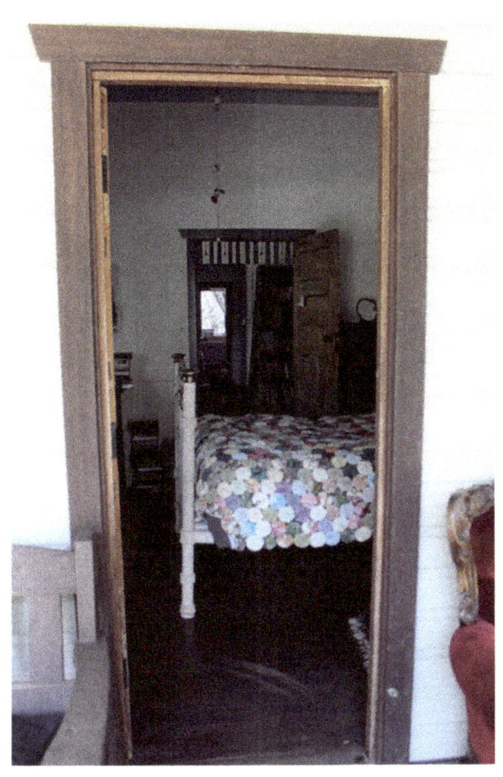

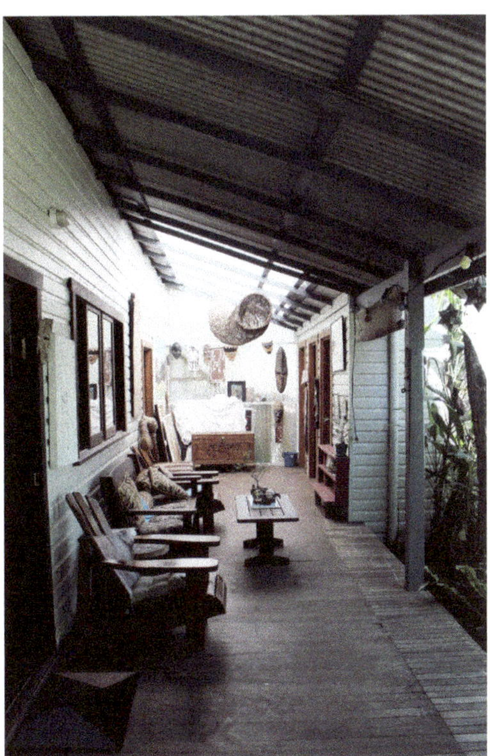

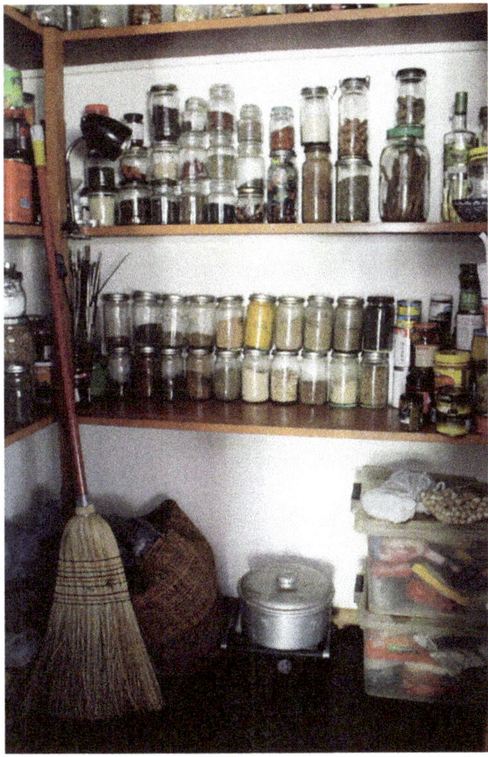

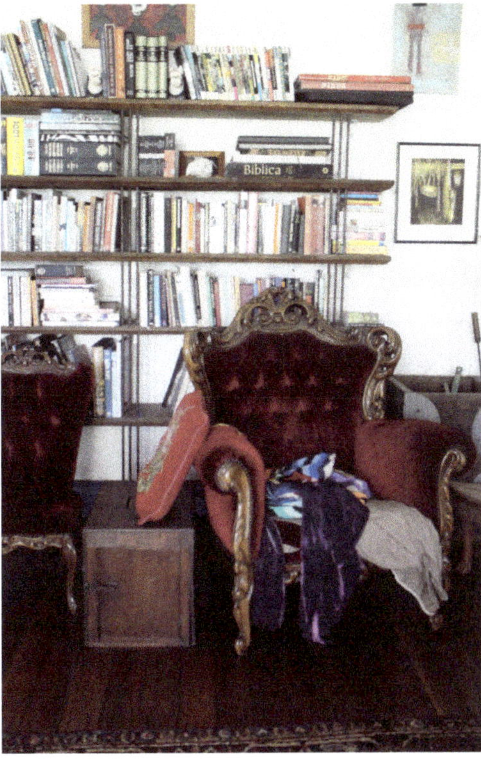
Biblica

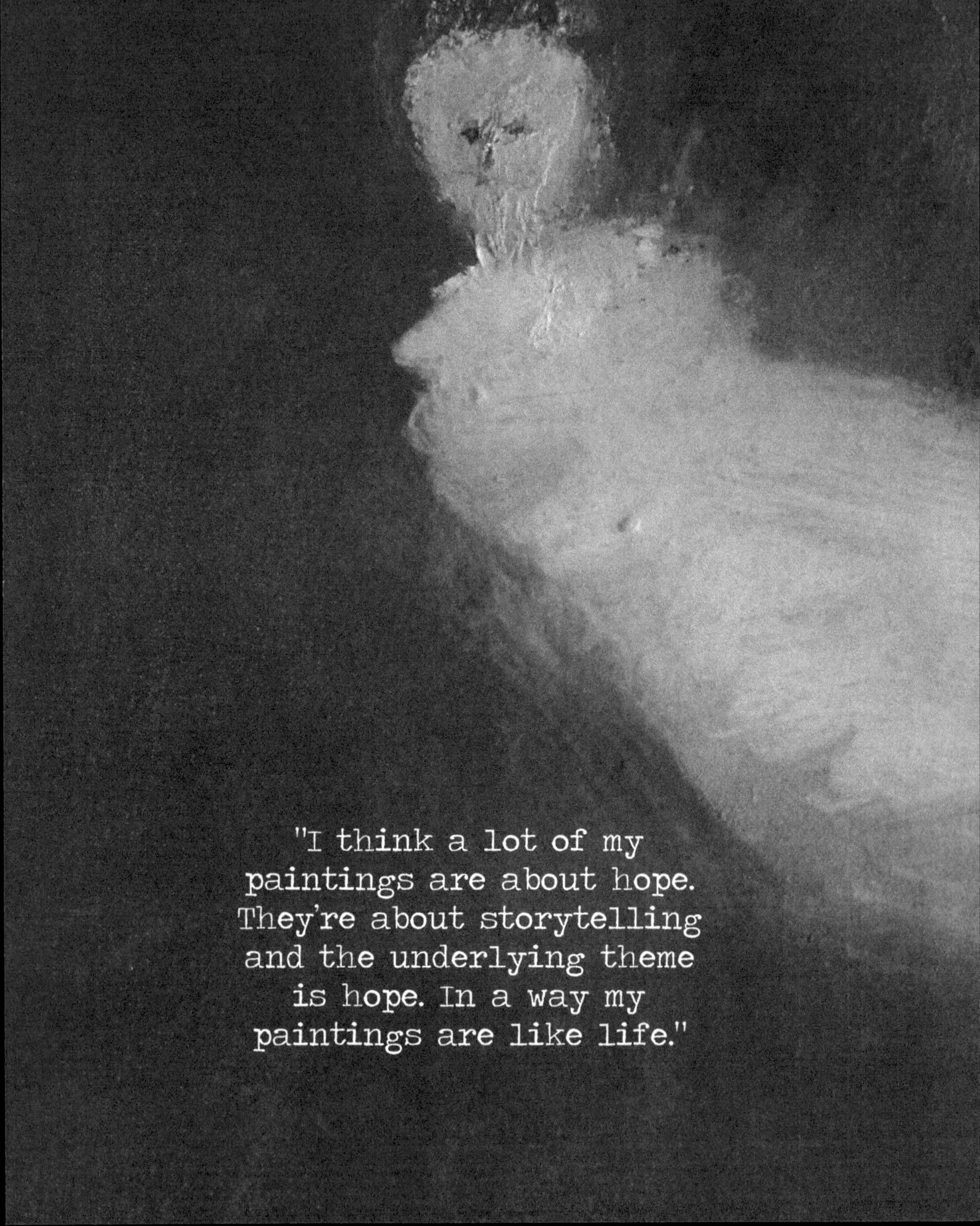

"I think a lot of my paintings are about hope. They're about storytelling and the underlying theme is hope. In a way my paintings are like life."

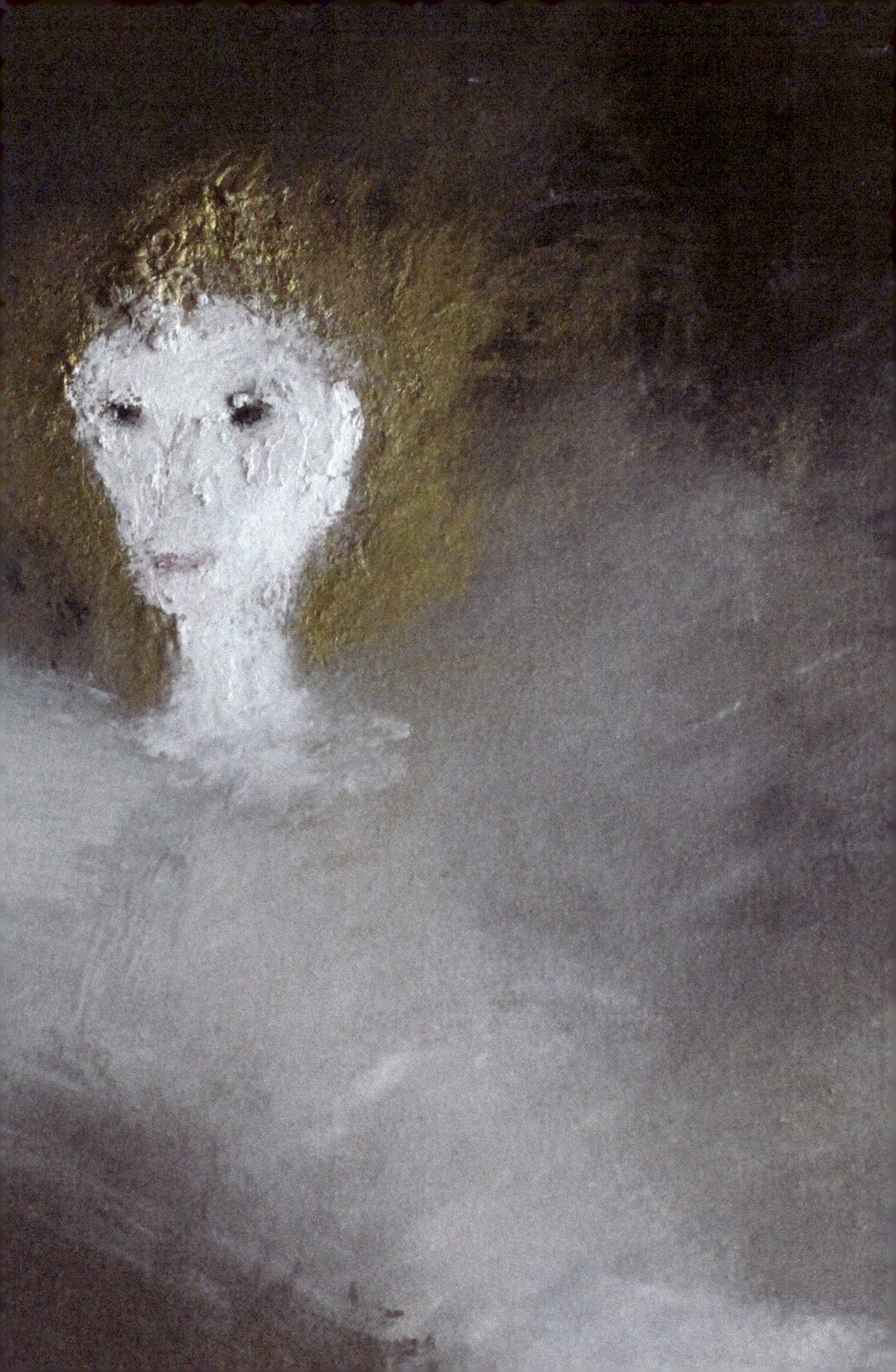

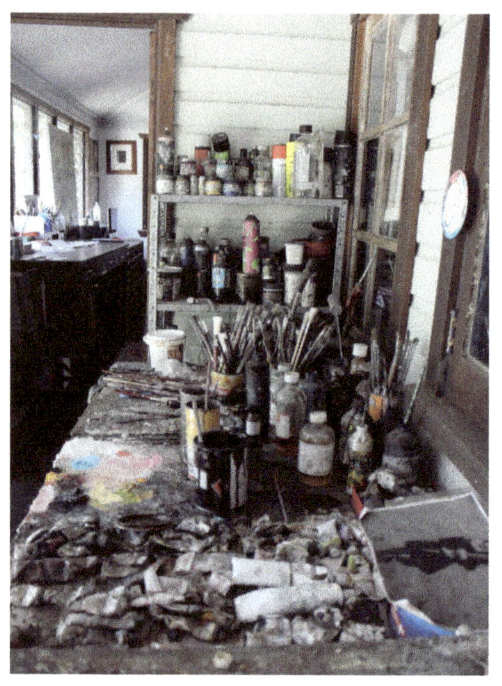

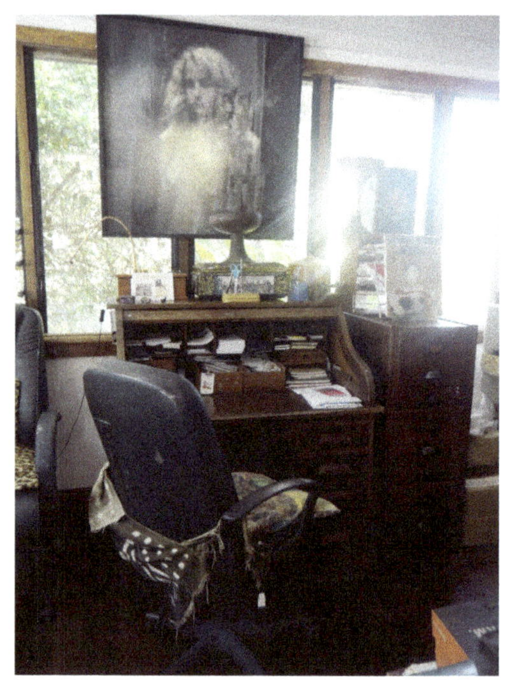

*A native frangipani tree is in full fragrant bloom, and French doors are thrown open to the breeze.*

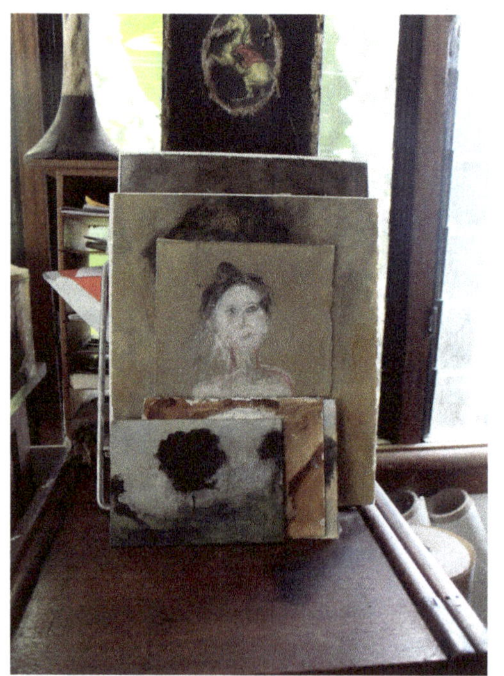

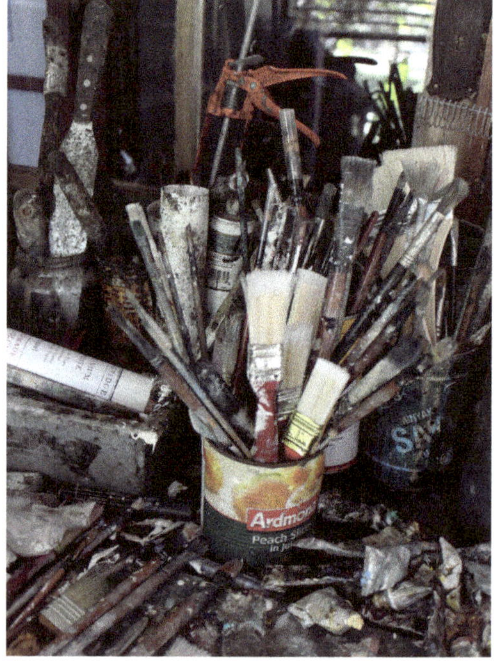

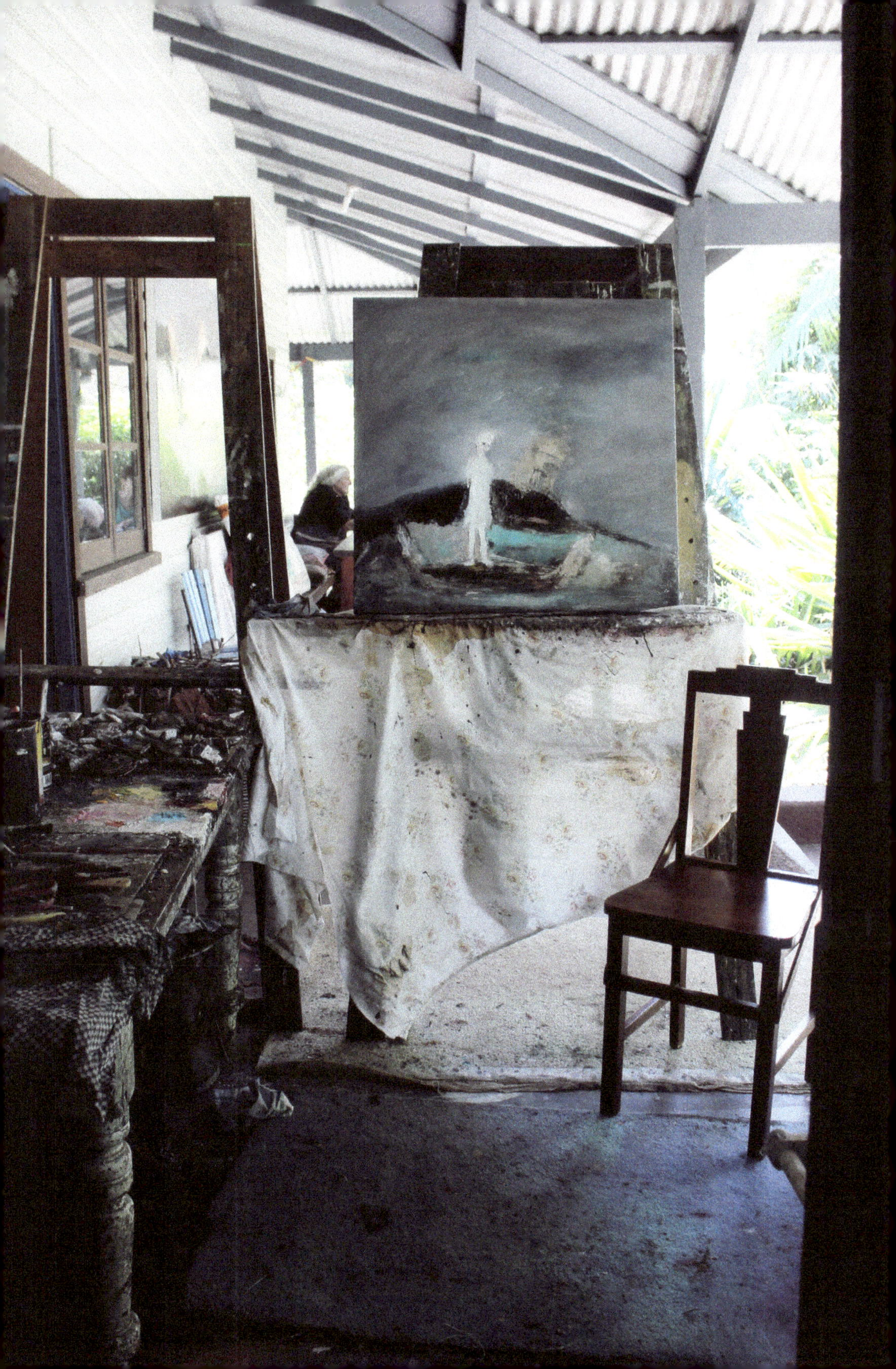

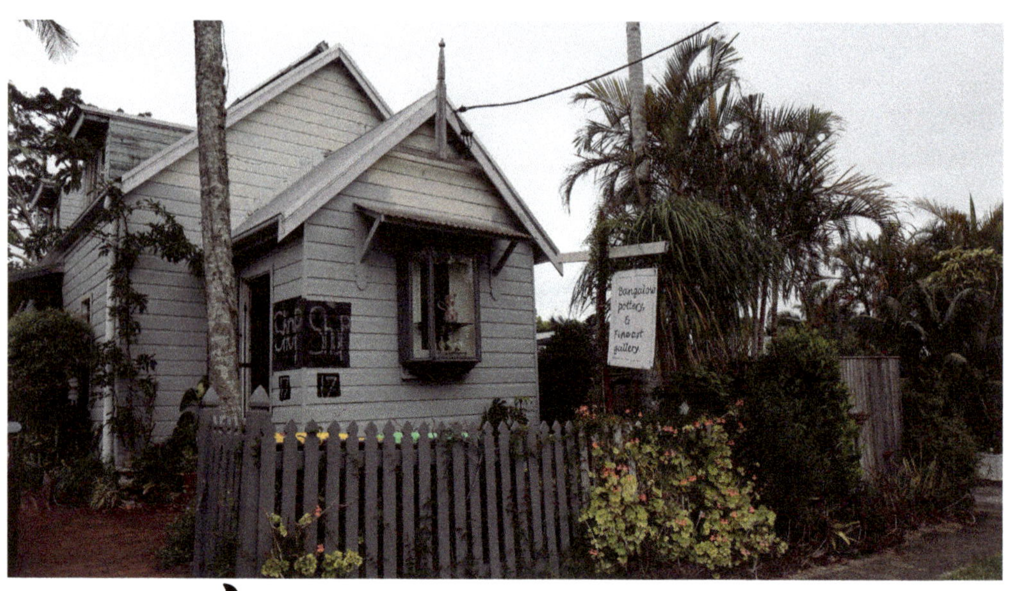


# Rebecca Ross

## By clay and kiln

The humble timber cutters' cottages of historic Bangalow are like beacons to hipsters, tree changers and holiday makers. As is the palm-fringed main street. Highlights include the Barebones Art Space, the green-tiled Art Deco hotel and Poet Store; home to loose leaf tea and the magazines *New Philosopher* and *Womankind*.

Thanks to the popularity of this pretty place, the properties here are worth a mint. But in the not-too-distant past it was an economic and creative refuge for many, including potter Rebecca Ross.

"Bangalow has been through a few phases in the 25 years I've been here," Rebecca says. "When I first came it was a real country town, there were only a few people here from the city. Then creative people began to move here, for the low prices and natural beauty and freedom to do what they wanted. And then came the people with money. Still, it's all been good I think."

Rebecca arrived in Bangalow from Victoria's Phillip Island, with two young children in tow. She was looking for some short-term rest and relaxation, and unexpectedly found home.

"I came up for three months but it was so nice, so easy to live here with children that I just stayed," she says. "At first I just worked from the verandah of the house I was renting and then this place came up for sale. I bought it without thinking too much about it, I just had to. At that stage it was just a shell with a bathroom and kitchen and I've been building it ever since."

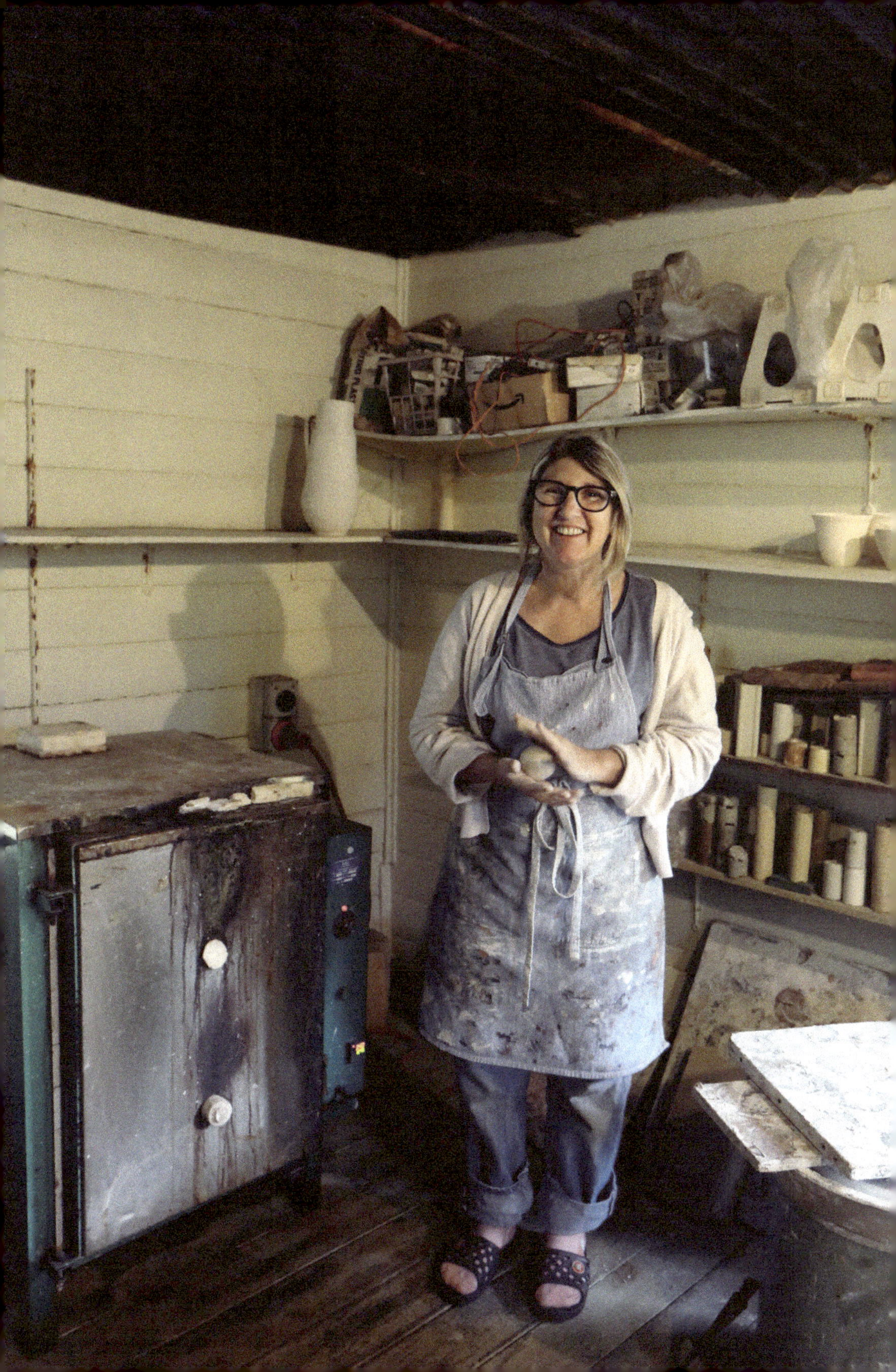

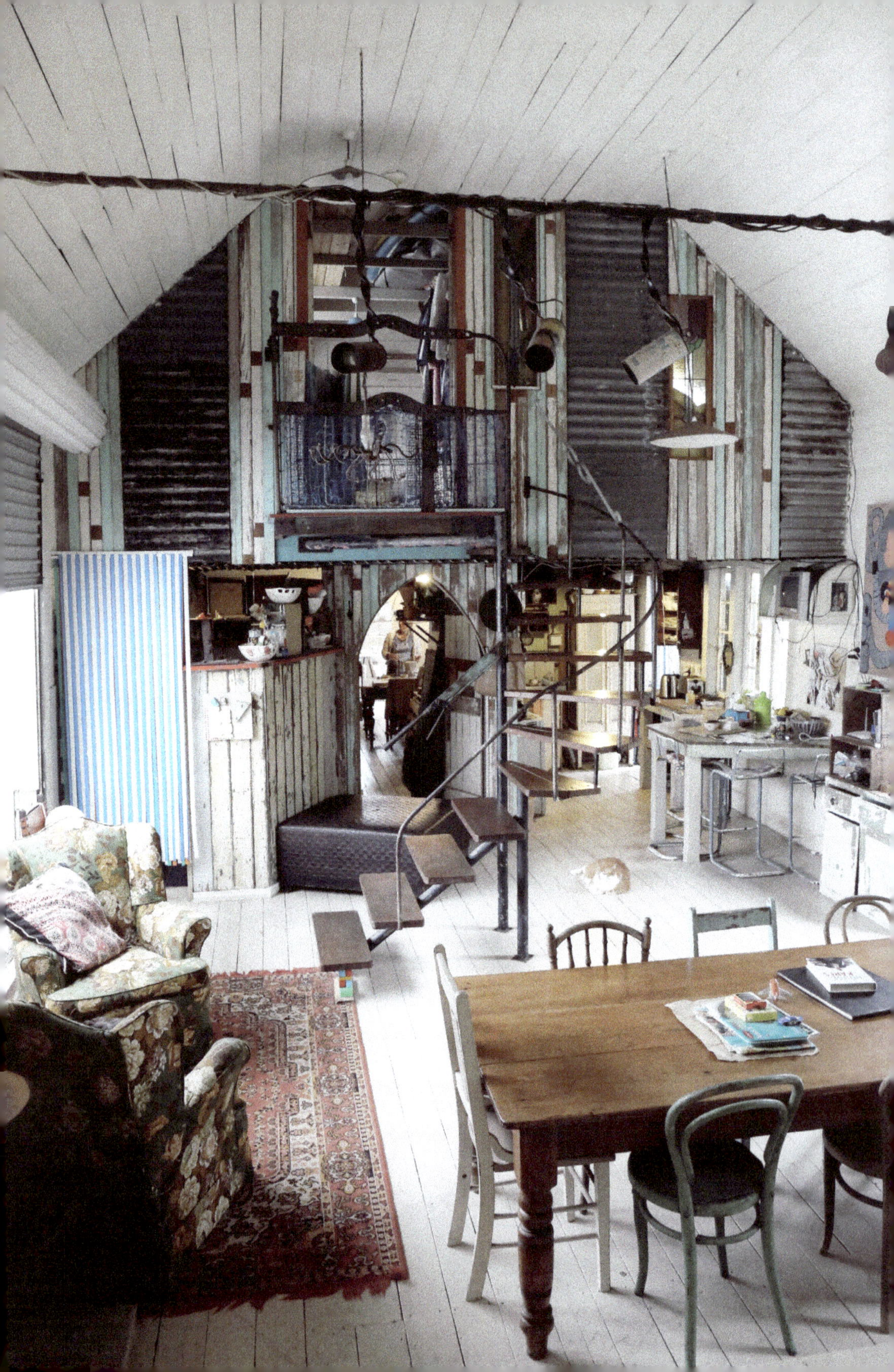

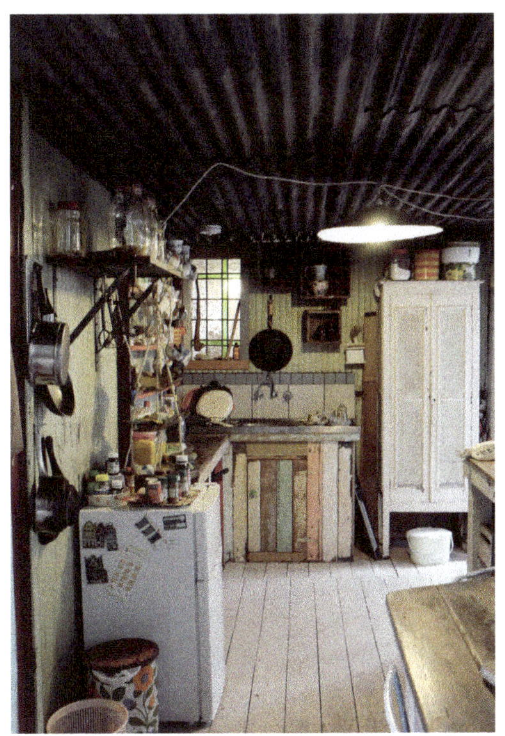

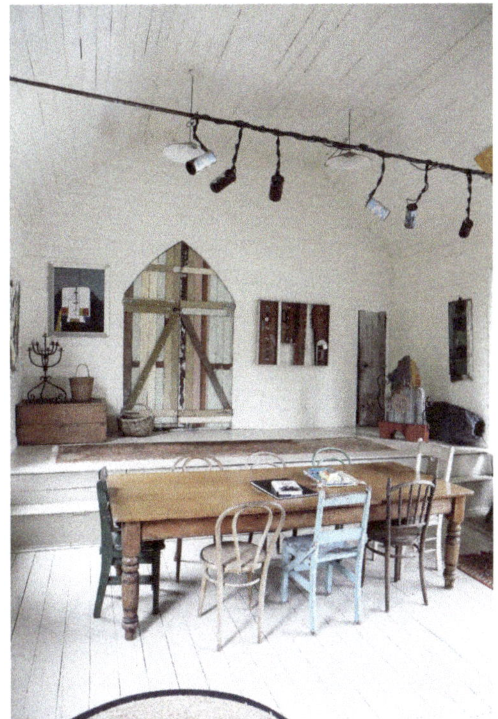

Rebecca's place is Bangalow's original – albeit briefly-lived – Temperance Hall, one block west of the shopping strip. "The religion didn't last long in Bangalow, the people have always liked a drink here," she says. "After that it just became the local party hall. For a while there it was a glass factory, and then my house."

As a home, it's a beauty. It's like a giant, handcrafted timber sculpture that's been added to and patched up through the wear and tear of life and love. Rebecca says she's spent years working on it, building its beautiful innards from scrap heap metal and other recycled bits and bobs. "That was because I had no money, but also because I liked it that way," she says. "Sometimes I think I might leave, but where would I go? I couldn't live in a house that was all plaster walls and low ceilings. I say I'm used to living like this, but if I go away anywhere I always come home and think, 'it's so peaceful here'."

Yes, this place suits Rebecca. She's crafted it to suit her life. The front entrance houses her Bangalow Pottery and Fine Art Gallery. A quirky little bay window frames a tall pottery pitcher, and the open timber shelves prop up plates and bowls and latte cups. They're stencilled and painted with Rebecca's signature mix of rose blooms, dots, dashes and retro comic strips. Very cool.

Rebecca has been making pottery since the age of 22, after studying a fine arts degree, majoring in ceramics, at Prahran College of the Arts. "I'd always wanted to do it," she says. "When I was a kid there was a woman down the road from us who did pottery and I'd go and hang out with her on the weekends for fun. I really liked her house and I really liked her lifestyle."

Rebecca's own life follows the demands of clay and kiln. She has a constant production line going to keep the gallery stocked, as well as her regular stalls at the region's craft markets. The works are all made here, in the room beyond the gallery, with a big old timber table at its heart. "I bought that on the drive back home from Melbourne, in some place like Gunnedah," she says. "I strapped it to the roof of the car and drove the rest of the way home with it. I was always going to fix it up, then I thought, why? I quite like it as it is. It's gotten better over the years, it wasn't as scuffed up as that when I first got it."

That table has seen Rebecca's style change greatly over the years. "Ceramics was a big thing in the 1980s and 90s, and that's when I was doing all that quirky earthenware. In the 2000s it went out of favour for years and years and now it's resurged. People have gone from really liking it, to being a bit shocked by it, to really liking it again."

Continuing the tour of the hall, past the pottery door is Rebecca's living space. It feels welcoming and communal, every bit still a gathering place, with a long dining table by the old stage. Hanging overhead, a pineapple can chandelier. Here, Rebecca's pottery is used daily, turning even toast into a ceremony. A spiral staircase leads to the bedrooms, and dainty dormer windows that peek over the neighbouring rooftops.

Double arched timber doors at the back of the hall hint at more, and there is. The rear section has been renovated as a gorgeous Airbnb, and here Rebecca welcomes guests from all corners. "It's always been there but I suddenly realised that if I shut those doors I could have two houses, so that's what I did," she says.

The apartment has two bedrooms, a bathroom and kitchen off a central living space that's lined with corrugated iron. The indoors is separated from the garden by a day bed and bistro blinds, so it gives the easy, breezy feeling of glamping (to borrow a Bangalow hipster term). And out back is a giant native fig Faraway Tree abutting the hall, dwarfing it in the familiar hug of decades-old friends. ■

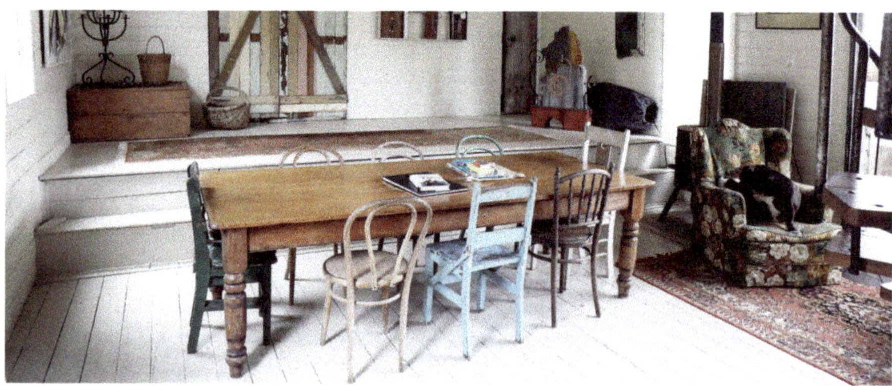

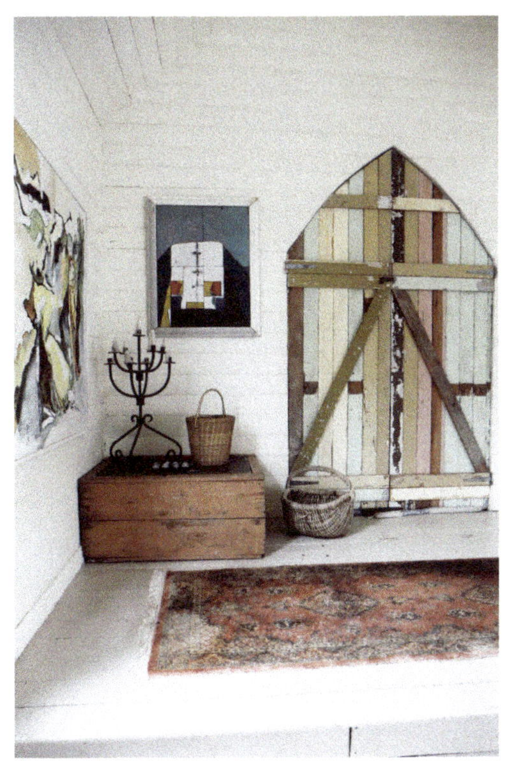
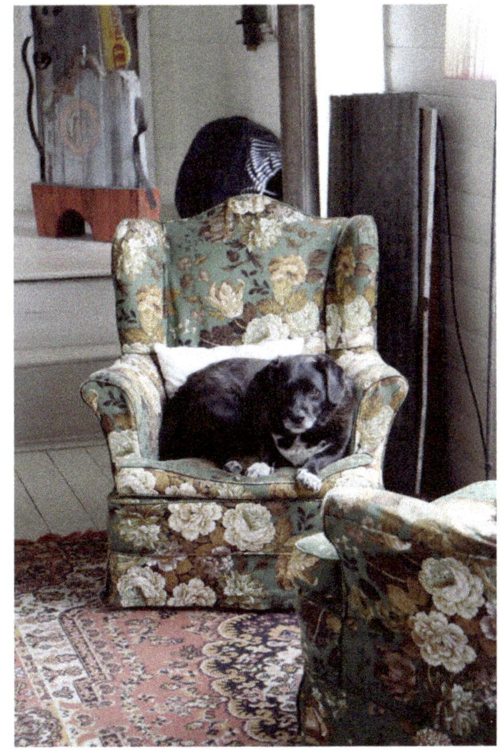
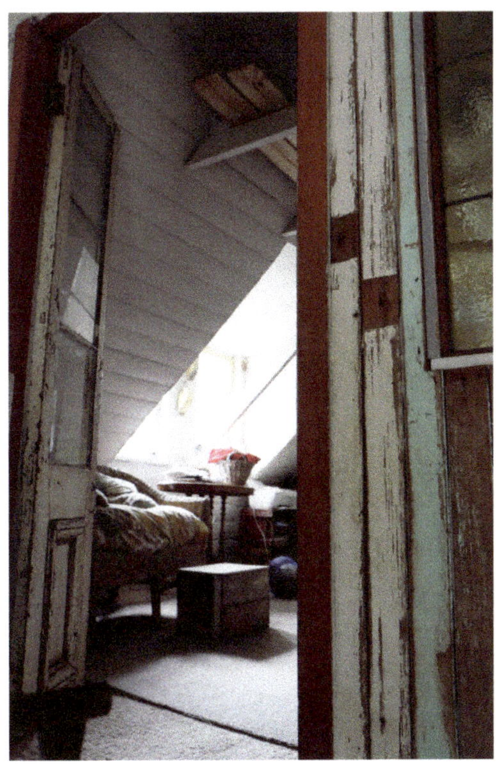
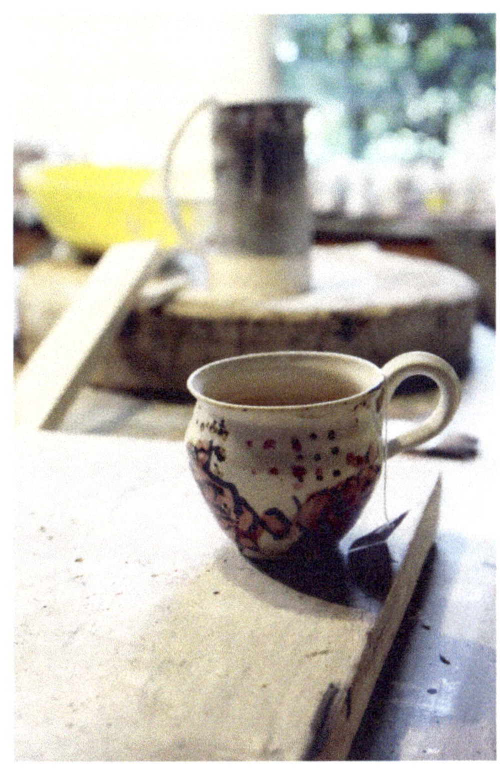

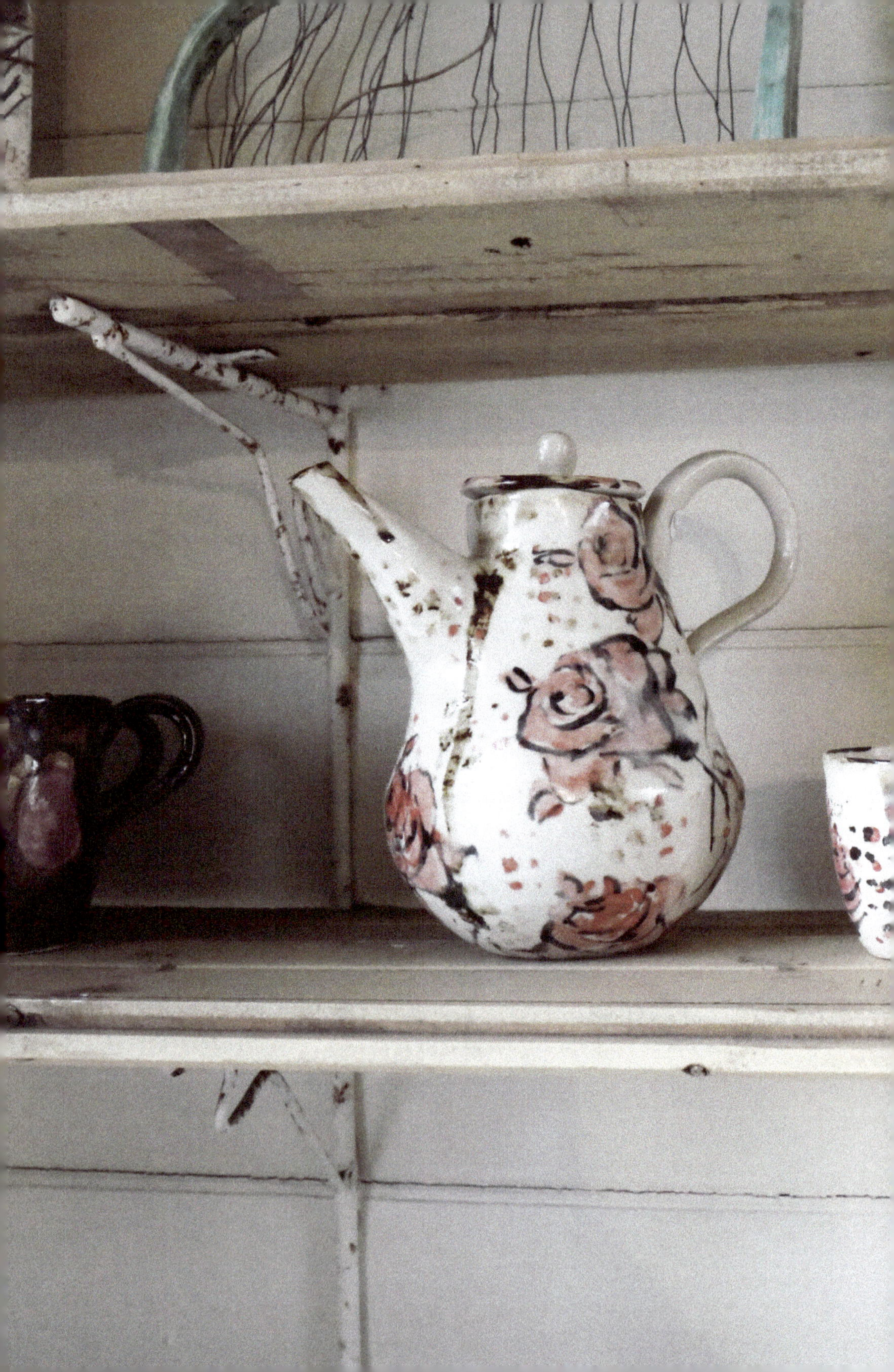

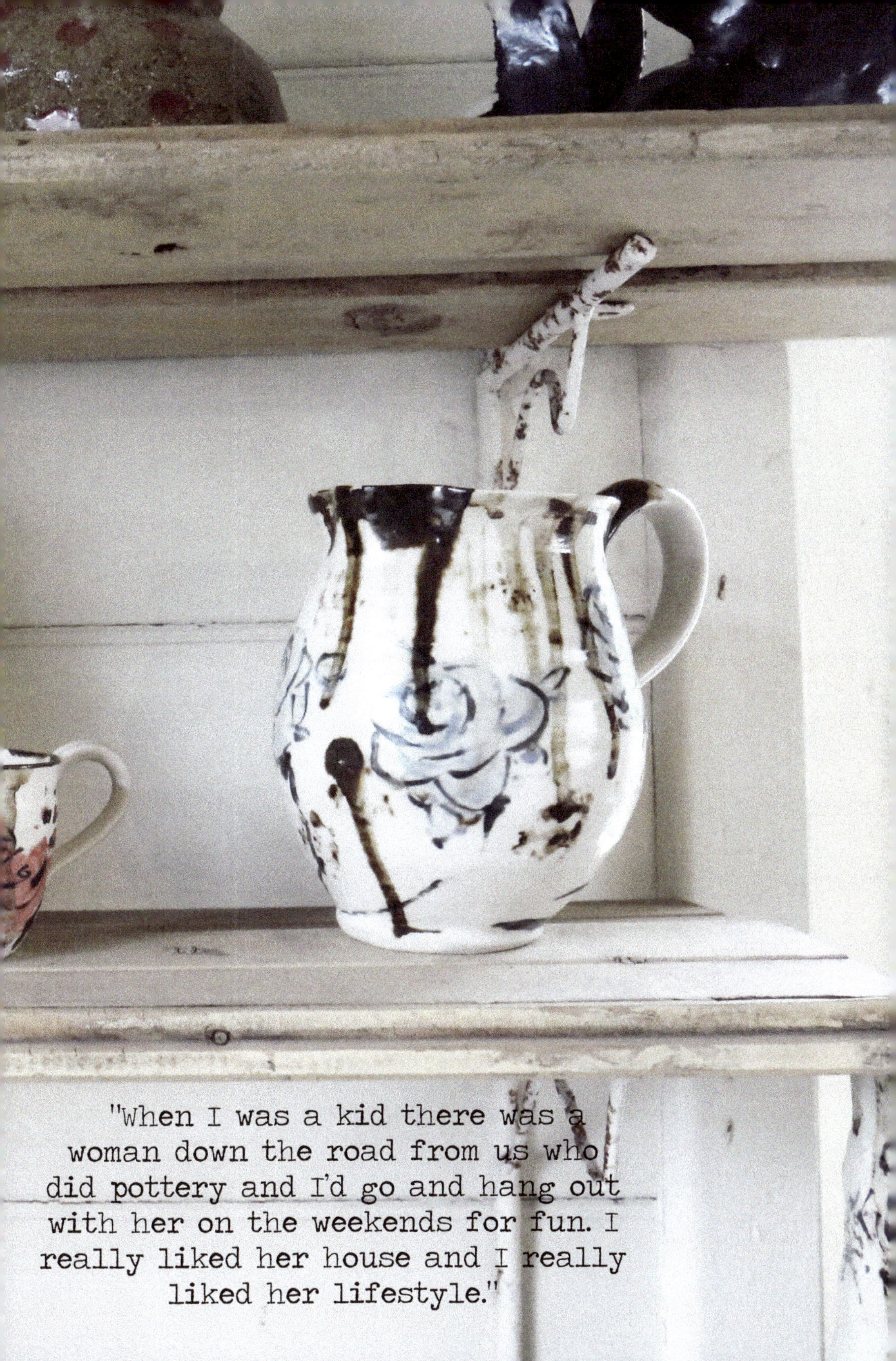

"When I was a kid there was a woman down the road from us who did pottery and I'd go and hang out with her on the weekends for fun. I really liked her house and I really liked her lifestyle."

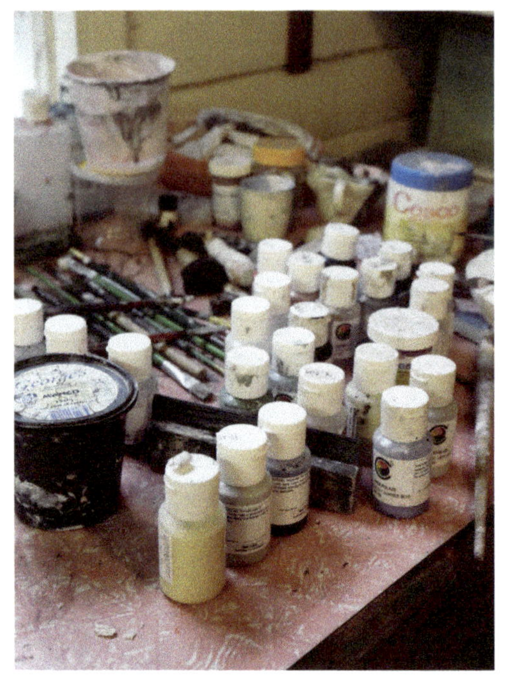

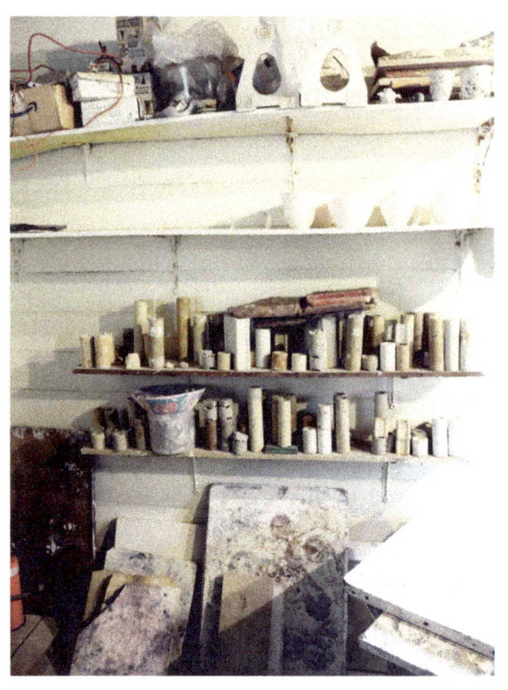

*As a home, it's a beauty. It's like a giant, handcrafted timber sculpture that's been added to and patched up.*

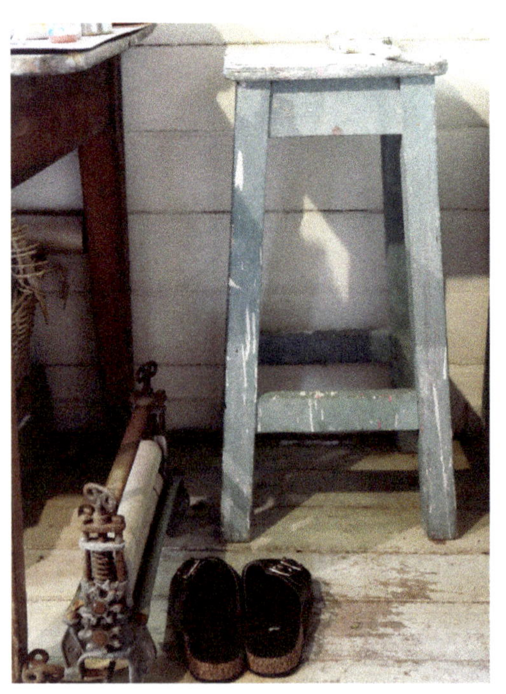

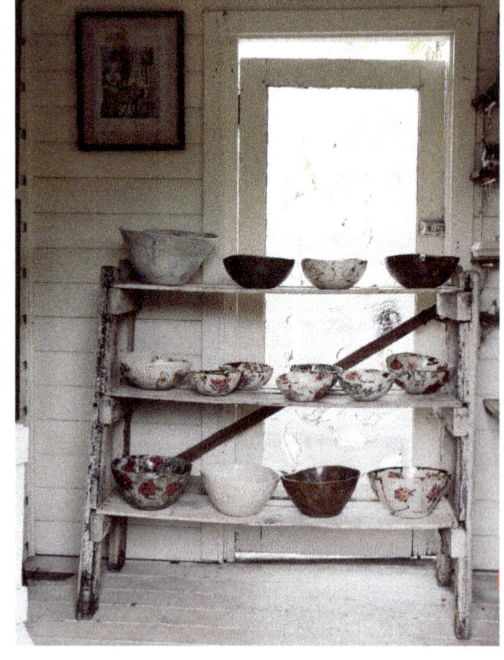

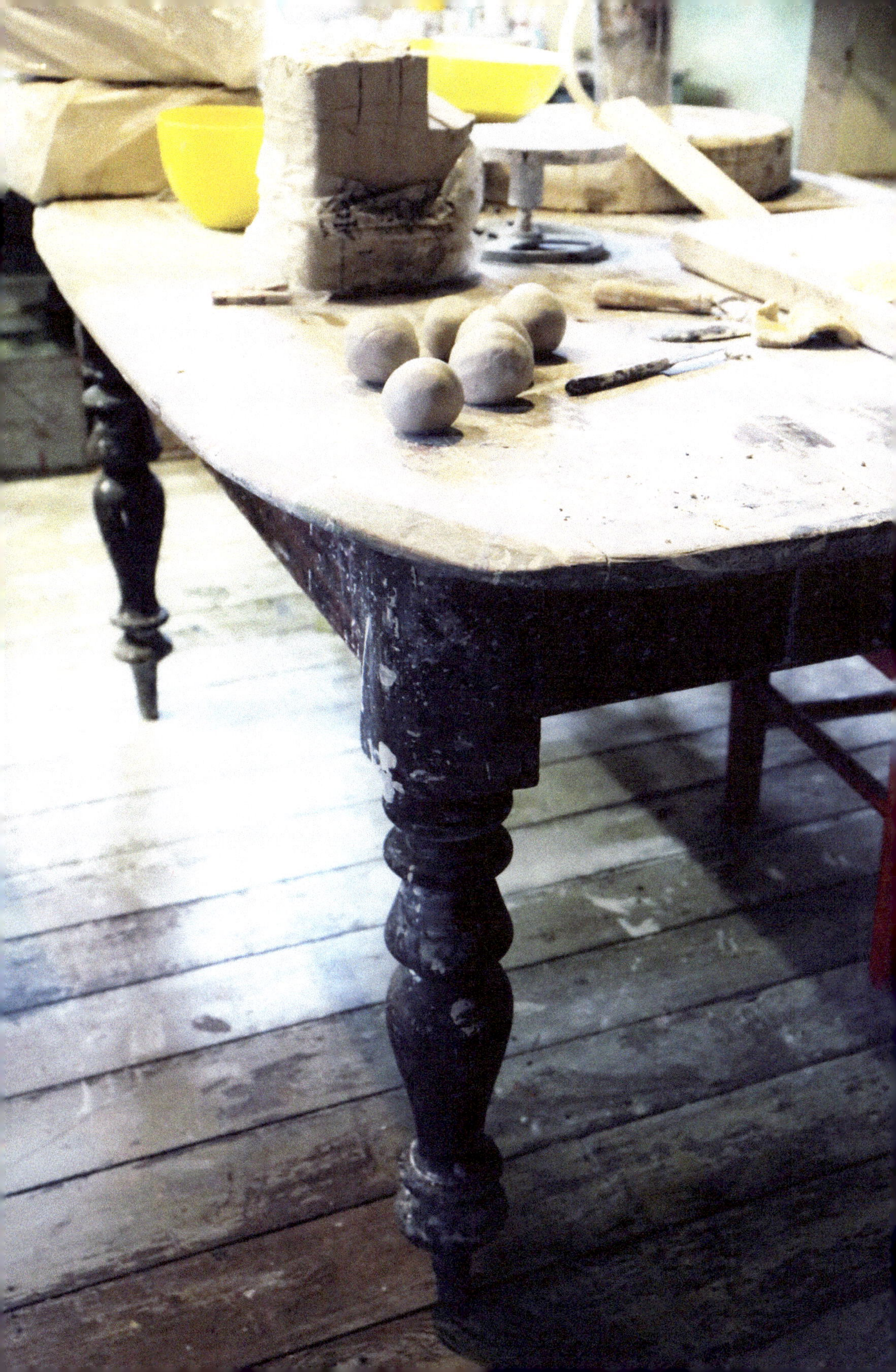

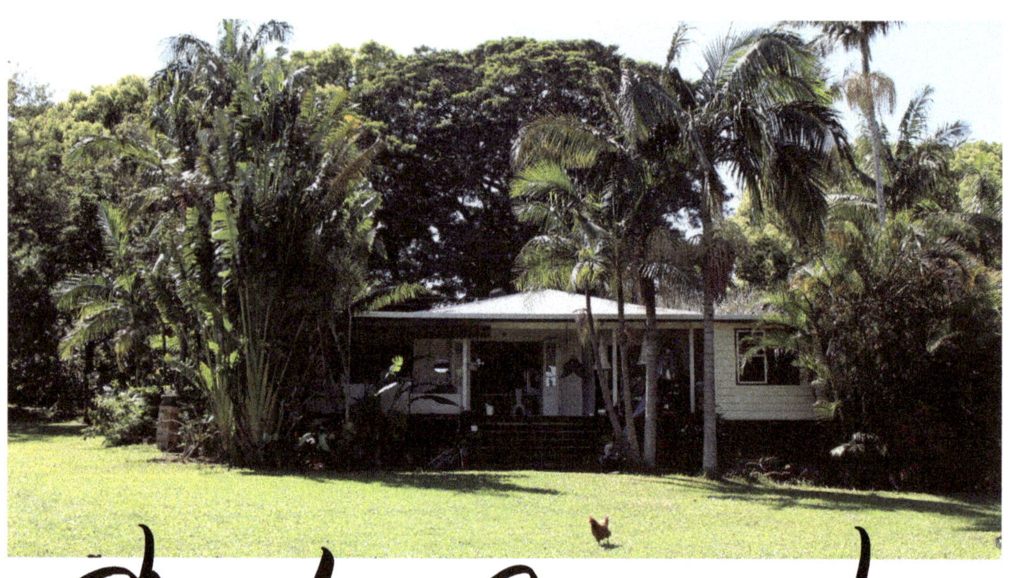

# Charly Wrencher

## On land and sea

Charly Wrencher emerges from his side verandah dangling a dead rat from its tail. It'd be a macabre greeting if it weren't for his school-kid grin, revealing one shiny golden tooth. "I'll just get rid of this," he laughs.

He's an expert at dealing with the critters these days, but it wasn't always so. When Charly, his wife Jane and their young children arrived on this Coorabell property in 2002, he says they were totally unprepared for life in the hinterland.

"We were so naive at first and it was really hard," says the former Sydney-sider. "We ran out of water and our septic system overflowed, all those things happened that country people take for granted." As well as snakes, rats, bedbugs, chicken pox and a dreaded family dose of whooping cough. But the couple was determined to make it work.

This 68-acre property is owned by Charly's parents, who run a boutique organic coffee farm where pine trees once grew. The land is also shared with Charly's brother and his family. "My parents were going to rent this house out and I said, don't get strangers to come and live on the property, rent it out to us. It was the right timing." Not only were the Wrencher's sick of city life, the tiny Coorabell community also needed them; numbers at the local primary school had dwindled to just 30 kids, so any new family made a big impact. And then there were the neighbours. "There used to be bikers on the property, so there was a lot of dark energy here," Charly says. "Margaret across the road started baking us cakes when we got here. She was so relieved that a family had moved back in."

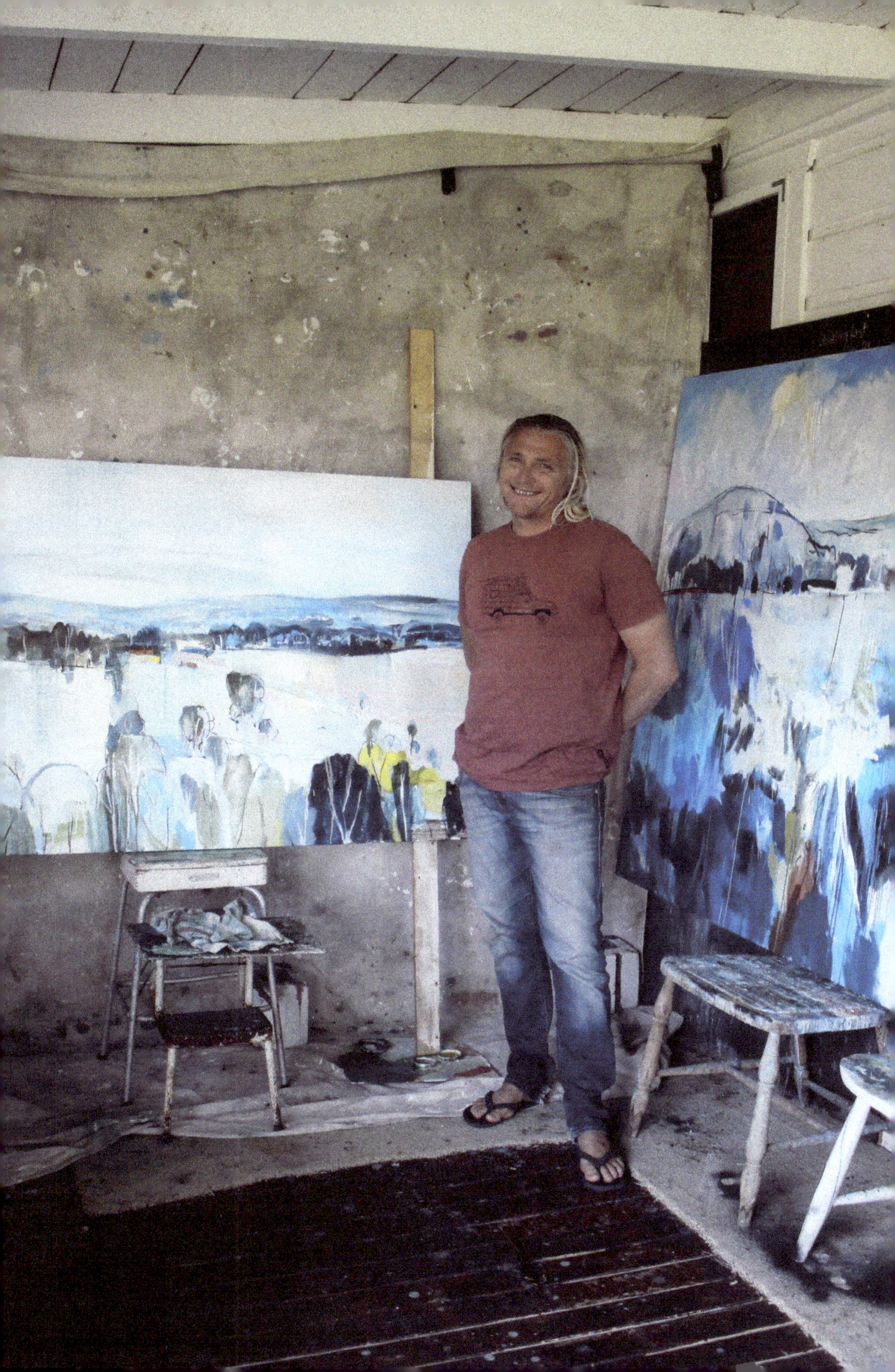

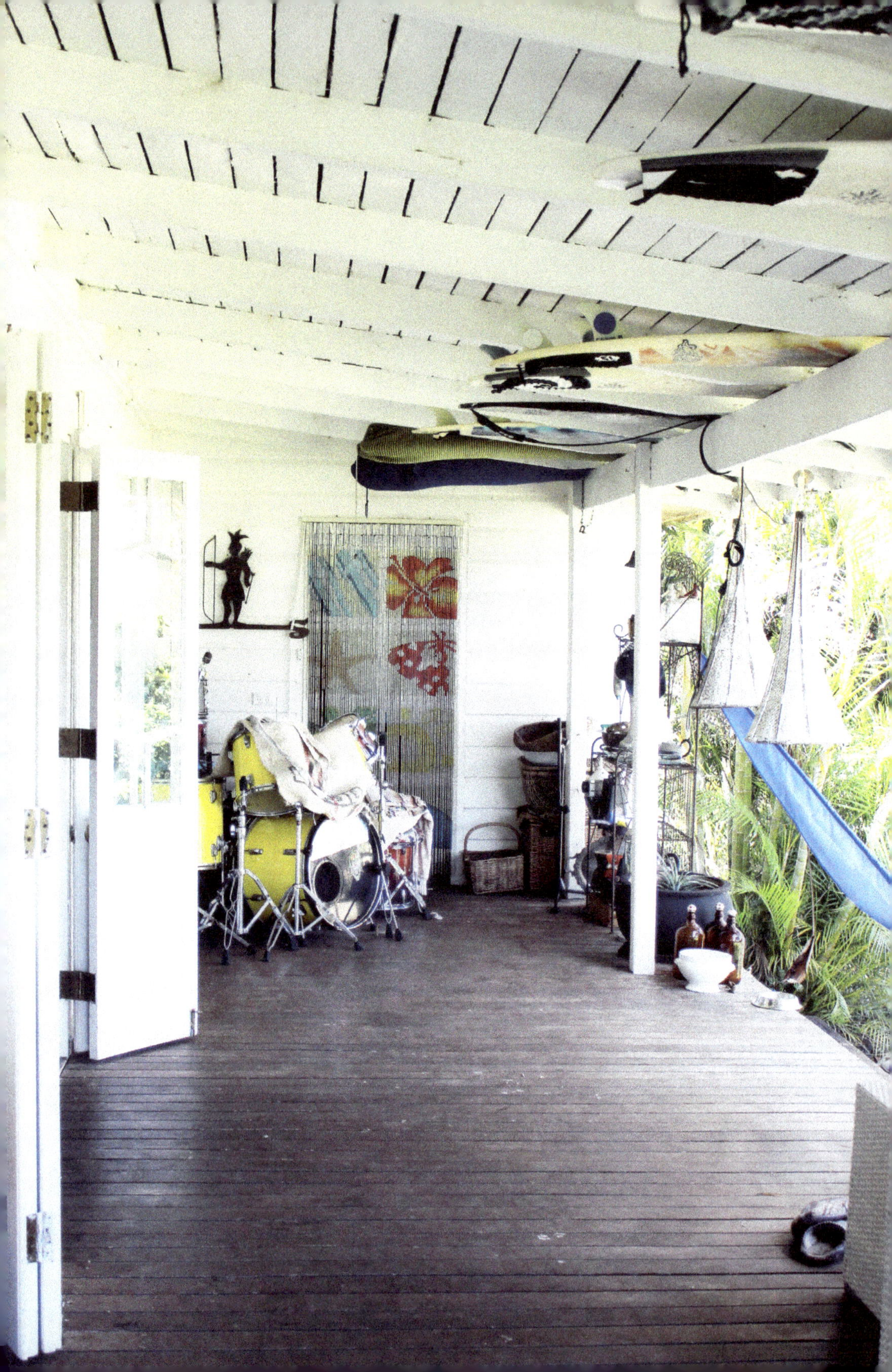

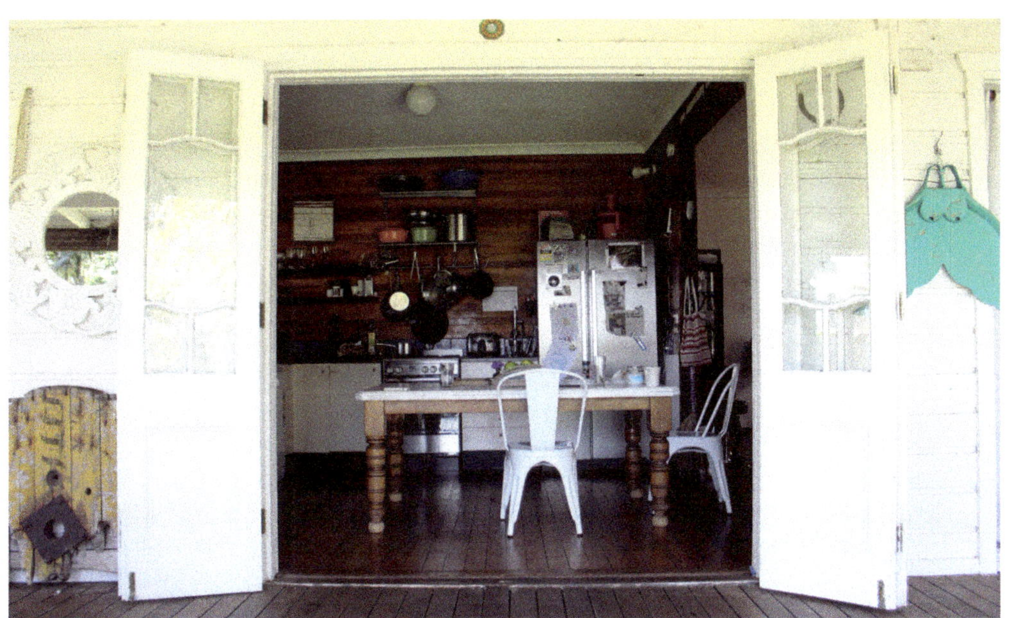

"It was very confronting, because it kind of felt like moving back to Mum and Dad's in my 30s. They've got six grandkids on the property now. We do live in close quarters, although we can have a week where we don't see each other. But on the weekend if you hear music at one of the houses you can go down and have a drink, so it's good socially."

Not everyone welcomed them though. Their classic Queenslander is the oldest house on Friday Hut Road. It'd had a colourful 100-plus year past and not all residents had vacated. "It's definitely haunted," Charly says. "We've come to terms with it now and we're okay. I was never superstitious until we had those experiences." Bumps in the night, waking to shrieks and coloured swirls. "One night I went into a room and it was the classic case of feeling like I'd walked into a refrigerator. We actually got a psychic to come in and she said there was definitely stuff going on. She said because we're from Celtic origins that we had to use Celtic remedies, like placing rosemary under the doormats." Charly and Jane still constantly 'cleanse' the house with sage sticks.

Sitting under the wide back verandah with a Friday Hut coffee, Charly's open-air studio beside, the family surfboards overhead and the Coorabell valley out yonder, there's only good vibes here now. It's easy to understand why this place has had a big impact on Charly's art. "Being a landscape artist I have to be in the landscape, the environment is what inspires me," he says. "Since I've been here I've never been so busy in my life. You'd think the Byron Bay area was chilled out. This is definitely a nice place to be creative, but it's a nice place to do nothing as well. For people to be creative here they have to be really driven."

The artist was born in London, and moved to Australia with his family when he was 11. Moving "from grey London to technicolour Australia" had a positive impact on the young creative, and there were family influences, too. His father was a photographer; his uncle an animator. Charly trained at Sydney's National Art School and graduated believing he would go on to paint large-scale abstract works. That was until he took a lap of the continent in the early 1990s.

"That's when I realised I was a landscape painter," he says. "I realised I was really passionate about the landscape and it was quite a surprise." Until moving to the Northern Rivers he said he'd largely paint his landscapes by memory, drawing on his regular travels, but here the fodder is literally spread out around him.

"Since coming here I'm not un-inspired yet," he says. His paintings are semi-abstract, elevated views of sea and forest, hills and valleys. "You'll notice when you're driving around here you're always looking out over the landscape." Same can be said from this verandah. "From here I can be in the landscape, and the whole house becomes my studio in a way. It's part of my life, the kids are connected to the paintings, everyone's connected." And not only through the art.

This is a close-knit family. They begin each morning at sunrise, taking the ten-minute drive down to the surf together, usually to Cosy Corner at Tallow Beach underneath the Cape Byron lighthouse. It's their daily source of exercise and inspiration. "It's everything from the drive down to the sunrise," Charly says. "I get a lot of inspiration from it. It's about immersing myself in the ocean. Diving into nature. Positive ions. It's forced meditation to clear your head."

Coming face-to-face with Mother Nature does have its responsibilities though. The week Charly shares his story here, the local papers are full of opinions on the latest shark attack. The victim is the best mate of Charly's brother's apprentice.

"There's so many sharks now," he says. "After 20 years of being protected they've been left to breed and they've got no predators. Their food source has been fished out off shore so the only place to feed is close to shore. It doesn't stop us surfing. It's about intuition. You feel it. You know when not to go there. I used to surf at 5.30am in the dark and not feel worried but now we stick together and look out for each other. That's just been in the last couple of years – but you don't want to get bitten by a shark, hey." ■

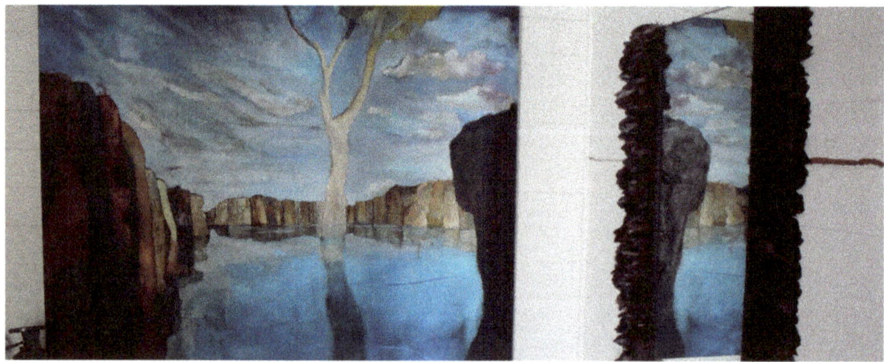

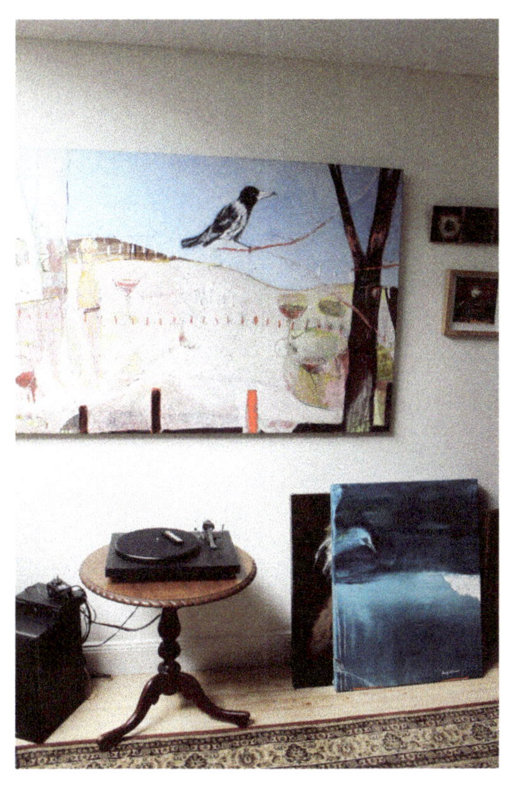

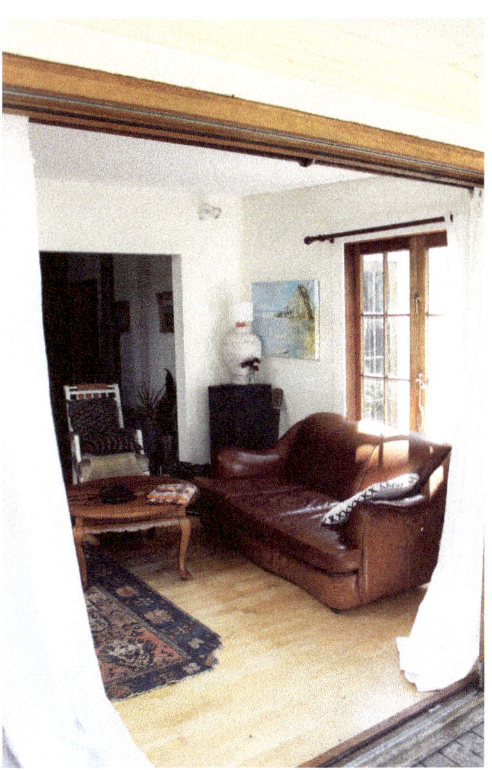

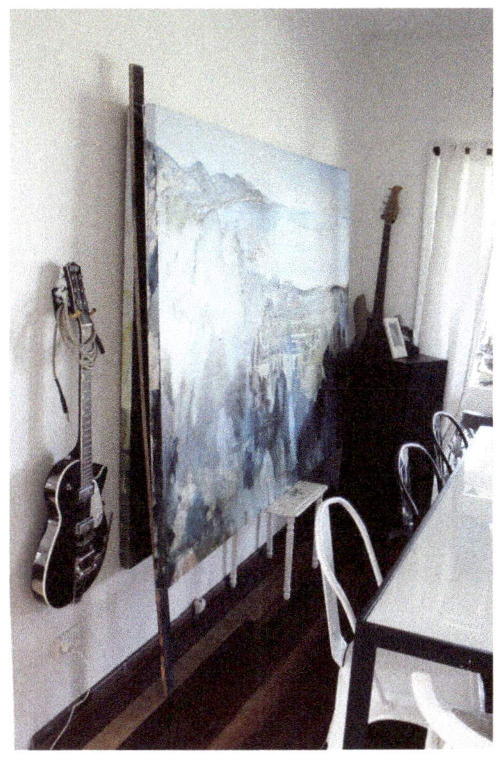

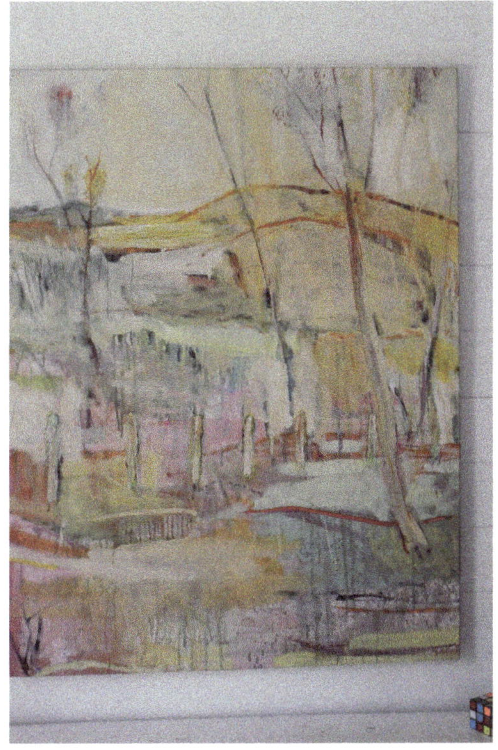

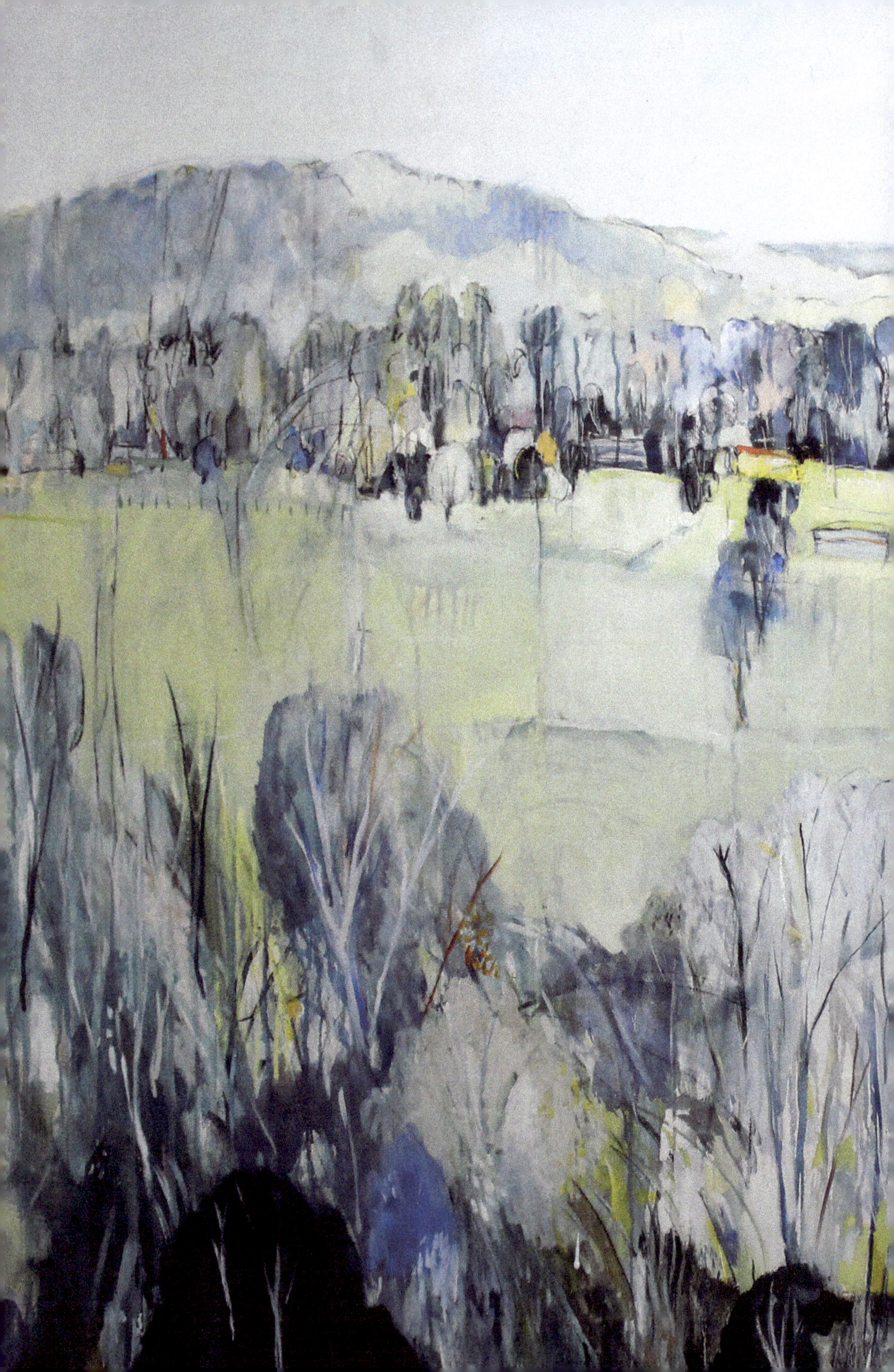

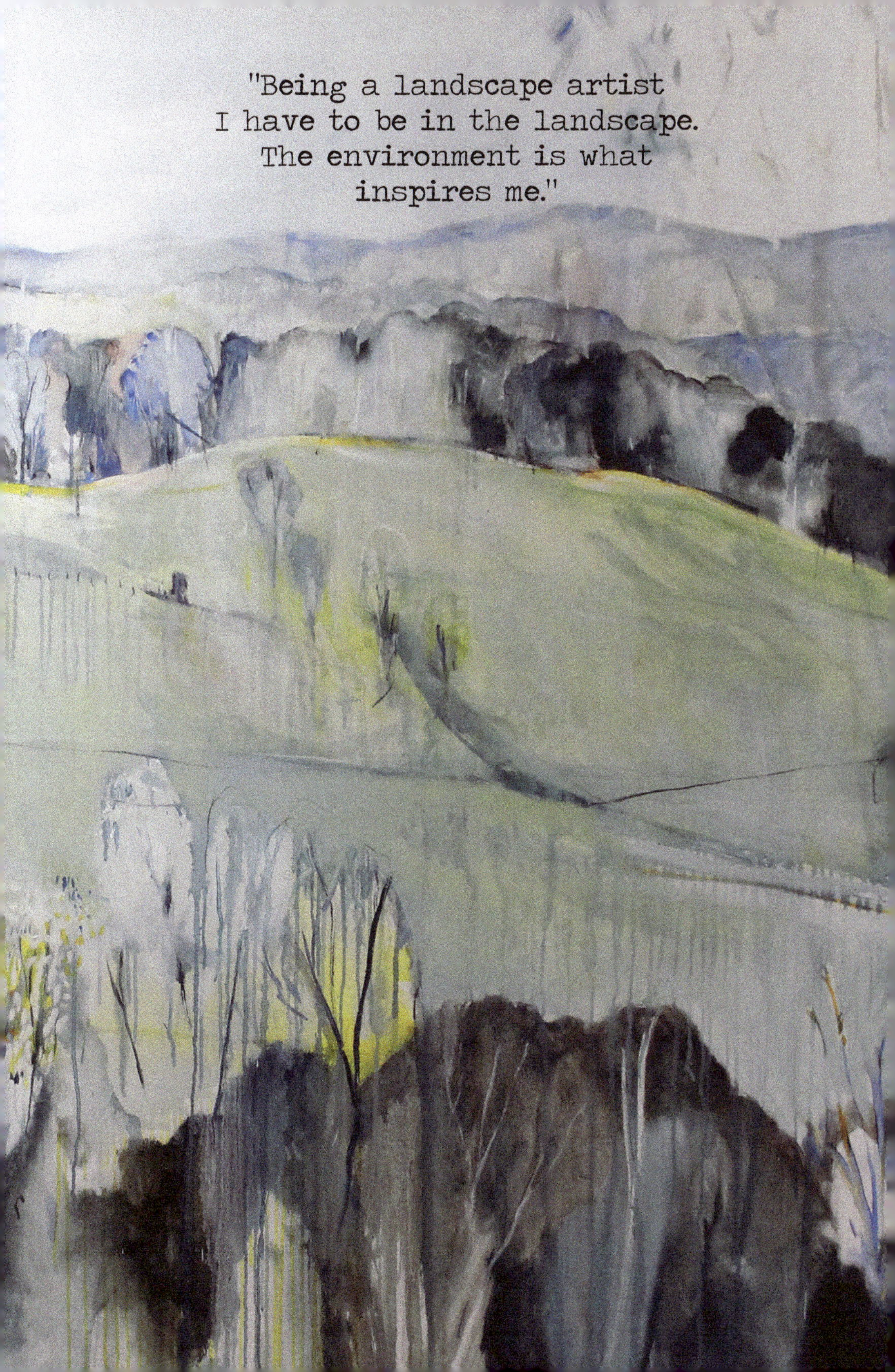
"Being a landscape artist
I have to be in the landscape.
The environment is what
inspires me."

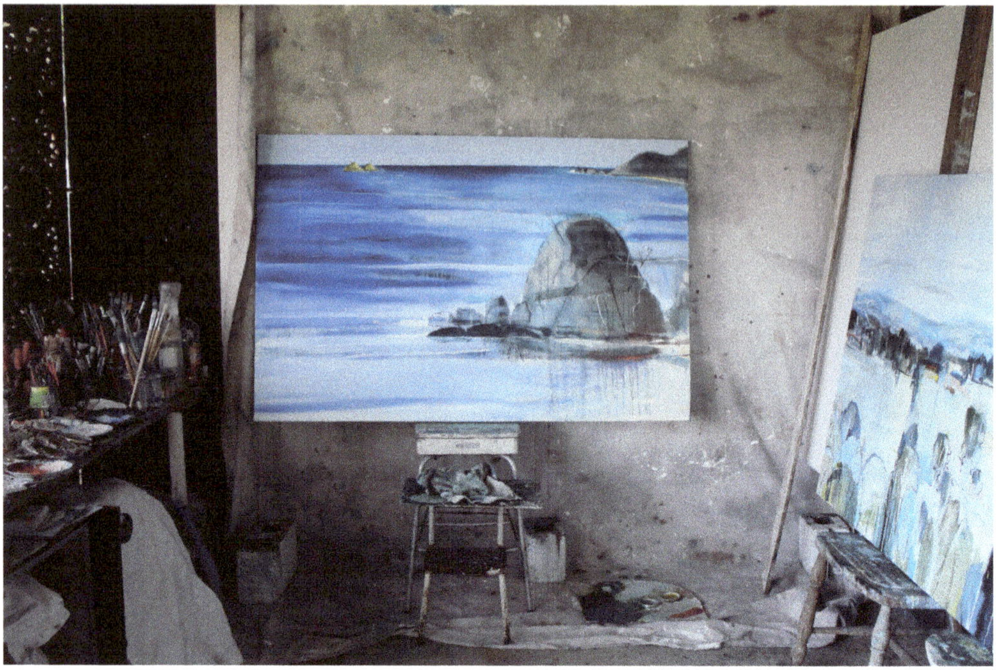

*The family begin each morning at sunrise, taking the ten-minute drive down to the surf together.*

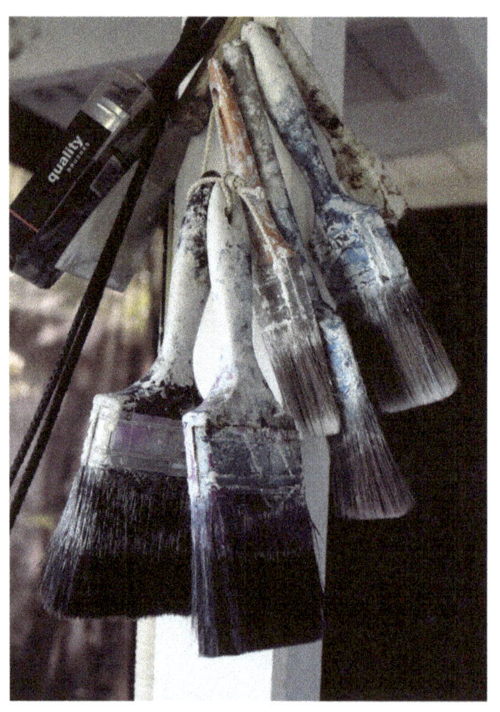


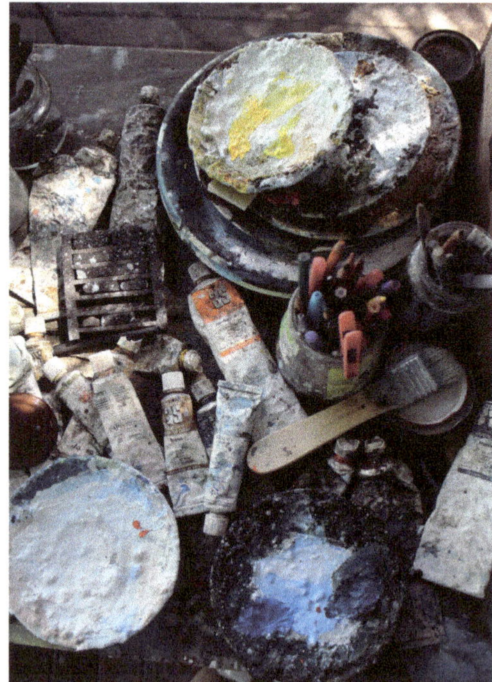

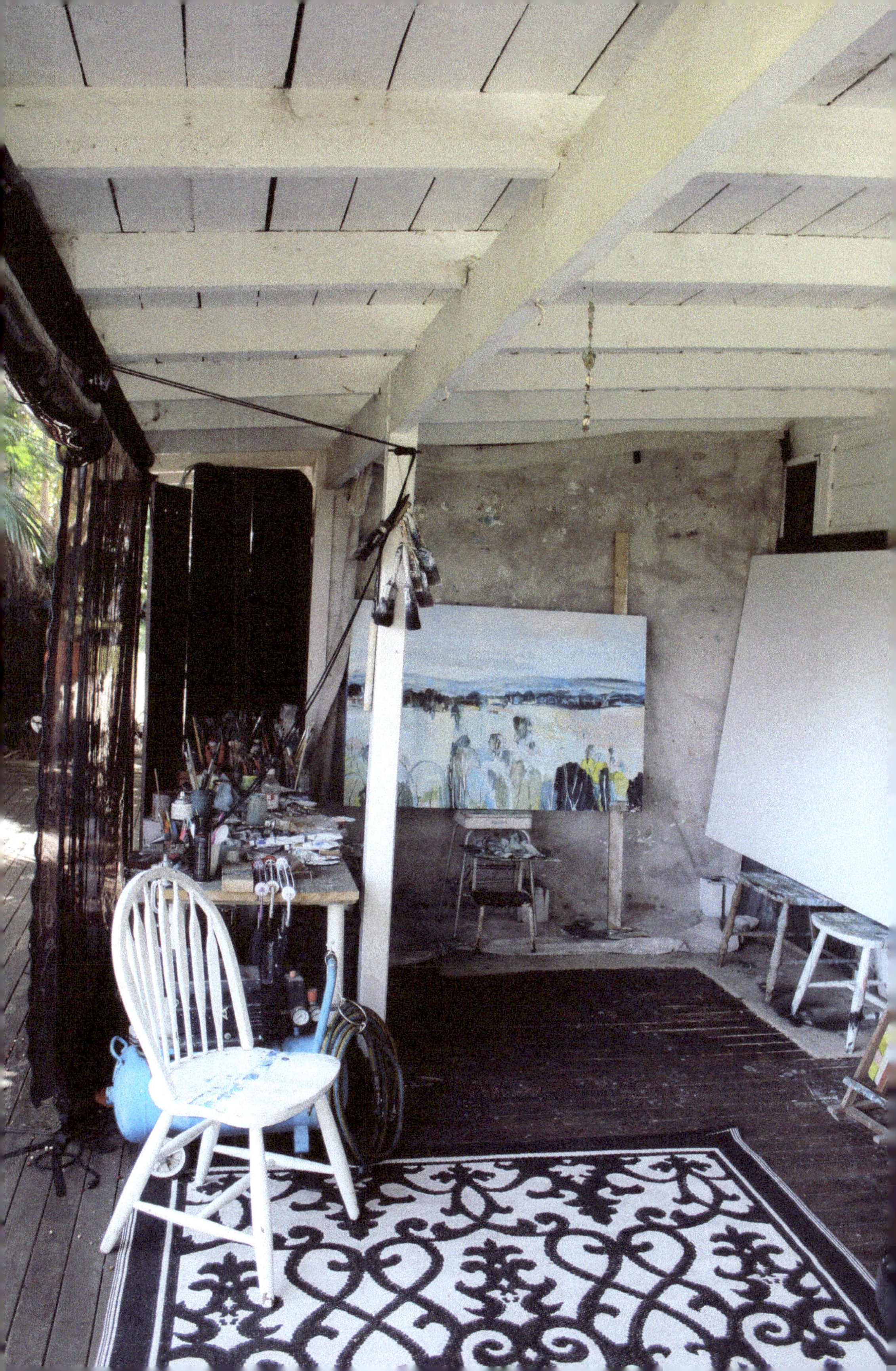

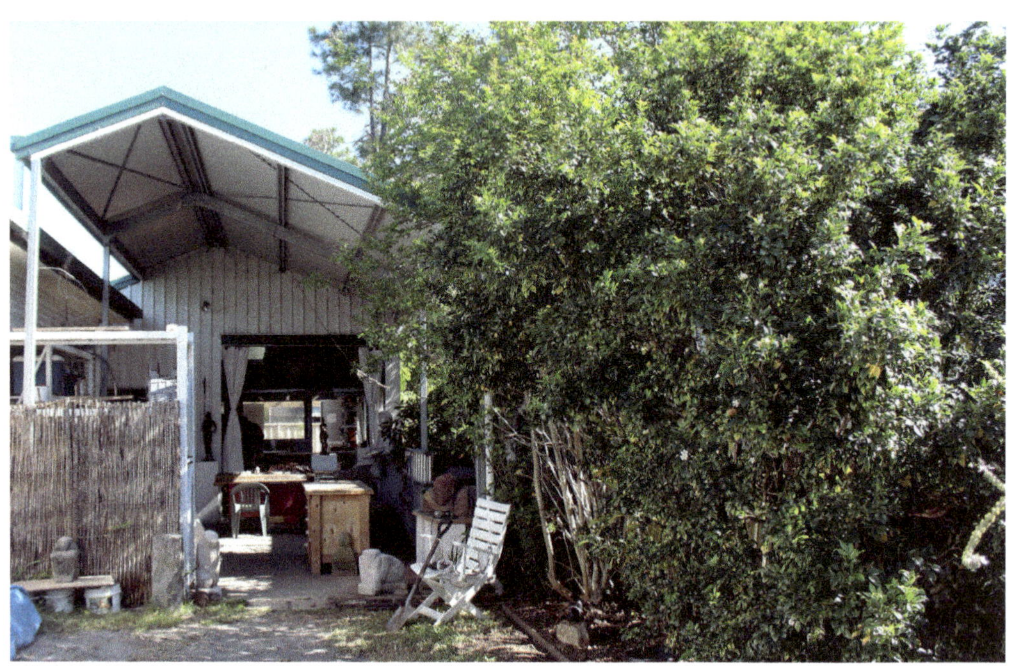

# Damien Lucas

## On social commentary

Past Lismore's Northern Rivers Hotel, under the railway bridge and opposite the servo is Damien Lucas' place. It's one of a strip of leggy 1920s weatherboards along Terania Street. Each a little world-weary, as is to be expected after almost a century on stilts. Past Damien's high picket fence, however, there's nothing predictable.

First of all, there's Florence of Terania; a brown and white border collie with a penchant for fetch and occasionally nicking off; hence the high fence. This is a place of characters, some living and breathing, others firmly set in stone. Or bronze, to be exact.

Damien bought this property in early 2015 for the shed. It's a great space where others may have parked a Holden or two. For the sculptor it had the bones of the perfect studio. "It was a bit of a cave actually," he says of its once pale brown walls. He painted those walls white and added clear panels on the rear wall to let in the diffused southern light, which is best for sculpting. Then Damien was ready to work here, plus welcome student sculptors and community life drawing classes. A daybed by the breezy roller door entrance has hosted a steady stream of willing models.

The studio walls are lined with miniature works. Scaled-down reliefs of large bronze sculptures dotted throughout the country. They're the perfect

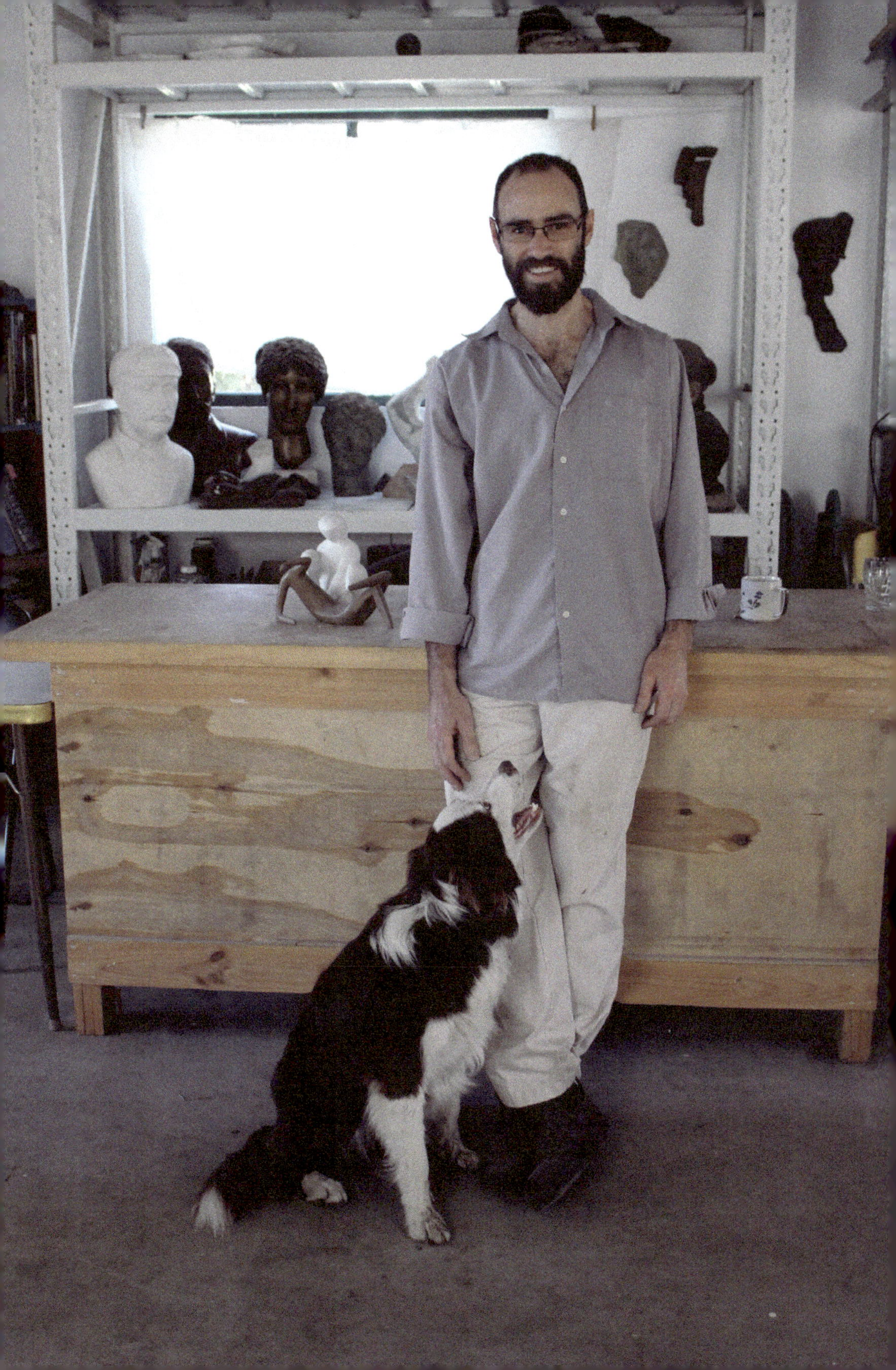

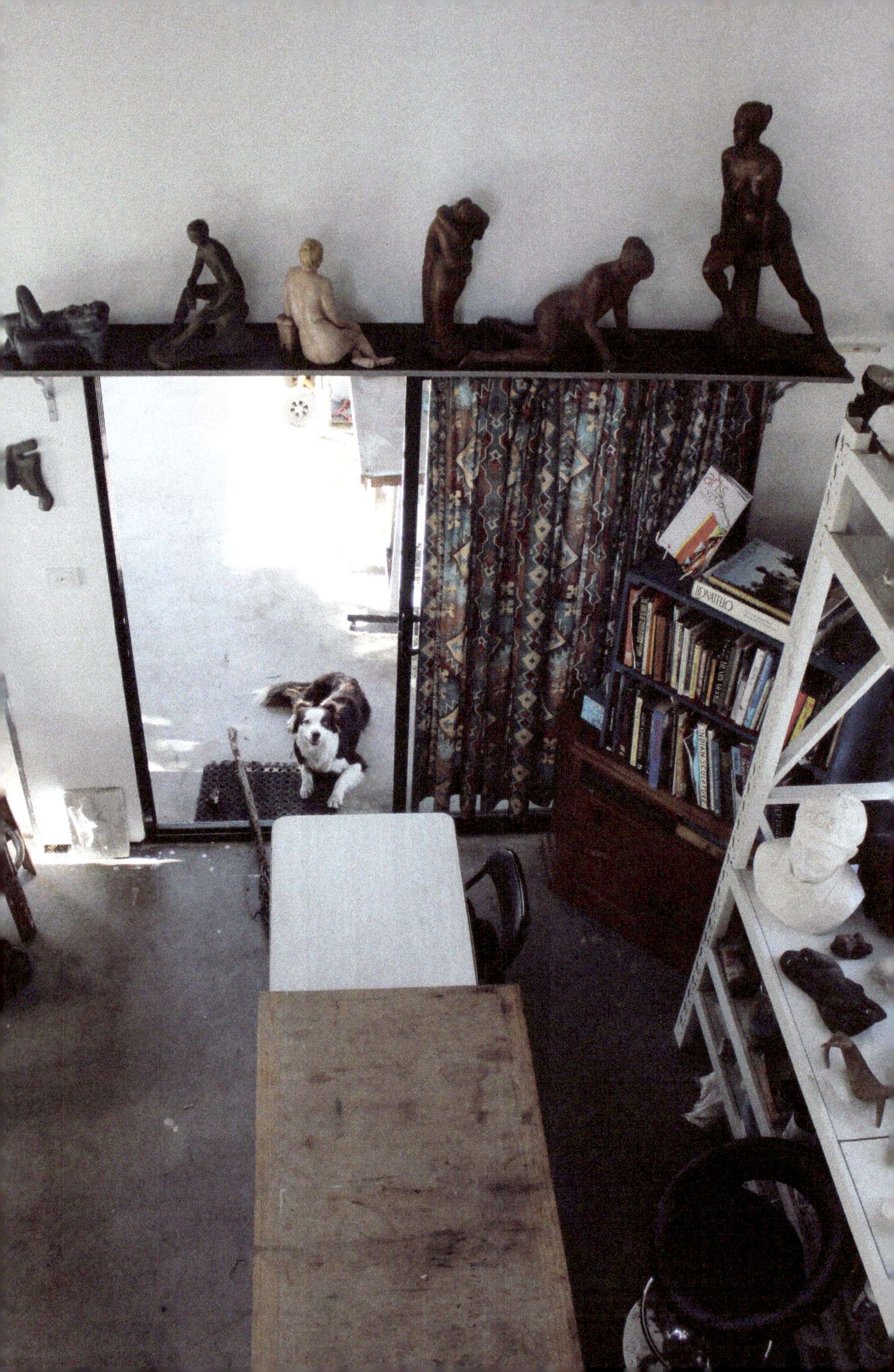
DONATELLO
INDIAN SCULPTURE

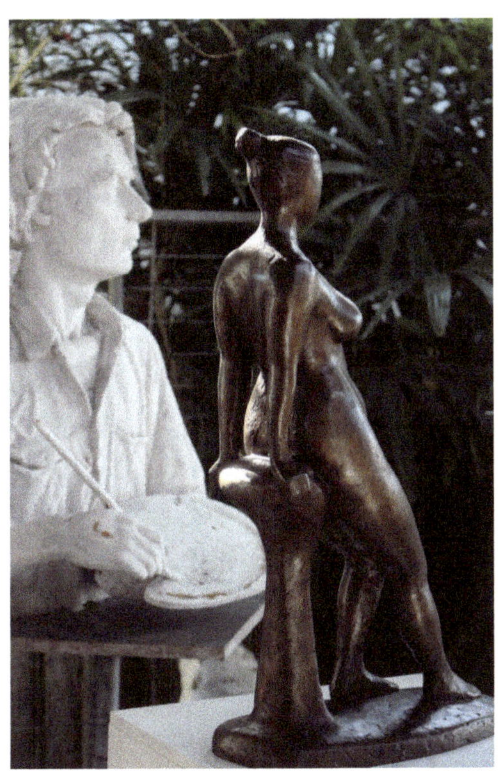

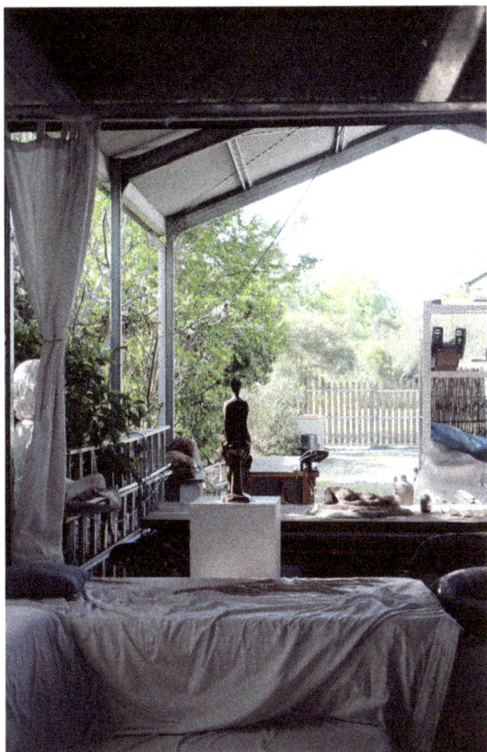

proof that from little things, big things grow. The same could be said for Damien's progression as an artist.

He was living in Bathurst in his 20s and working as a meter reader when he first started taking painting and drawing classes in his spare time. His teacher commented one day that he drew like a sculptor, and his curiosity was piqued.

The teacher handed Damien a brochure for the Tom Bass Sculpture School in Sydney and said it was worth the weekly train ride to attend classes if he could manage it. The school is Australia's oldest and most respected institution dedicated to teaching sculpture in the classic atelier tradition. At that stage its founder, Tom Bass, was 81 and still very much active in teaching. He was to change Damien's life.

Damien says it was a leap of faith to eventually quit the security of a full-time job to pursue an ancient art form. "It was one of the few times in my life that my mum said, if you don't do it, you'll never know." Damien's family saw Tom had made a career out of being a sculptor and that he was willing to nurture their son.

"It awakened a calling in me," Damien says. "Tom was 81 when I went to study with him and he lived to almost 94. I studied and worked with Tom for most of that time under an apprenticeship model. It's pretty rare. I was only planning on going for a year. I thought I could learn all I needed to know about sculpture in that time."

Damien has followed his mentor's ethos of making sculpture for communities, rather than galleries, as it was always intended to be. "Sculpture used to be a social communicator. Even people who couldn't read could 'read' the symbols in a sculpture," Damien says.

Damien received his first public commission at just 27 years of age, when he was enlisted to create the 'pioneering woman' for the Stockman's Hall of Fame in Longreach. She was to represent the sisterhood among the cowboys of central west Queensland.

"Some people said the pioneering woman should have been made by a woman," Damien says. "But in the end I felt I became more empathetic to the women of that time in a way." For research he read the poetry of Banjo Paterson, looked at historic photographs of period clothing and enlisted a live model.

Subsequent commissions have included a piece for a Steiner property at Mittagong and the busts of cricket captains in situ at Cootamundra and Sunbury, such as legendary Englishman Ivo Bligh, who played in the first Ashes. Damien says he doesn't follow cricket, but no doubt his nanna's second cousin, Don Bradman, would have approved.

Public works aside, some of Damien's favourite pieces are the more abstract sculptures he creates purely because they're calling him. At an average of 100-to-300 hours to complete one piece, that's a loud calling, but the ideas keep coming.

Damien says he loves the thought of one day making a sculpture for his adopted home town.

"I really like the idea of making something for Lismore because this place hasn't really got traditional or even abstract sculpture. It's a bit lacking in that sense," he says, even though the area boasts a higher-than-average percentage of people who make art or music. (When Damien put a call out for a housemate, painter Robyn was the perfect fit. She has a studio down the road, but the front deck of this house has also proved a great place to paint.)

The artist says his ideas for Lismore may seem lofty, but this place needs something big, à la David of Florence. "A spirit for the city," he says. Because it's certainly got spirit in spades. This was proven in early 2014, when Damien joined the protest against drilling for coal seam gas at nearby Bentley.

"On my first night of protesting there were three of us sitting in the driveway to this property and when I went back a couple of weeks later there were 7000 of us," he says. "It was farmers, business owners, Indigenous people, everyone who cared about the water and the land and it was a really unifying event."

The protest camp went on for several months, disbanding only when the New South Wales Resources and Energy department suspended the drilling license. It was seen as a triumph of community over multi-national company. A real David and Goliath battle. David of Lismore. That's got a nice ring to it, actually. ■

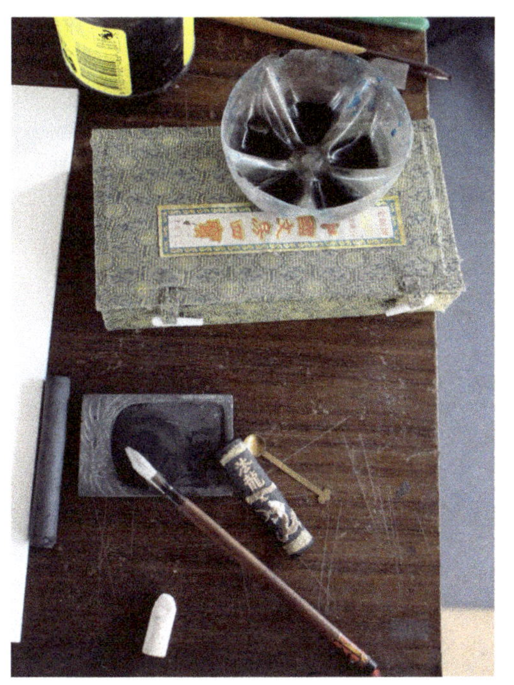

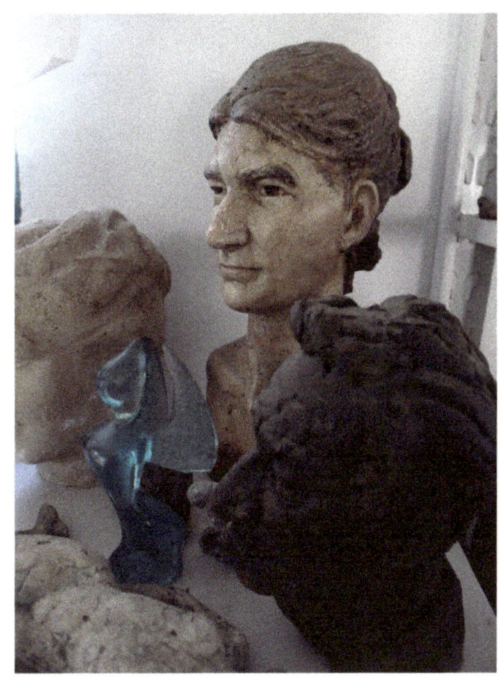

*The studio is lined with scaled down reliefs of large bronze sculptures dotted throughout the country.*

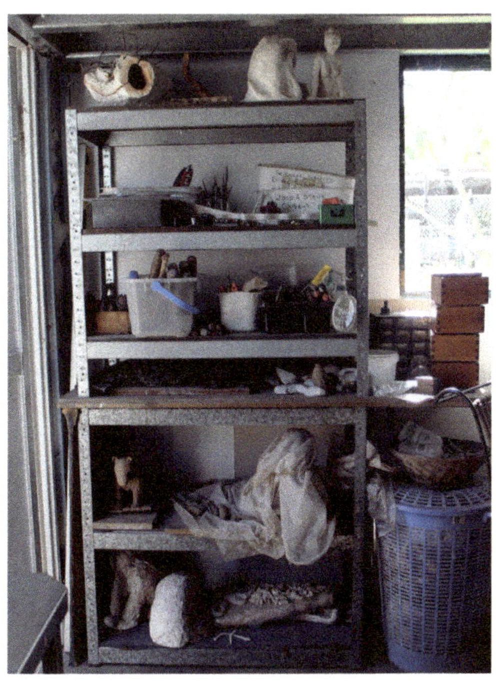

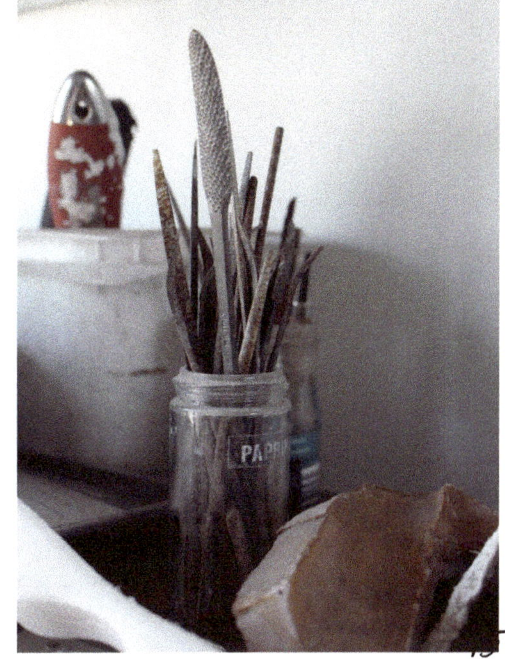

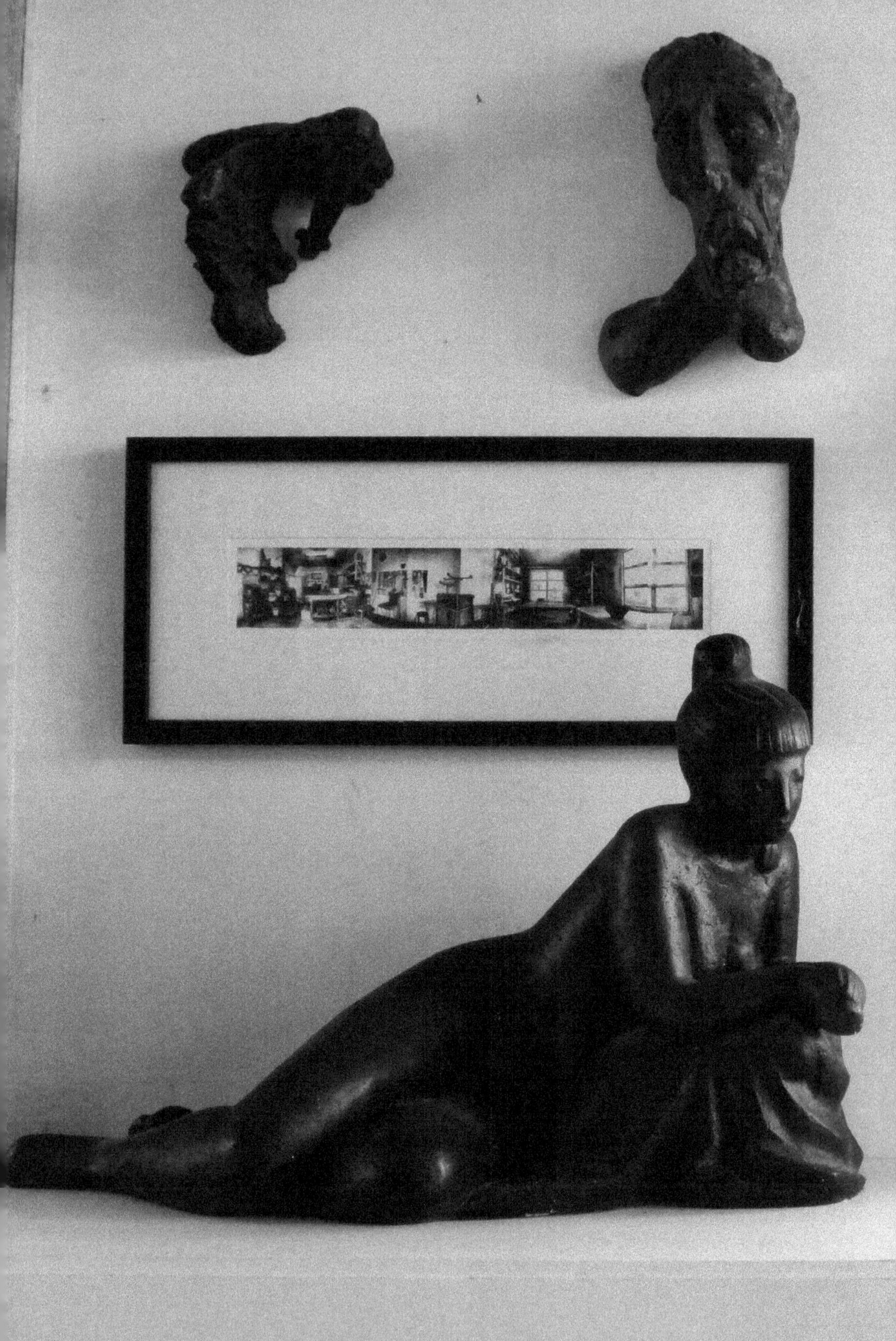

"Sculpture used to be a social communicator. Even people who couldn't read could 'read' the symbols in a sculpture."

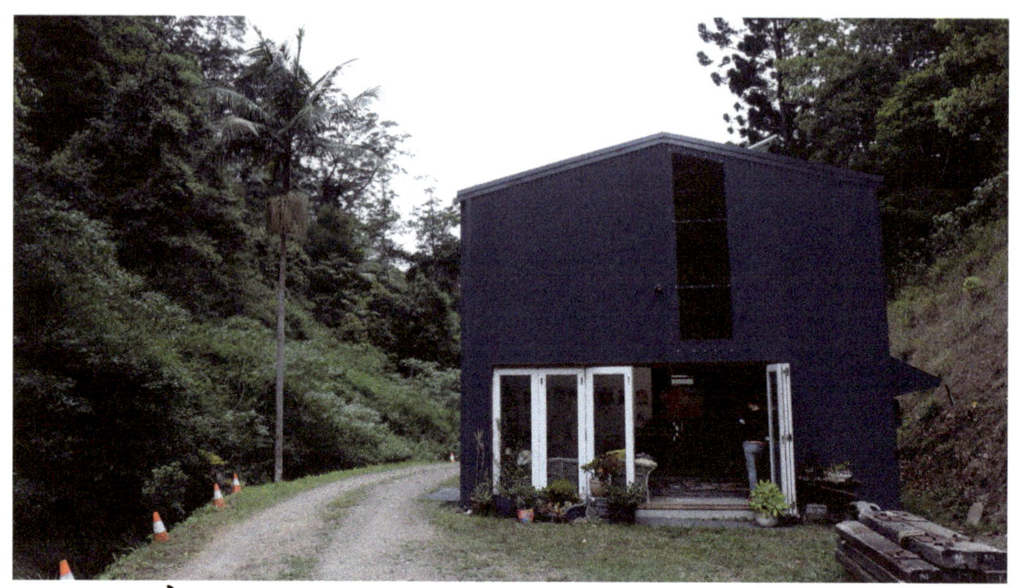

# Alex Hudson

## Under creation's canopy

There's a long way 'round in most of life's endeavours, and it's worth taking on the way to Main Arm. Drive the Pocket Road with your windows down and inhale liberally. This place has a scent you could bottle and bank your house on. Mint leaf lollies, toothpaste and sweet damp earth, taken and stirred.

Then again, tiny Main Arm has been commodified enough. Thanks to a generation spent cutting timber, much of the forest here is new growth, and on the road in to Alex Hudson's place, quarry trucks continue to take the very soil from its roots.

Alex, however, is more interested in what this place gives her. "It gives me a lot of time and space," she says. "And it gives me nature. The tranquillity of nature has always been good for me because I've always had a lot of mental and emotional clutter and this just seems to empty me out – the inspiration it gives is endless, its colour and forms. I've been here for 12 years but I grew up in the area. I was born in Lismore, grew up in Byron and lived all around the hills. I'm lucky to have grown up in such a beautiful place."

Alex lives on this off-grid five-acre property with her partner, Moses, and their young son. Their home is a couple of pavilions; one for sleeping, one for cooking and living, clustered between the folds of Main Arm mountainsides. Rising high on three sides is dense rare remnant forest, so steep it couldn't be felled.

At the base of the property, just off that quarry road, is Alex's studio. It's the only structure in proportion to the forest; lofty and stretching up to meet the sunlight. "My partner built this studio for me two years ago but before that I rented people's garages

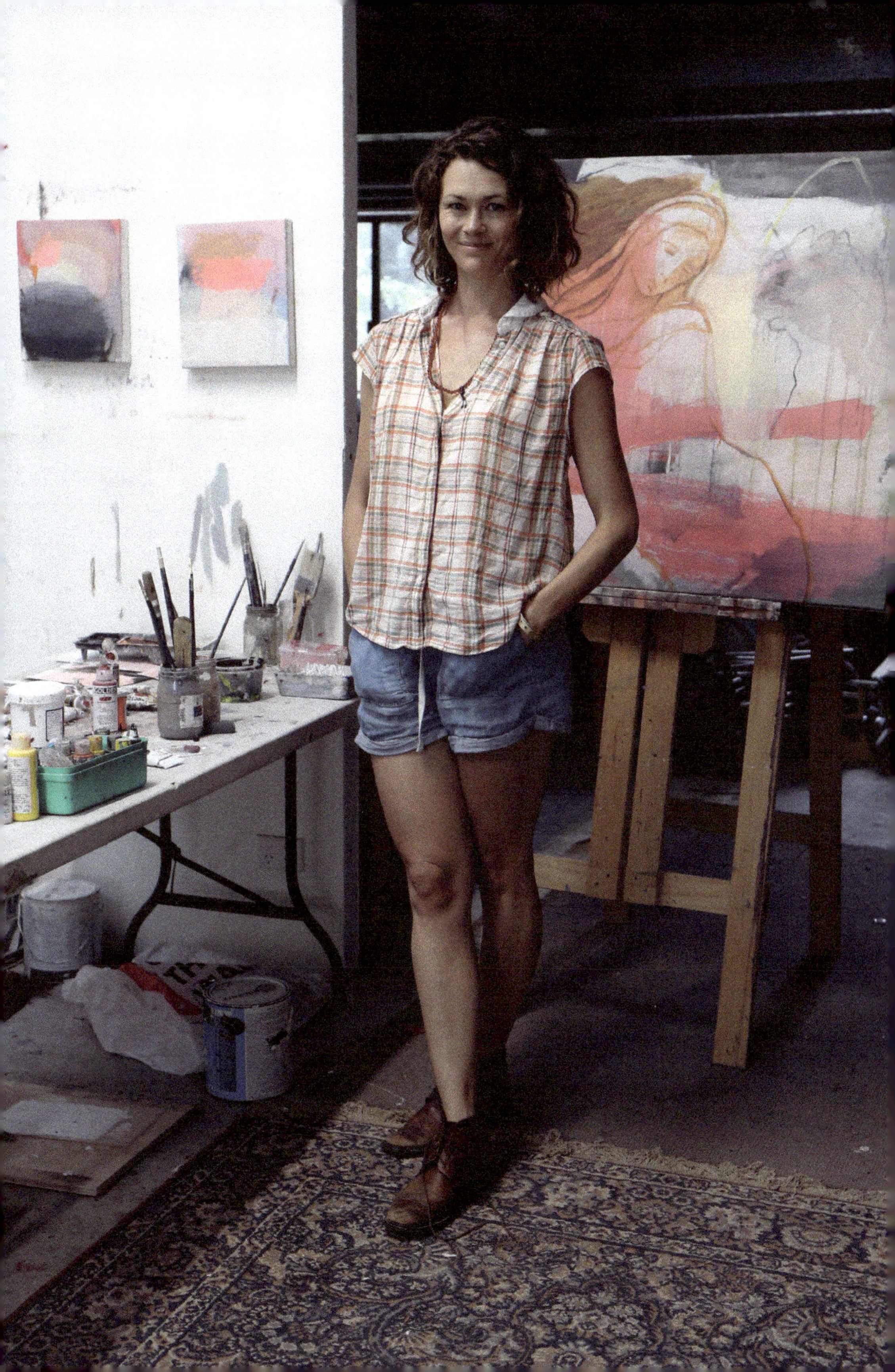

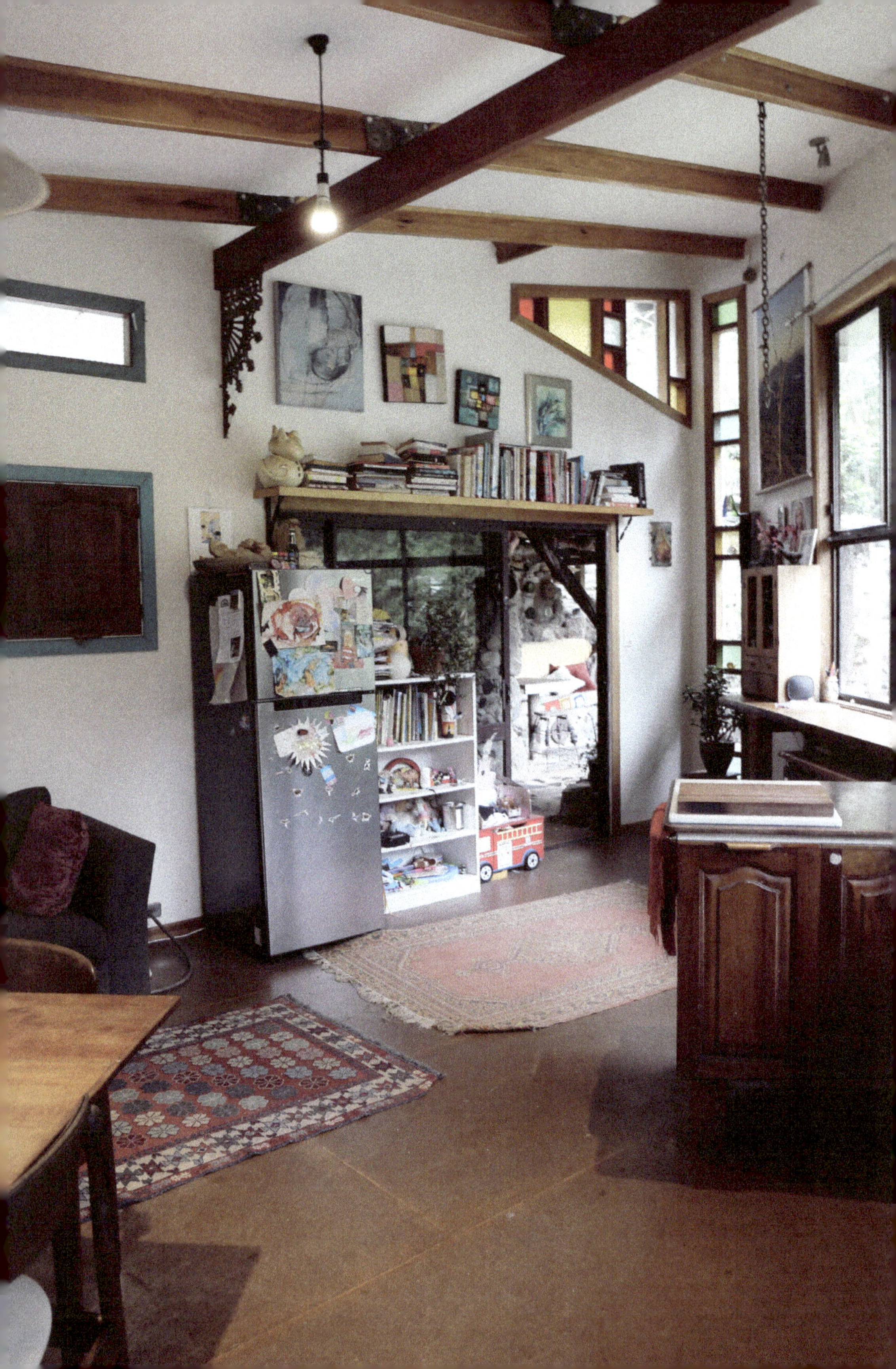

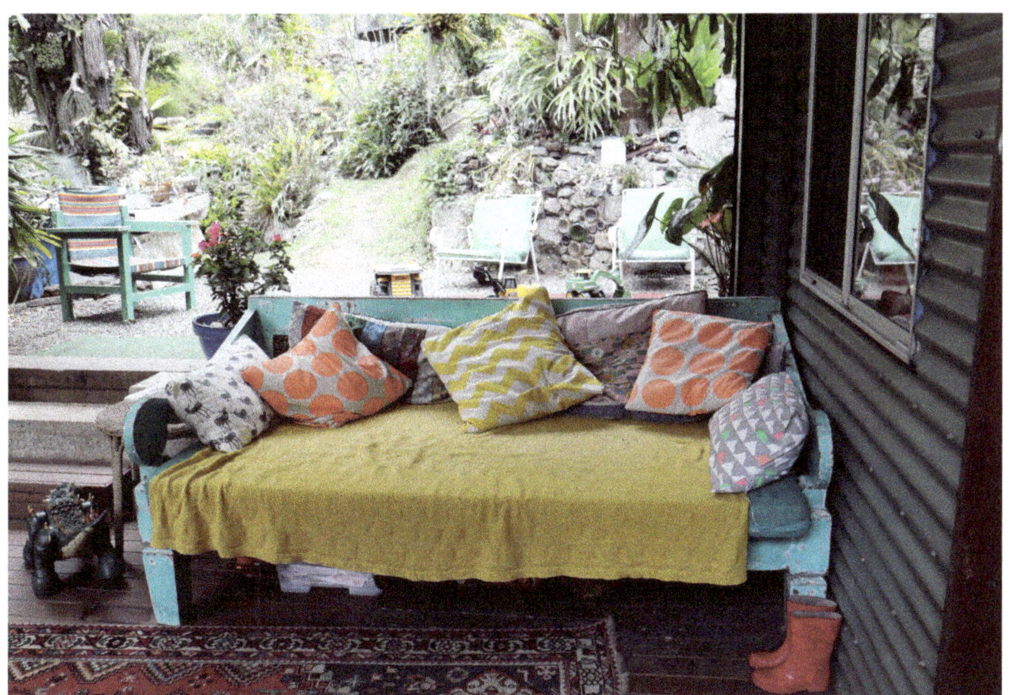

for a while," Alex says. "It's really nice to have my own space." It's a relaxed, lived-in space of rugs and daybeds, plants and paintings. So many paintings. Abstracted works created in a pursuit to delve deep and find an inner truth via art. For Alex, this quest began in her teens.

"I had a bit of a hard time at school – emotionally, not academically," Alex says. She had planned to study computers at university, but was also craving some breathing space. A local TAFE teacher caught wind of her art and convinced her to explore her creativity. "I did a year of Drawing Fundamentals at Lismore TAFE and I didn't look back," she says. It became a short-cut to success. "I was really lucky in that I started exhibiting early. I had my first solo show when I was 20."

Over the next ten years, Alex exhibited in a long string of successful group and solo shows around Australia. Then, life happened. Alex took a five-year hiatus from her art to care for her mum, who was terminally ill.

"I had already started to burn out creatively and with the constant worry and pressure of Mum's illness, I eventually put it aside to be with Mum for the last period of her earthly existence," Alex says. "I ended up living and caring for her with my sisters during my pregnancy and she passed days after my son, Oscar, was born. It was an incredibly difficult time, but also gave me the most deeply profound, beautiful and truthful life moments I have, and probably will ever, experience."

Alex's son was born right here on this property, just as his dad had been. The family connection to this place runs deep. "My partner's father bought this property 40 years ago," Alex says. "He was part of the alternative movement, which was what brought him here from Luxembourg."

Moses' father, Jean-Pierre, followed the philosophies of Friedrich Nietzsche, who was interested in the enhancement of individual and cultural health through creativity and down-to-earth realities, rather than those imposed by the wider western world. "He believed the way to get to know your true self was to strip yourself bare of everything society wants and expects of you," Alex says. There was no better place to do that than right here, with a freshwater spring for bathing, timber for fuel and sun, moon and fireflies for light.

Jean-Pierre built water tanks and retaining walls out of recycled bottles, and dug the ultimate tiny house out of the hillside, featuring stone walls, recycled windows and a slow combustion stove. "This was our everything for the first six years of our relationship," Alex says of the single room. Later, Moses added the living pavilion and deck.

"It's pretty magical, really, but I do sometimes have issues with the isolation and the work of it. There are times when I just want to be in my studio and not worry about the gardening. I have moments where I struggle with the lack of contact with people. The suburban dream of smelling other people's food and hearing their morning routines can seem appealing. But I've worked out I just need to travel each year to get the balance."

Alex speaks about her recent travels to Greece. "Being in a different environment, landscape and culture was really invigorating," she says. It was also a great escape from winter, when those steep, timbered mountainsides allow for just four hours of sunlight a day.

For Alex, art is a distilling and outpouring of life's experiences and emotions. It's been a way to help comprehend life's happiness and tragedy. A way back to herself. "A couple of years after my mum died I found myself asking, 'Wow, where am I? And what about my art? How do I get that back? I needed to get back into my practice but I felt very isolated from it, as though it was a long way away. All I can say is thank god for the Byron School of Art."

Alex was one of the first students to enrol in the new school in 2014. "The one-year course I enrolled in turned into three years," she says. "Life's a lot better now because of it, that's for sure." As she speaks, Alex is preparing for a show at Yellow Brick Studio, an artist-run cooperative in Murwillumbah. Since having her first solo show in ten years in 2015 she has continued to exhibit frequently. She's back on track with her art, in more ways than one.

"The creative process has become a way for me to navigate the world, especially my inner experience and relationship to it," she says. "I view my work as psychological and emotional landscapes. For me, it's where the material and immaterial meet. This presents endless possibilities and questions, and the work becomes a vehicle for reflection, frustrations, possible reconciliation and hopefully, the odd revelation."

Some of those revelations are scrawled on Alex's studio walls, such as the profoundly simple, 'what I am is enough'. It's certainly a truth worth travelling for. ■

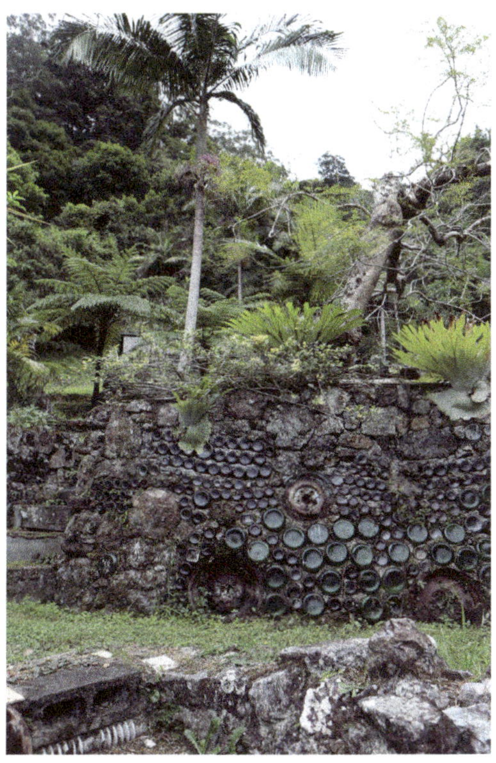
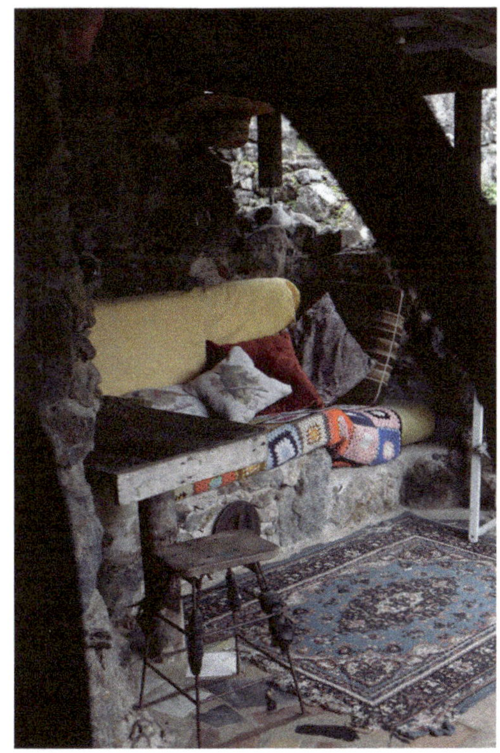
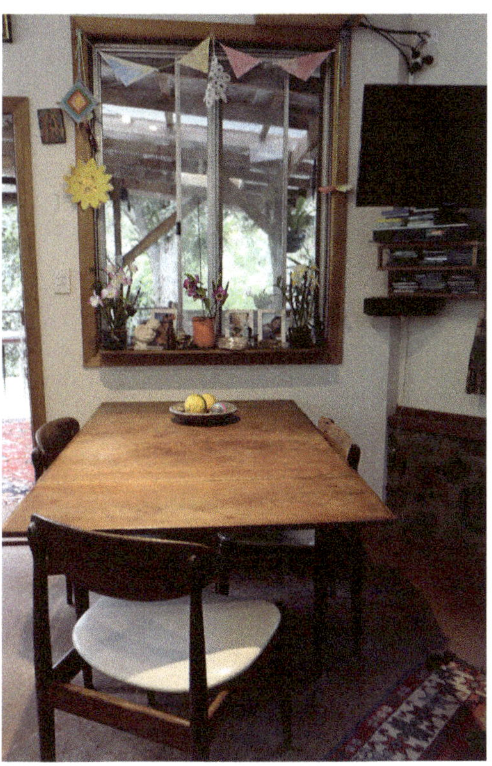
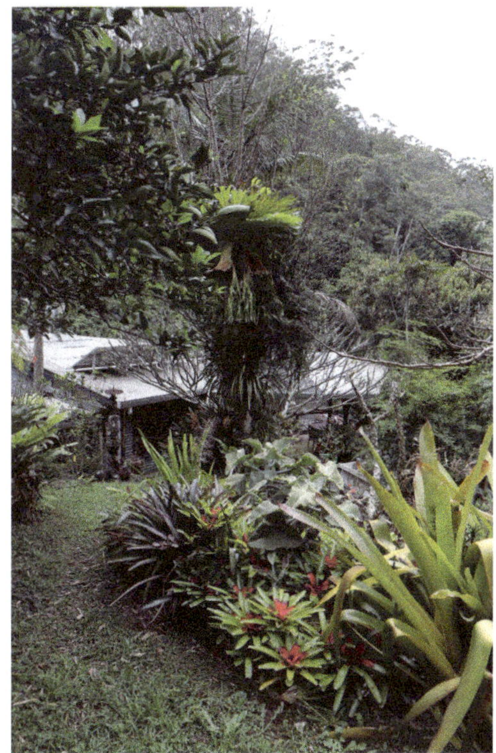

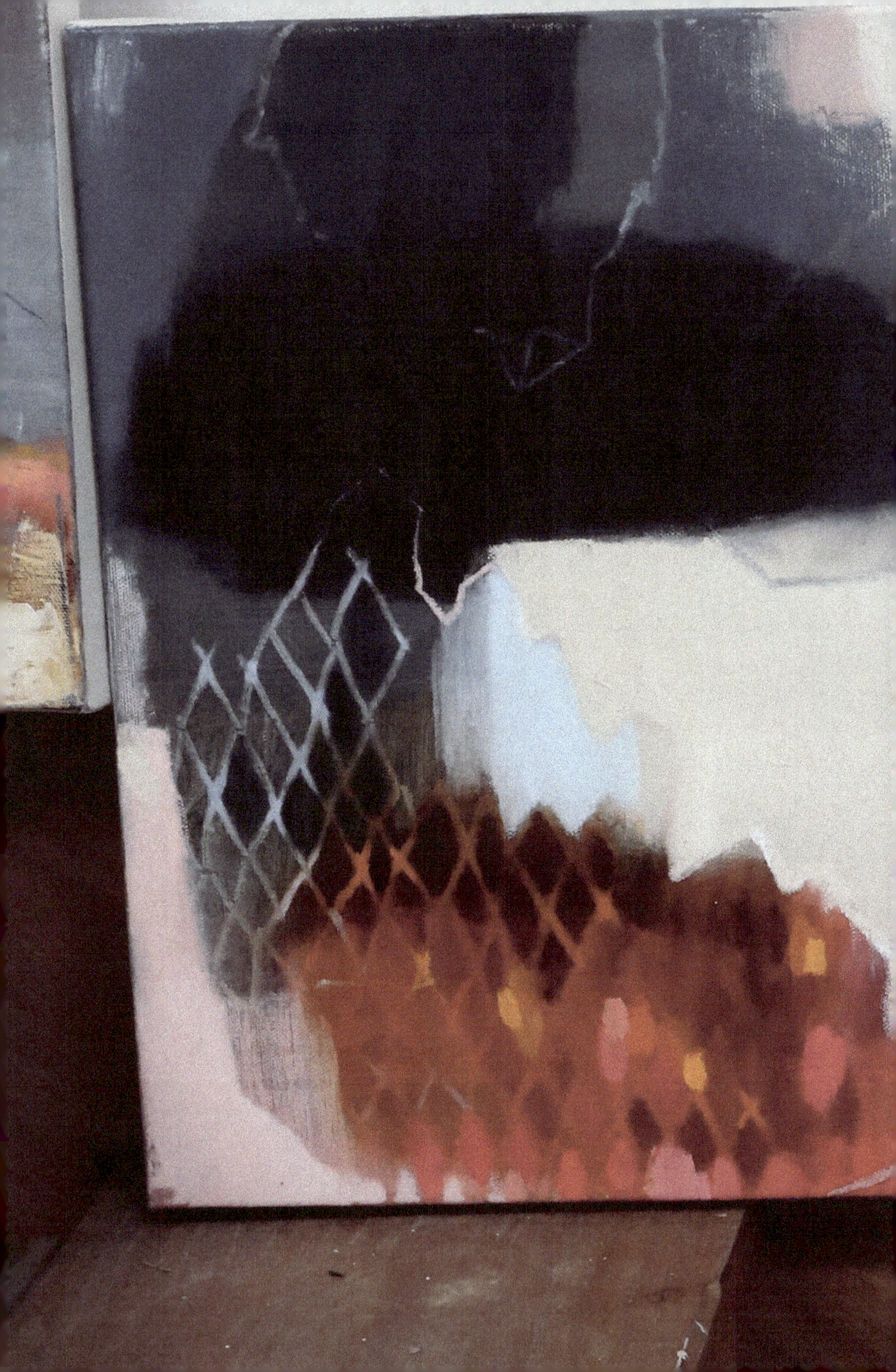

"For me, art is where the material and immaterial meet. The work becomes a vehicle for possible reconciliation and hopefully, the odd revelation."

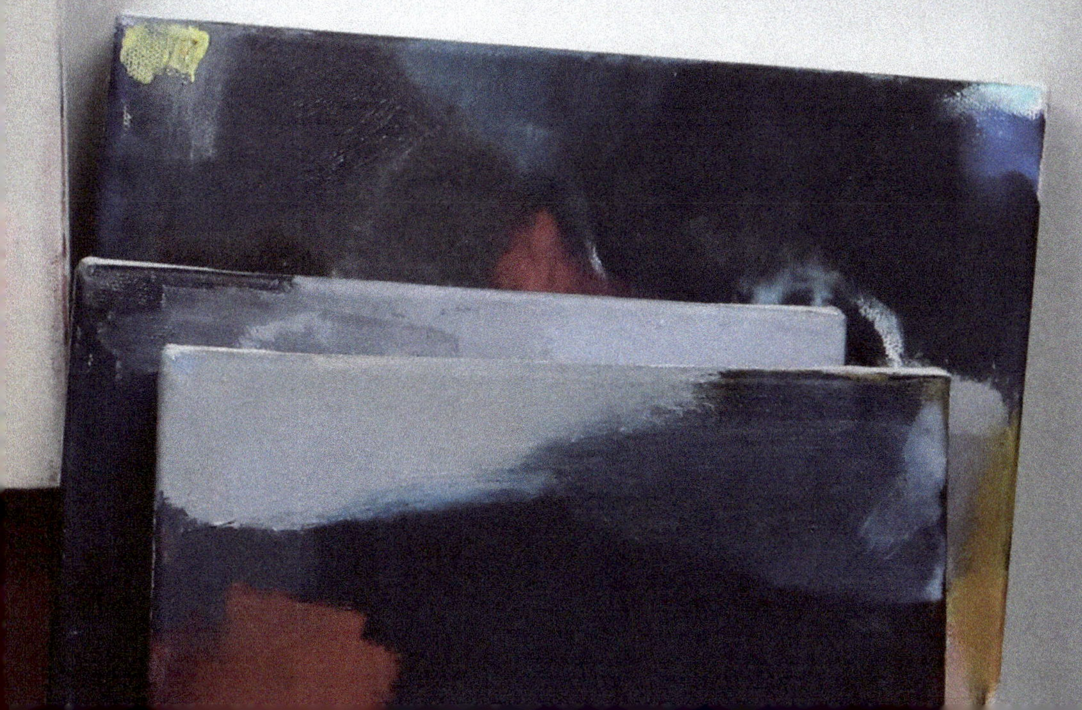

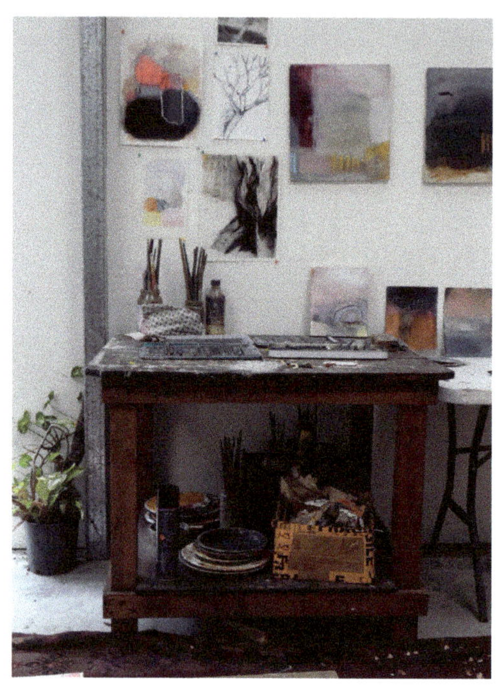

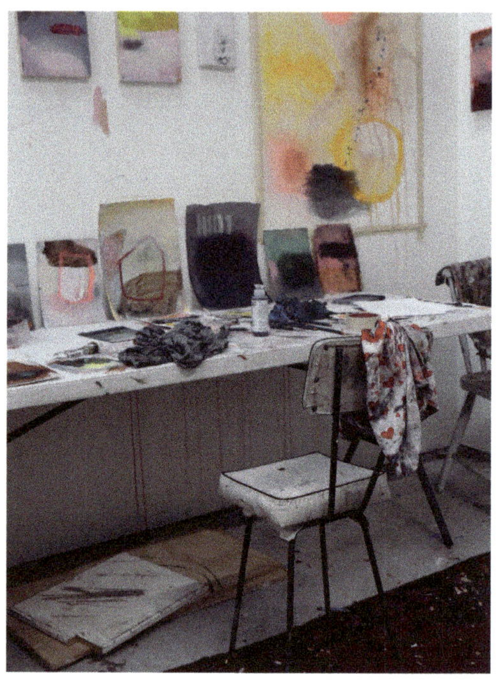

*Alex's studio is the only structure in proportion to the forest; lofty and stretching up to meet the sunlight.*

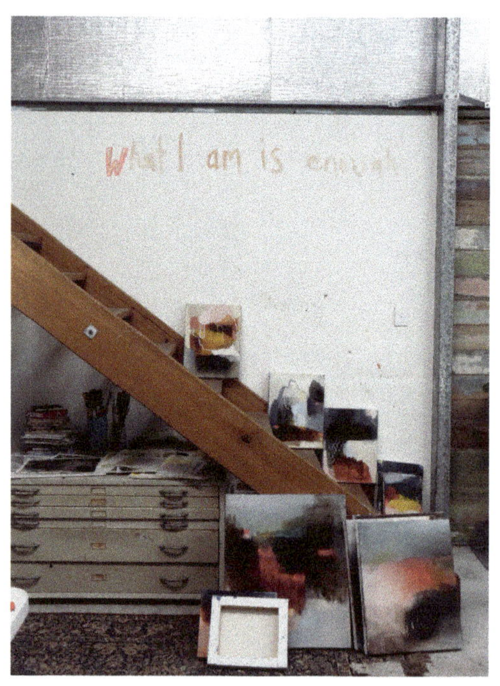


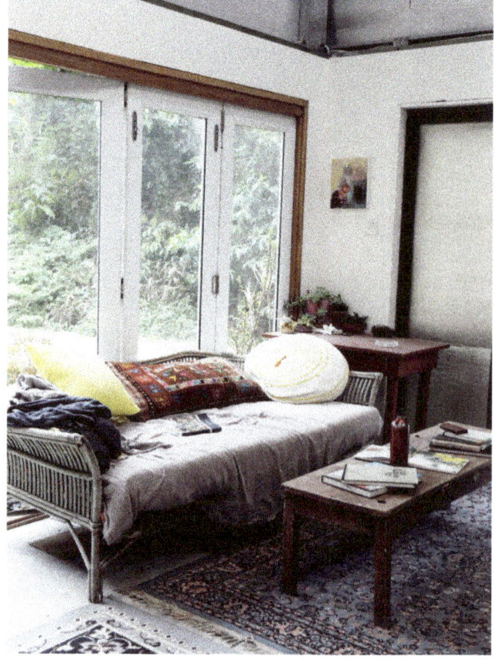

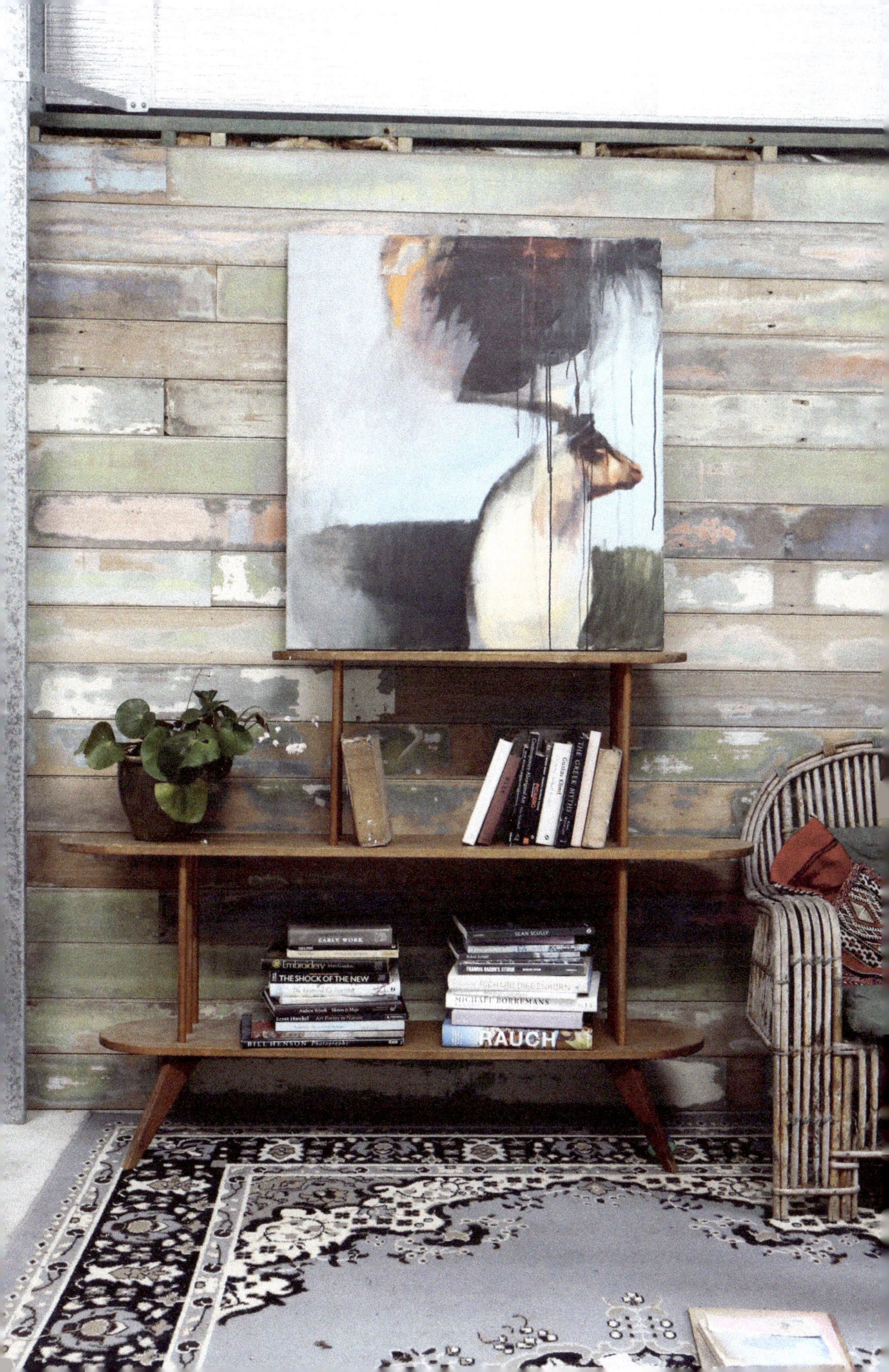
Gustav Klimt
THE GREEK MYTHS
EARLY WORK
Embroidery
THE SHOCK OF THE NEW
Ernst Haeckel Art Forms in Nature
BILL HENSON Photographs
SEAN SCULLY
RAUCH

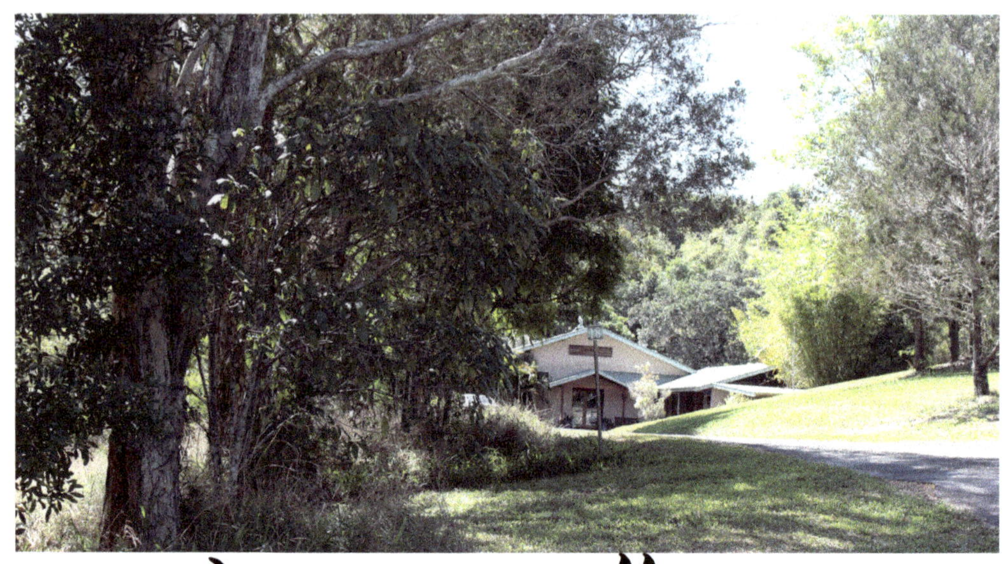

# Gatya Kelly

## On poppies and pomegranates

Gatya Kelly lives on a 400-acre community title in the hills between Mullumbimby and the coast. The road to her home is really one big driveway, breaking off to secluded pockets beyond banks of solar panels and fantastic fruit and vegetable gardens. There are around 35 dwellings and 100 people living here.

"Everybody has their own little private situation, but it's one property," Gatya says. "It means you have space around you but you're still part of a neighbourhood. Some communities like this are more connected than others. Some pitch in with working days or breakfast mornings, and some have nothing to do with each other. This one is in-between. It's nice to have people around you who you know.

"It's a nice place to live. It's near the beach! I go to Brunswick Heads sometimes twice a day. It gets quite hot in here in summer, and when that happens I just bail and go swimming."

She's referring to bailing from her studio space; a spare bedroom on the ground floor apartment of a large house, beside a remnant Australian teak tree. It's a rare thing, as most of them were felled for cedar, then dairying, then bananas. Here, Gatya paints still life. Magnolias, pomegranates and opium pipes... but more on that later.

Gatya is one of the region's most respected – and newest – artists. Although her paintings have whispers of the great European works of old, she only started painting in 2009. What else to do while housesitting in

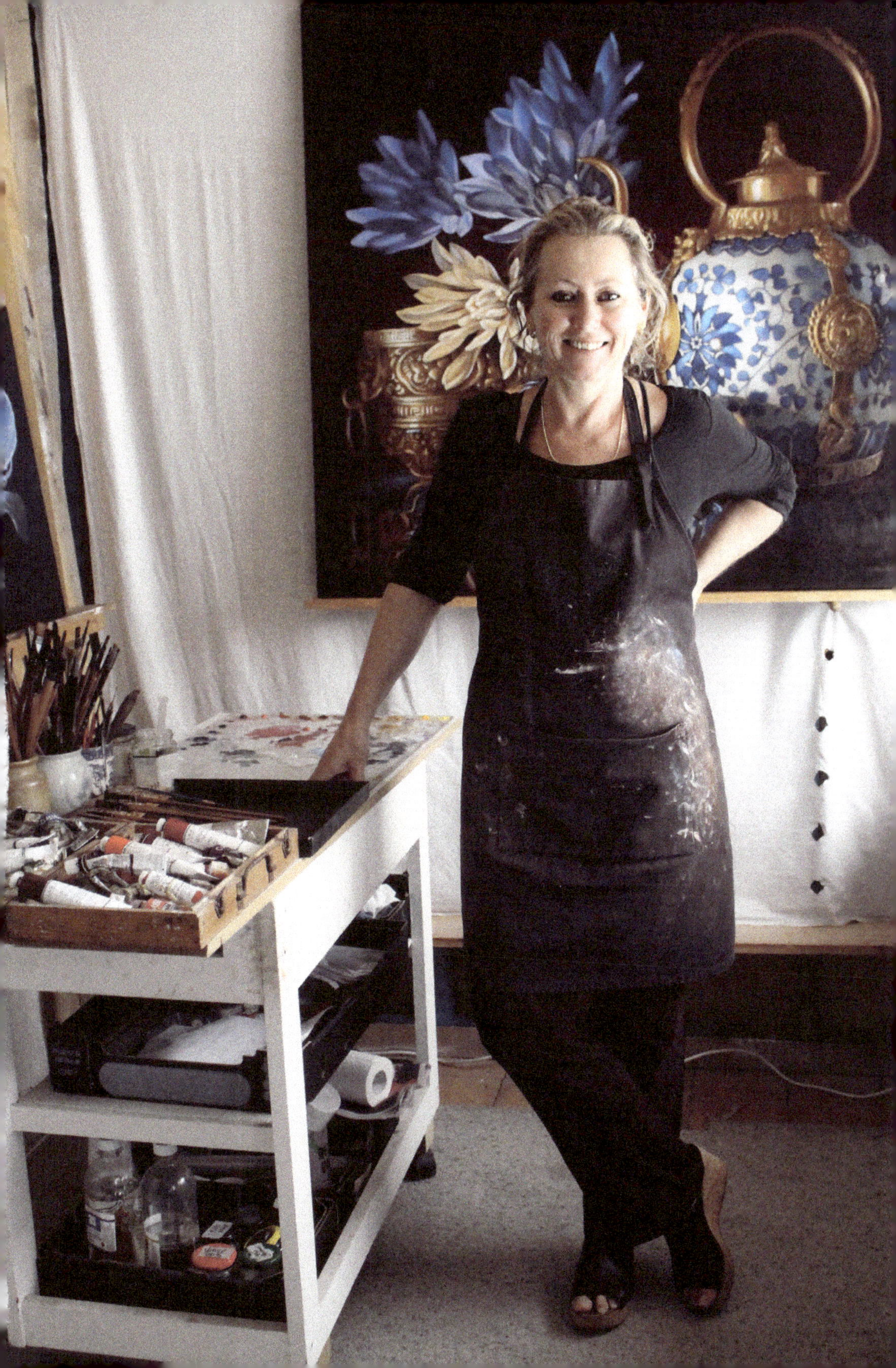

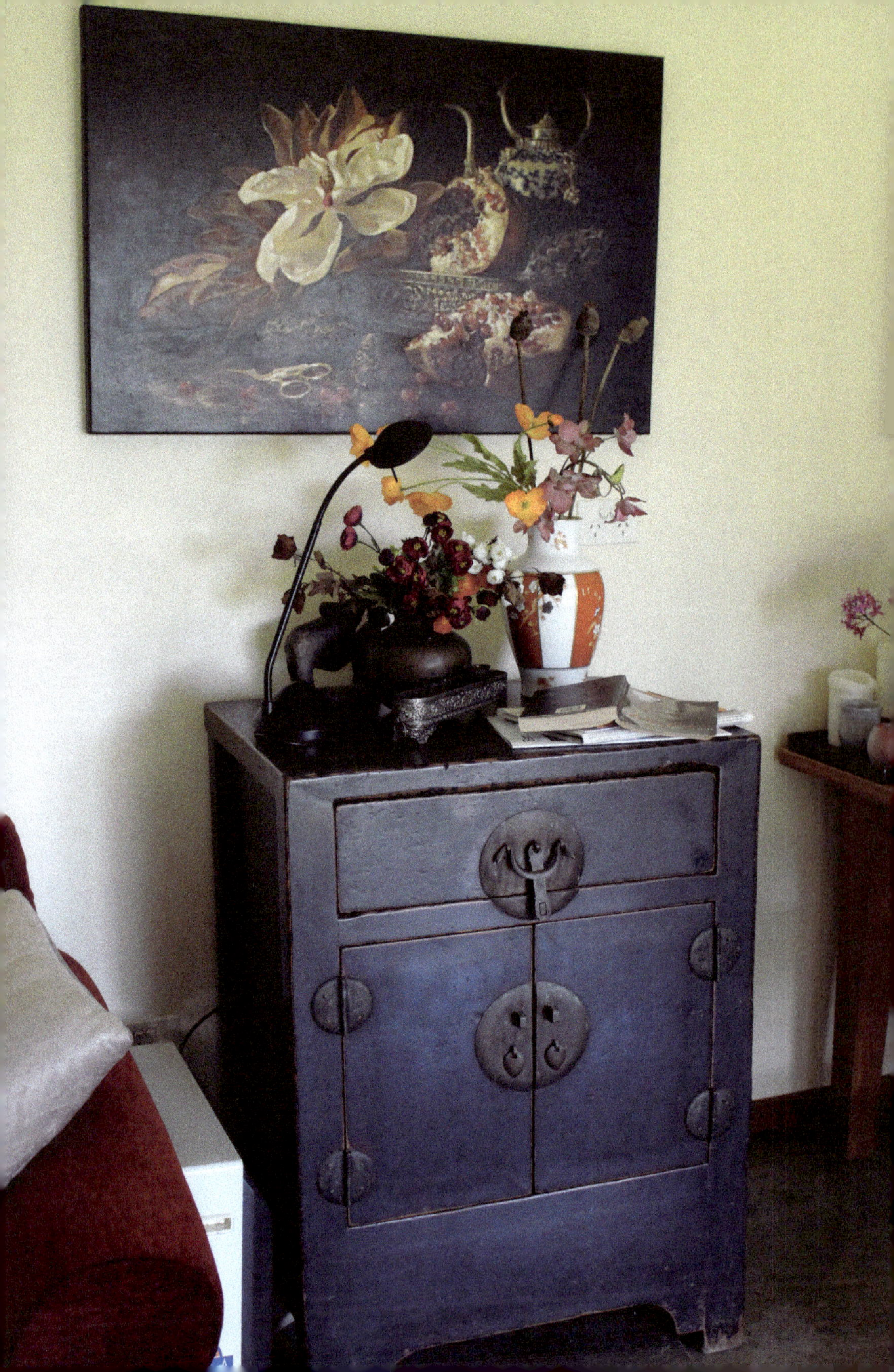

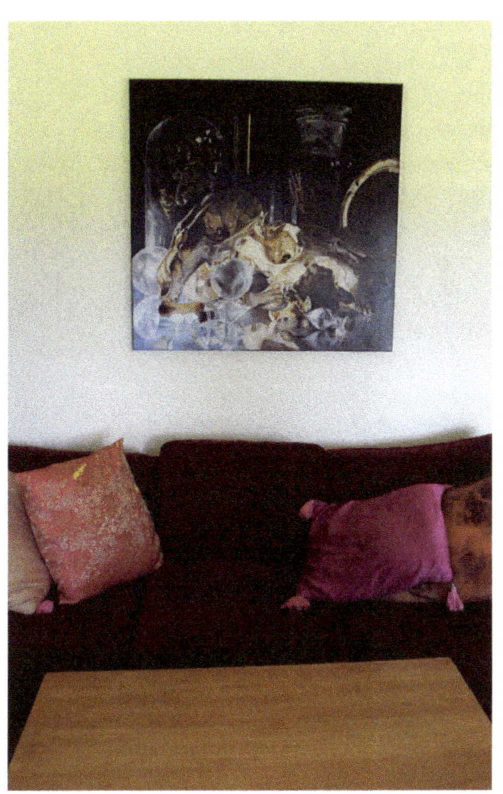

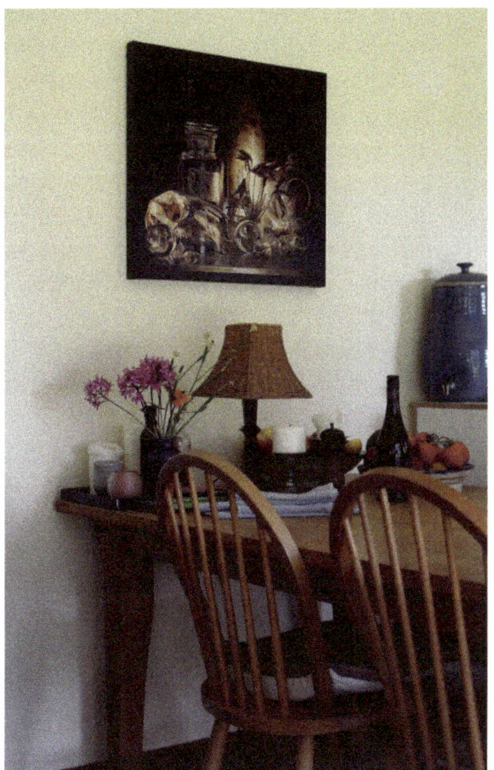

Tuscany over the winter months? Gatya says she needed a project, so picked up brushes. It was to be the next phase of her creative career.

Gatya's working life began as a graphic designer in Sydney, designing books for publishers such as Random House and Trans World. "I became a graphic designer but I wanted to be an artist," she says. "I just didn't have the courage to step straight into it. I needed to make money and that was the substitute for being an artist, and at that stage it wasn't a bad substitute. It was good work for a freelancer. That was until ten years ago when my work turned to websites. I was doing back-of-office stuff, paypal buttons and shit like that. The internet really killed it for me."

She says it wasn't until she started travelling that she found the time and space to play with painting. The Tuscany stint led to other travels through Corfu, France and Spain. Gatya used that time to amass a small collection of still life. She was encouraged to leave them with a gallery in London, where they sat, still. "After a couple of years I had them shipped back here and put into storage. I thought no one wants them, they're no good." The locals, however, disagreed with her.

Good friend and local ceramicist Suvira McDonald asked Gatya if he could use the paintings as a backdrop to a ceramics exhibition. Ruth, of Barebones Art Space in Bangalow, was at that exhibition. "She loved them and really wanted them," Gatya says. "She took them and one-by-one she sold them all."

It was just the encouragement Gatya needed to return to her art. She did so with bravado, applying for artist residencies to fuel her creativity. "Residencies and moving around are really good for an artist, to take yourself out of your environment," she says. "The next great thing that happened to me was when I applied for a residency at Tweed Regional Gallery. It was a small miracle getting that. I was batting out of my league when I applied for it but I was too naive to know." The experience led to a sell-out solo show in February 2016. "That was a real bolster to my confidence."

Just six months later, Gatya found herself on another residency in the goldfields township of Hill End, in an 1850s house once owned by the precociously talented Sydney artist Donald Friend.

"In the 1940s all the Sydney artists took an interest in Hill End," Gatya says. "It's accessible to Sydney but remote as well. There was a big, bohemian arts scene in Sydney and they wanted to escape that to make work."

The house is also famous for hosting the likes of Margaret Olley and Russell Drysdale. "Hill End is an artistic place and it's got this heritage to it," Gatya says. For our artist, it was the sense of alienation she felt in the town of 170 people that dominated her month there. She got thinking about the Chinese people who flocked to the goldfields, and how strange it must have felt for them. The idea has led to another solo show, titled *Alchemy*, and bound for Brisbane gallery Jan Manton Art in 2017.

"There's a Chinese thread running through the Alchemy show. I've got opium pipes in there and I also wanted poppy seed heads. I had a lot of trouble getting them. I looked all over the world online but there's no online trade because you can make an opium tea out of them. And then they showed up at the Mullumbimby florist."

The seed heads now bob by a vase of faux poppies on Gatya's kitchen table. They are the perfect example of her aesthetic melding of beauty and darkness. "It's very difficult to make something beautiful without making it chocolate boxy or syrupy," she says. "I like a little bit of darkness in there. I do."

Gatya's paintings are scaled-up, magnified representations of still life vignettes; of objects she collects, arranges and photographs. Of flowers and fruit, butterflies and bones.

"Anything I paint I have to have a personal liking for. As much as I love the beach, I just don't get the same feeling about it as I do about pomegranates and magnolias. Not everything beautiful is of interest to me. That is my indulgence and one thing I love about being an artist rather than a designer. I can indulge my likings.

"For me, the pleasure is in making the painting and once I'm finished I'm not that interested in it. It's a totally selfish pursuit. I do this for my own pleasure and enjoyment and the fact that someone wants to buy it is a wonderful by-product. It's a very wonderful pathway. The paintings go from my pleasurable experience to someone else's pleasurable experience... and that makes room for the next one." ■

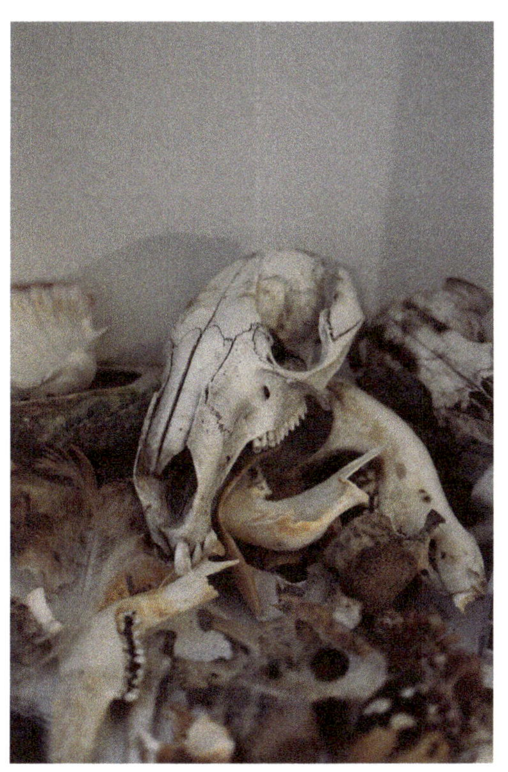

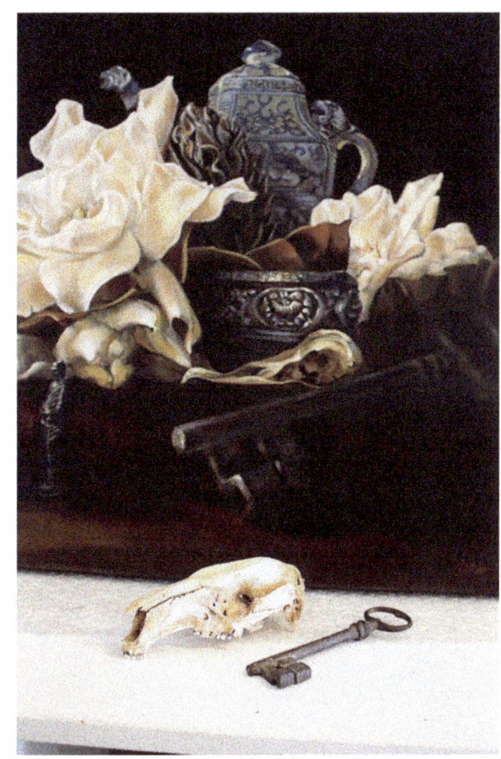

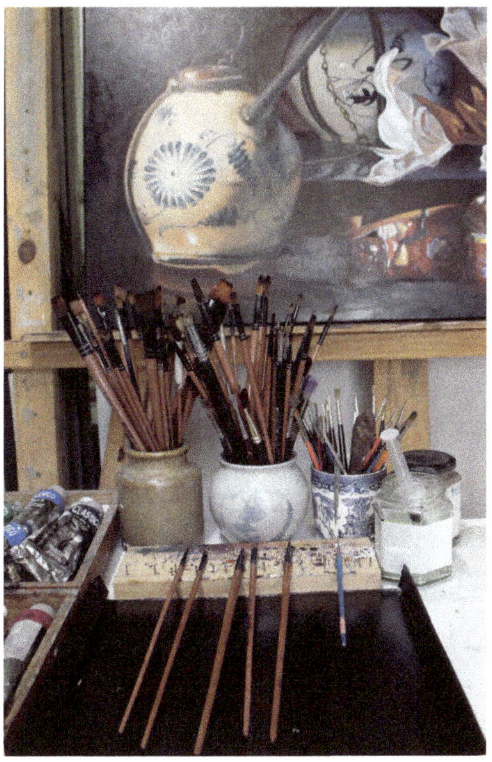

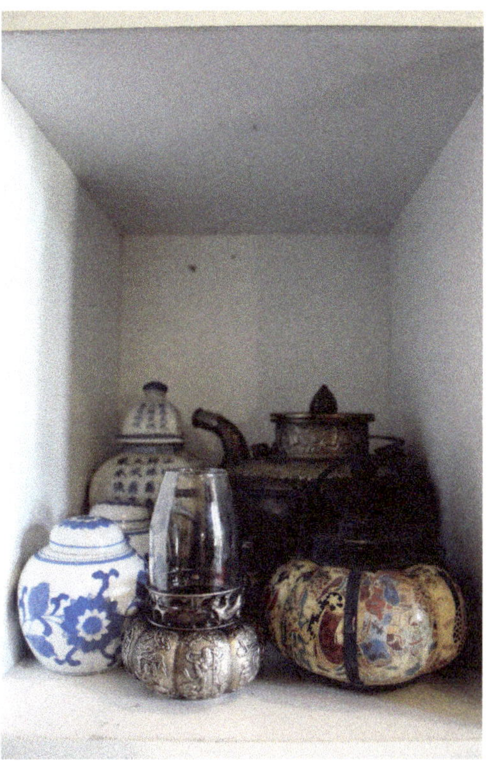

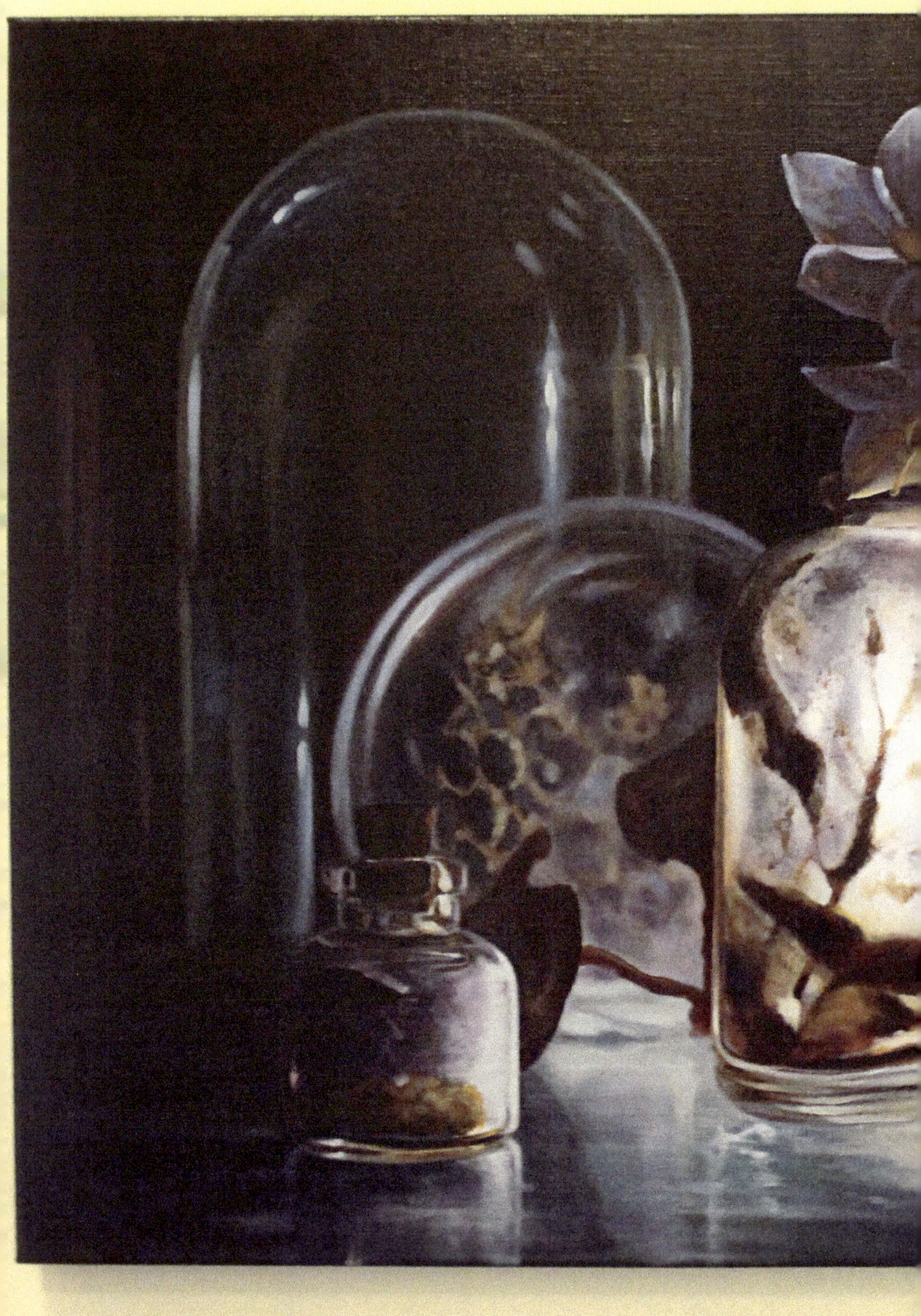

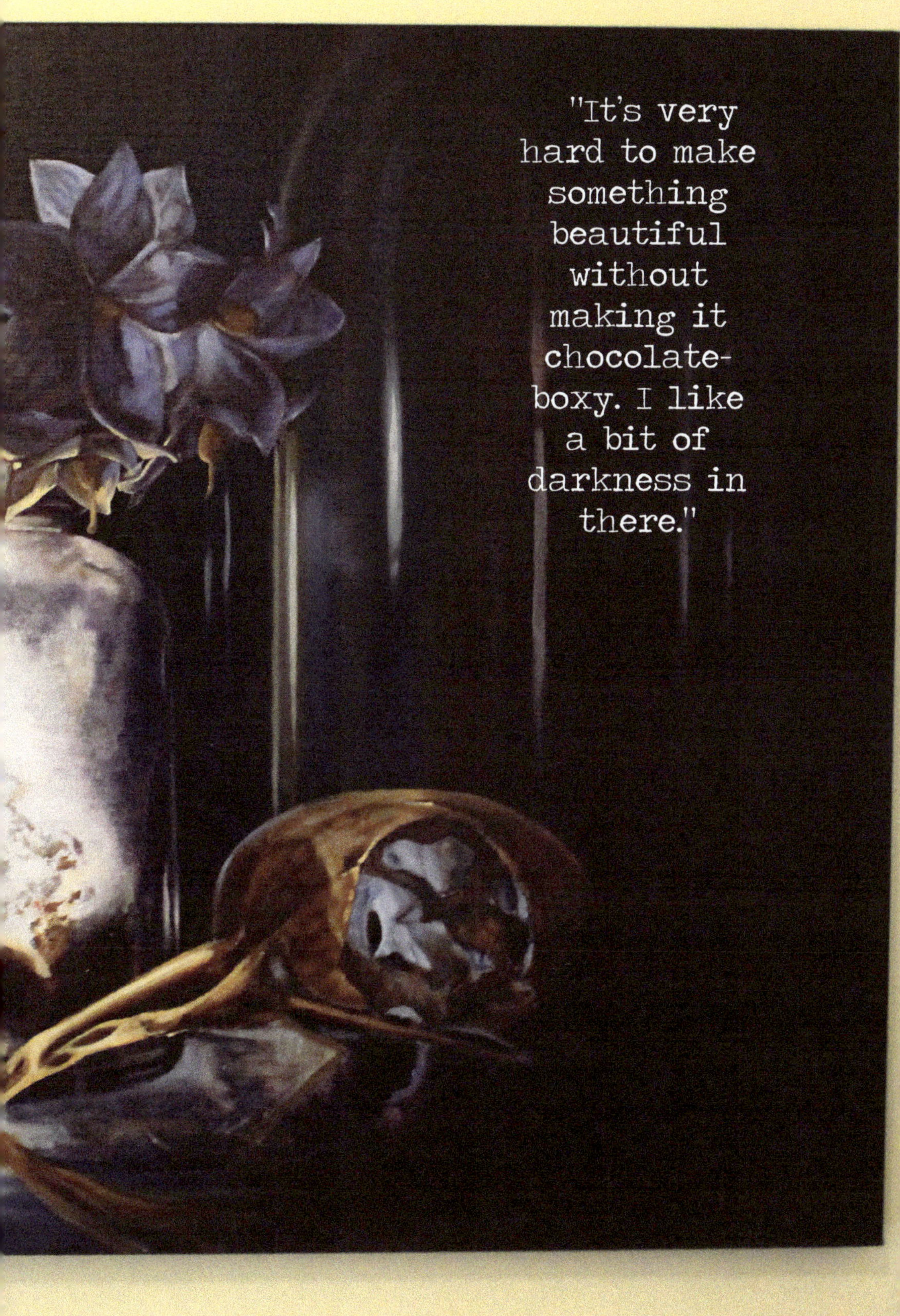
"It's very hard to make something beautiful without making it chocolate-boxy. I like a bit of darkness in there."

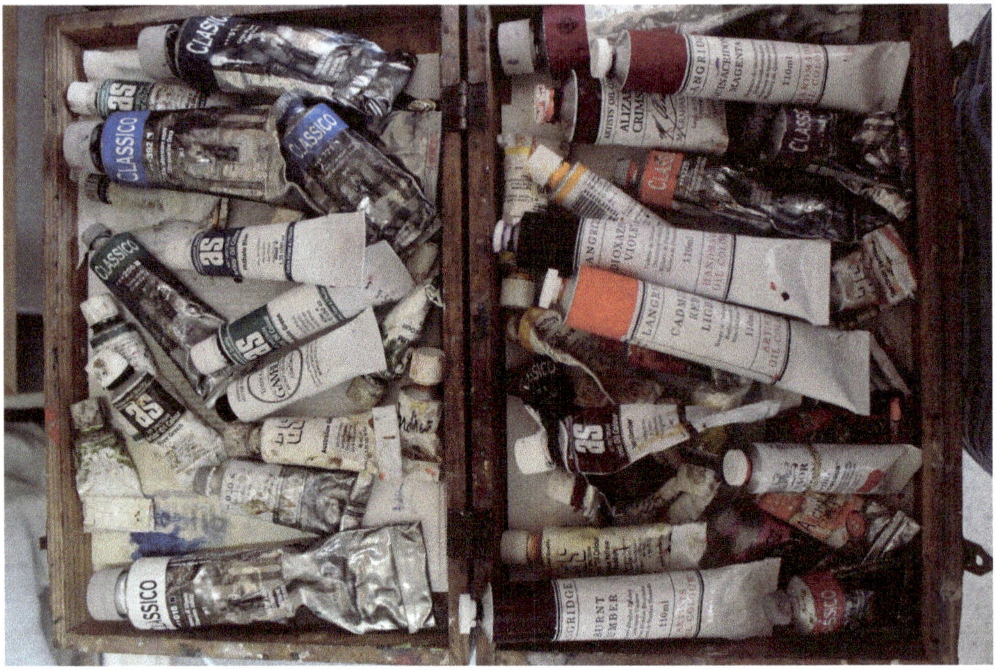

Here, Gatya paints still life. Magnolias, pomegranates and opium pipes.

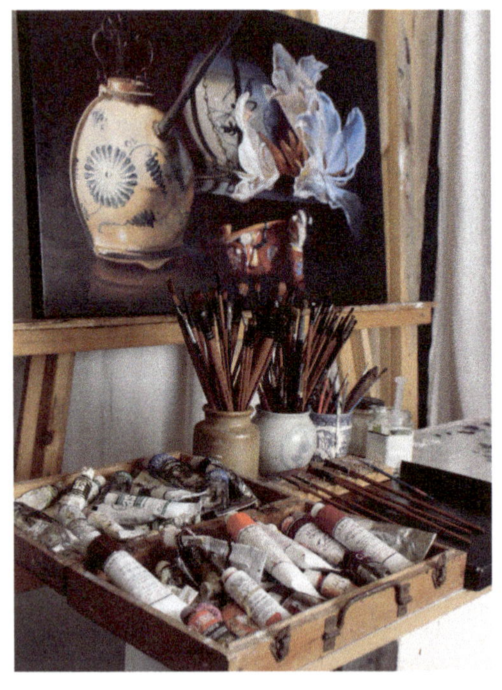

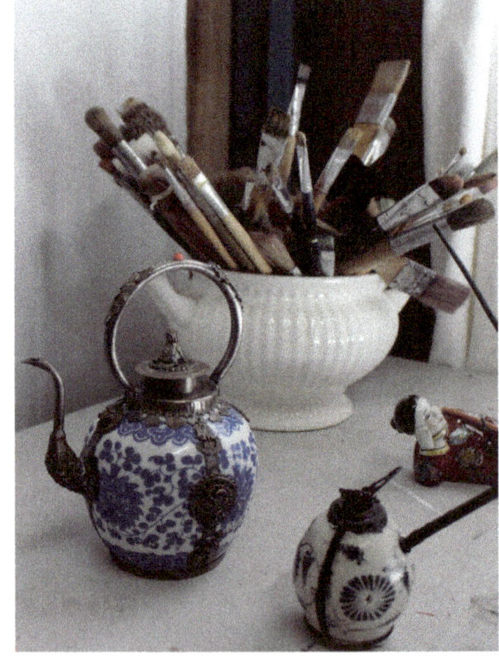

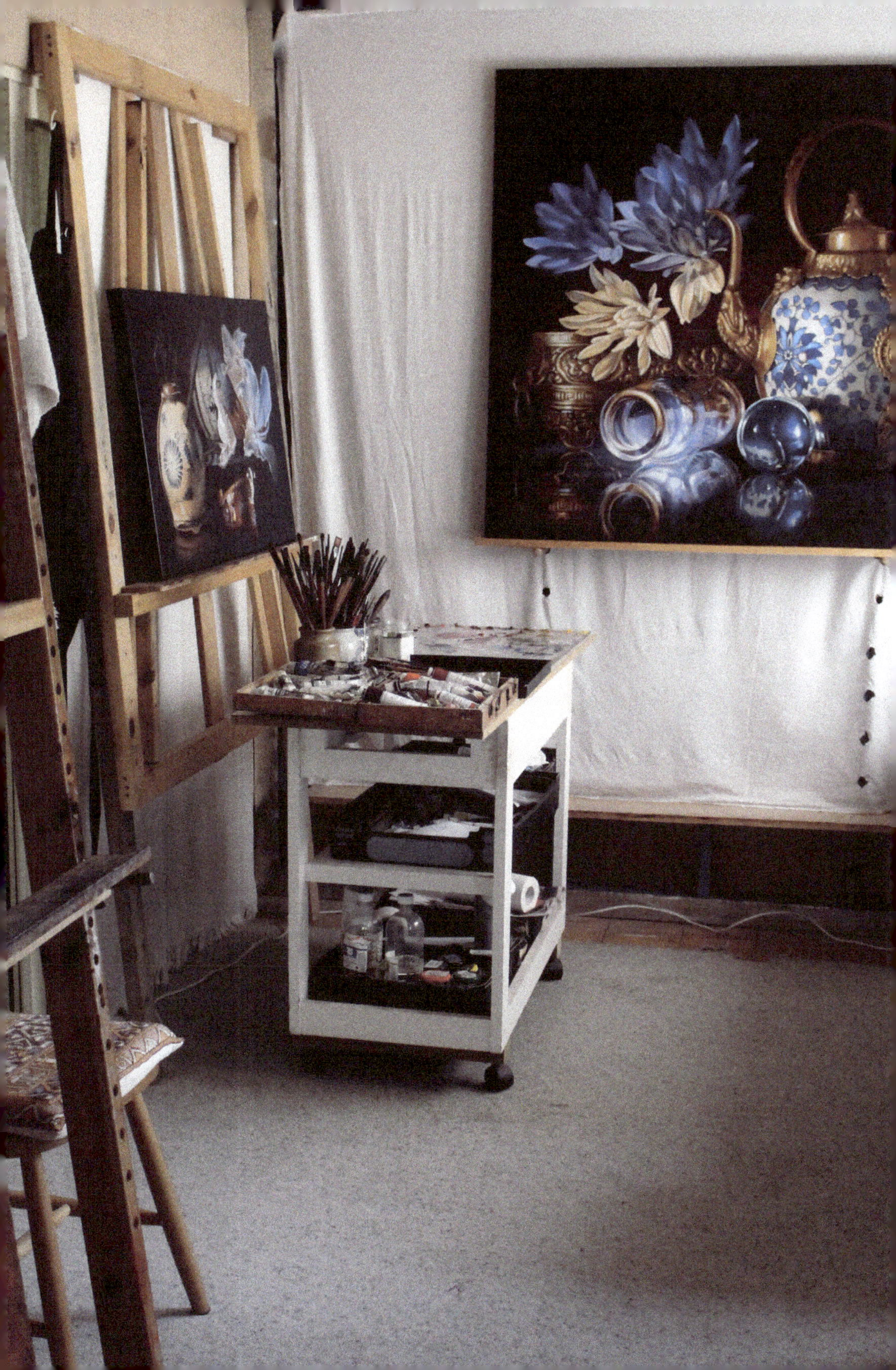

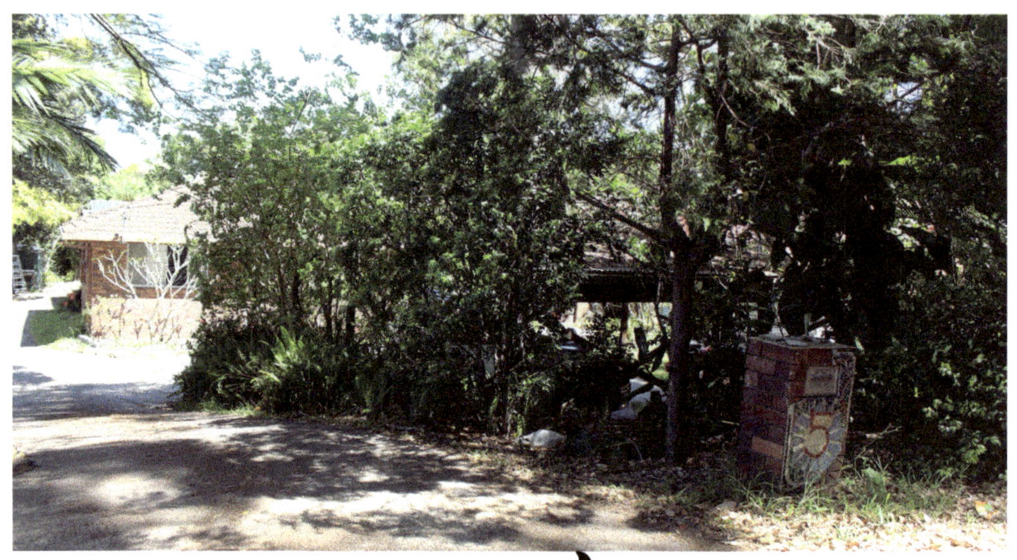

# Leora Sibony

## Bits, bobs and butterflies

Mullumbimby shoulders the Brunswick River at the base of Mount Chincogan, nine kilometres inland from the coast. It's a truly beautiful pocket of the Northern Rivers. But for Leora Sibony, it's what lies underground that most interests and perhaps inspires her. Rose quartz.

She says Mullumbimby is built on a bedrock of the soft pink stone believed to awaken the heart and provide a deep sense of personal fulfilment. Leora believes those deep down reefs of rock may be responsible for drawing in the unofficial gatherings of creative souls to this place.

Second only to infamous Nimbin, Mullumbimby also played a crucial role in the 1960s hippy movement. Unlike its alternative counterpart, today there's very little evidence of flower power in Mullum, save the odd dreadlocked hitchhiker. But there are lots of makers and creators, quietly plying their skills and finding fulfilment in hideaway places. Leora is one of them.

She arrived here in the late 1990s with her Israeli partner. "We met in Israel, and he knew of this area from travelling," she says. "It just so happened that my sister was living in this area, so we moved here too. And soon after that our first baby was on the way."

Leora set to make a home here, welcome more babies, start a business, and in the throes of a busy life, discover her inner artist. "I had a sense that I really had to do something for my own sanity," she says. At the time Leora and her partner had two children, aged three and one. "I started working

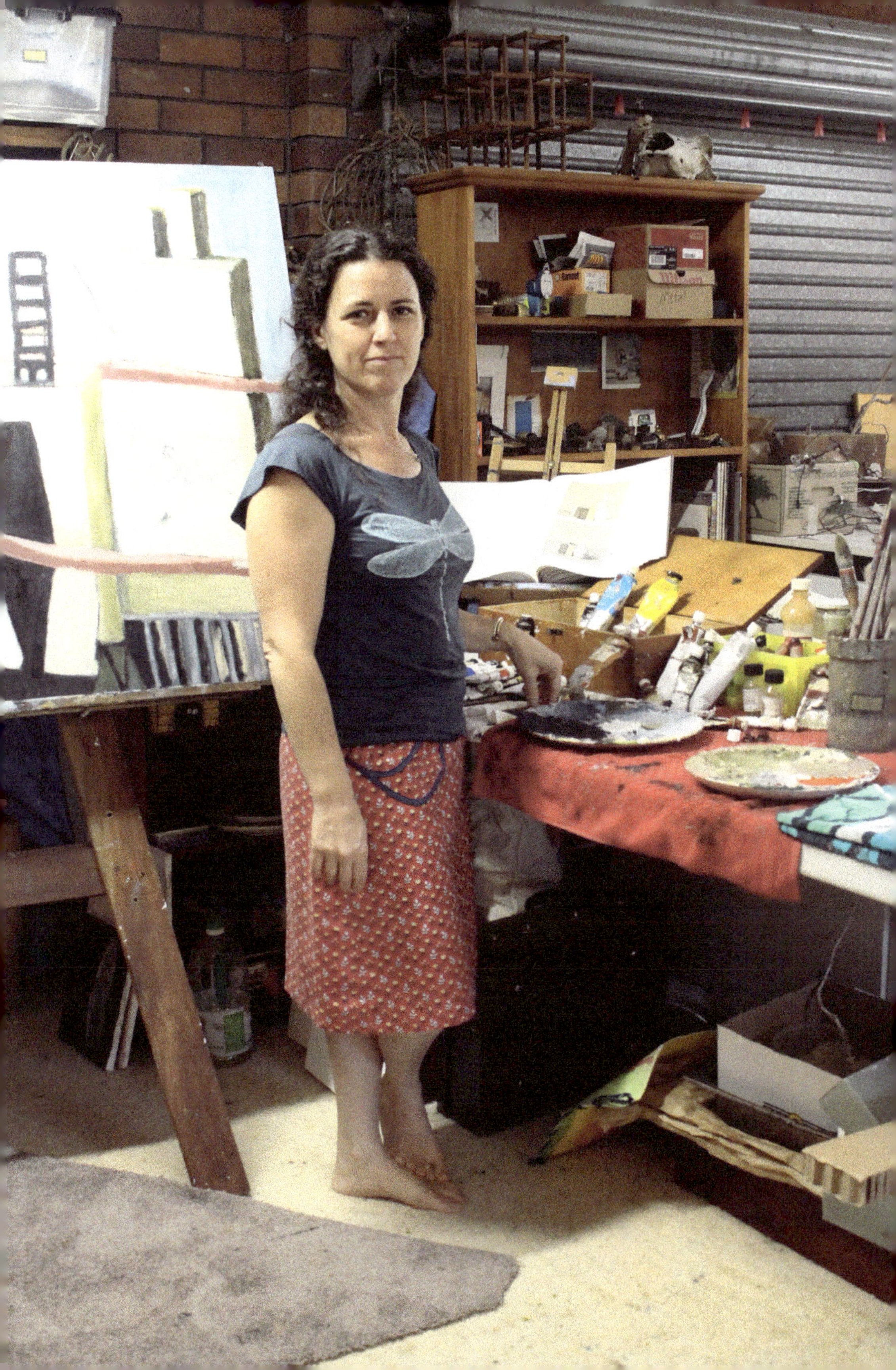

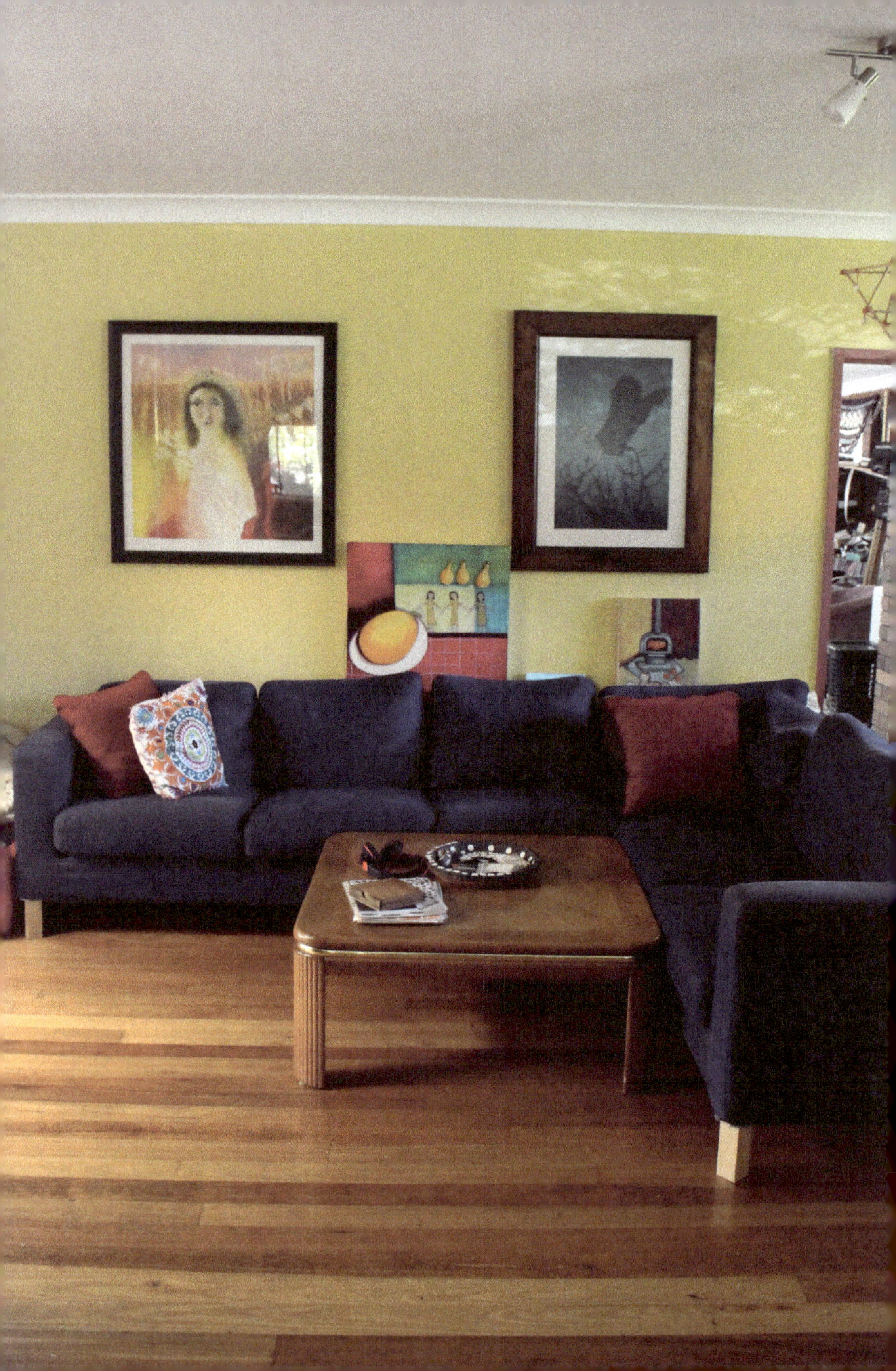

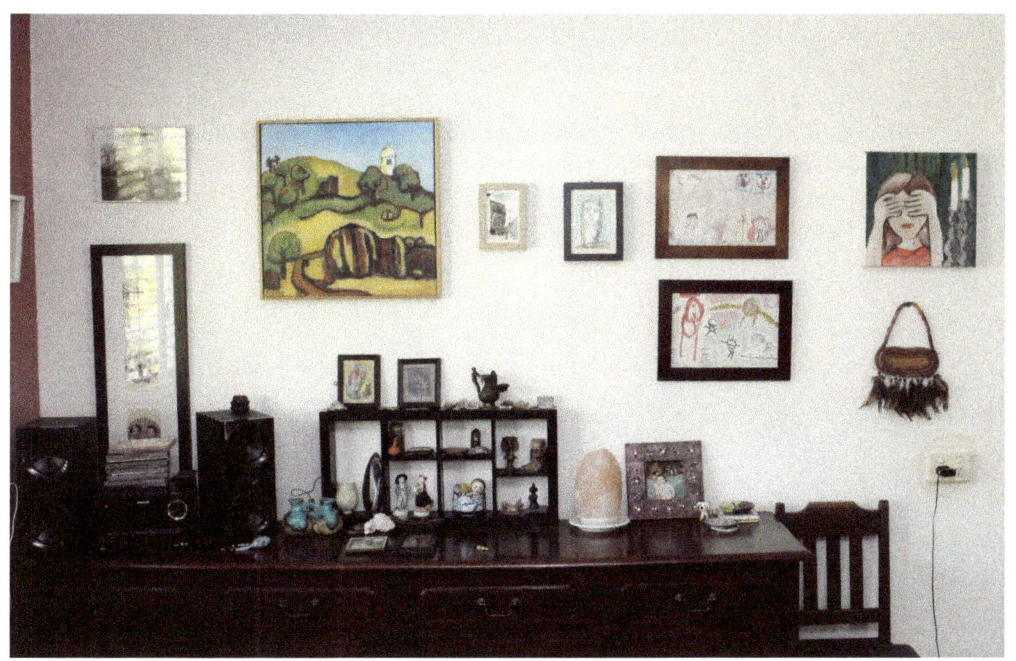

with an artist I know and from then on painting became a life or death situation. I think when you're creative if you don't express it, you have this build-up of energy in you and it has to come out, and the only way for it to come out is through creative expression."

The work happens in the garage attached to the back of Leora's home. This house was chosen for that garage space, although initially it served an entirely different purpose; as storeroom for Leora and her partner's retail stores. They own two shops, here and in Burleigh Heads, called Shanti Town, selling imported clothing and soft furnishing from Nepal and India.

"But I don't want that to define me," Leora says. "I just want to be an artist. I just want to do that, every day if possible." That quest became easier once a warehouse space was found for the business, and Leora moved her home studio from a spare bedroom to this cavernous space. "It was open slather from then on for me," she says.

After she'd been painting for 12 years, refining her style and adding her works to the colourful walls of her home, Leora enrolled in the newly-launched Byron School of Art. "I was scared at first that if I went to art school I wouldn't be able to paint like I used to," she says. "It seems so naive now because it's just expanded my view of art and the way I see all things." It also expanded her mediums. "I was always a maker and collector and I've always loved to repurpose things. I always did that as a child. All of a sudden I saw how I could apply all of that into 3D work."

As *Artist Spaces* visits, Leora has just launched her third solo show, at the Yellow Brick Studio in nearby Murwillumbah, in one of the town's original Art Deco buildings. The gallery itself is another example of how the art school has enriched her life. Leora is one of five graduates to be a part of this space, which is owned and managed by fellow graduate Lisa Arronis. “Lisa had this vision of a space for workshops and art supplies, which would support our art,” Leora says. “We all have a similar vision. When you work from a regional area you’ve got to expand out and be part of what happens nationally and internationally. I think all of us are in it for the pure love of it. We’re not making things because we think they’re going to sell, we’re making things because we have to. Of course, selling them is great too.”

Leora’s latest show, *Castles in the Sky*, was influenced by a recent trip, where she met up with a friend in New York City. “She’s also got three kids and we were just pinching ourselves every day,” she laughs. “I saw art every day, music, food, comedy, and then I started noticing these water towers…” Only when Leora returned home did she draw parallels between those leggy tanks atop the New York buildings and the structures on stilts back home. Much of the Northern Rivers infrastructure is built to withstand flood; homes and outbuildings, tanks and silos sit up high to allow for seasonal moods.

“The works in that exhibition were a response to the industrial structures in the landscape here, drawing parallels to the water towers in New York,” Leora says. “My work is also about reinvigorating the objects that are discarded and left to decay. I’m interested in taking the time to illuminate these objects and bring them back to their majesty.”

She says after New York, the art poured out of her. She speaks of finishing three large canvases in three hours. With a busy life Leora has got to work fast when she can. “As most mothers or women artists will tell you, if you’ve got 15 minutes, you get in there for 15 minutes. If you’ve got two hours, you know you can start painting.”

Beside Leora’s easel and paints is a U-shaped workbench of tinkering tools and found objects. Pieces she picks up on walks around her home town, bits and bobs from op shops and garage sales. Underneath are boxes, labelled ‘dog bones’ and ‘sheep bones’. They’ll all get used here eventually, as fragile sculptures, assembled in unison with the paintings.

“The 3D work I make is really part of my thinking process about the ideas I’m trying to communicate,” Leora says. “The 3D work informs the painting. The works are not mutually exclusive, they happen at the same time to communicate the same ideas.

“It gives me butterflies in the tummy,” she says of this pure act of creating. “What is exciting in our life as adults? I think artists have that.” ■

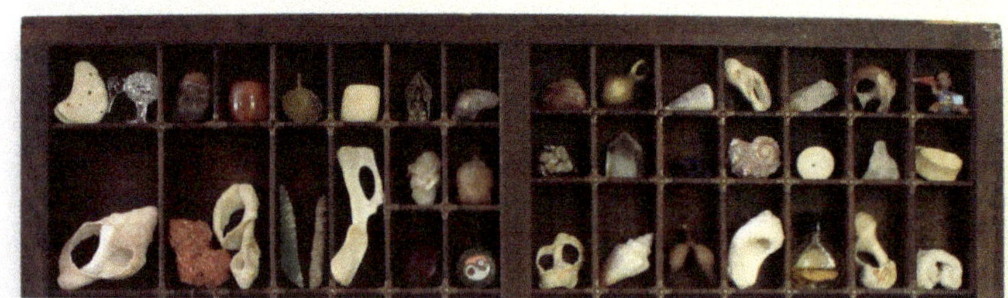

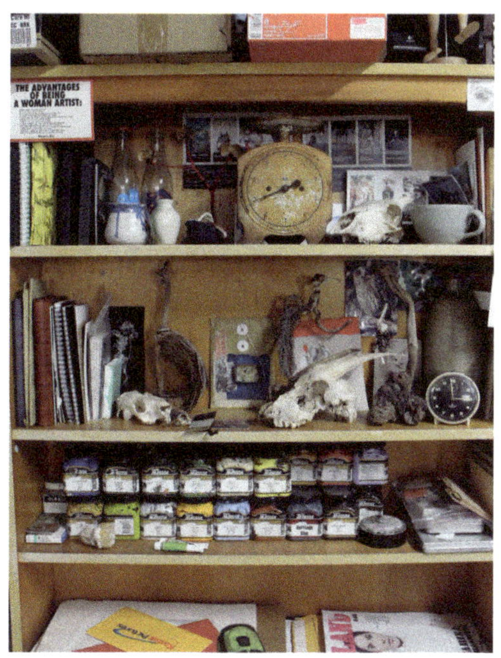


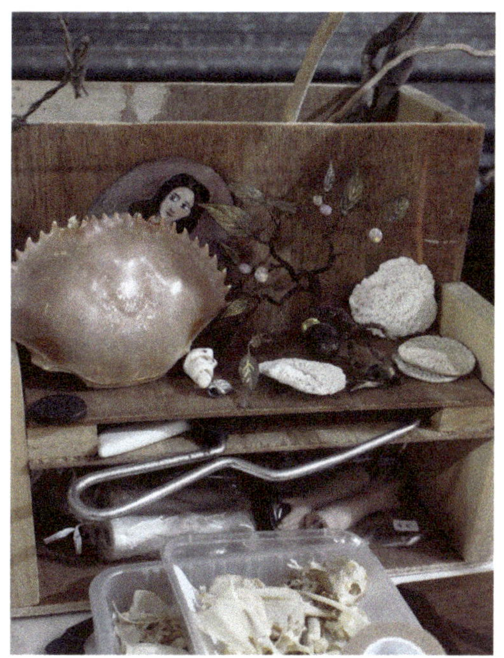

*There are lots of makers and creators here, quietly plying their skills and finding fulfilment in hideaway places.*

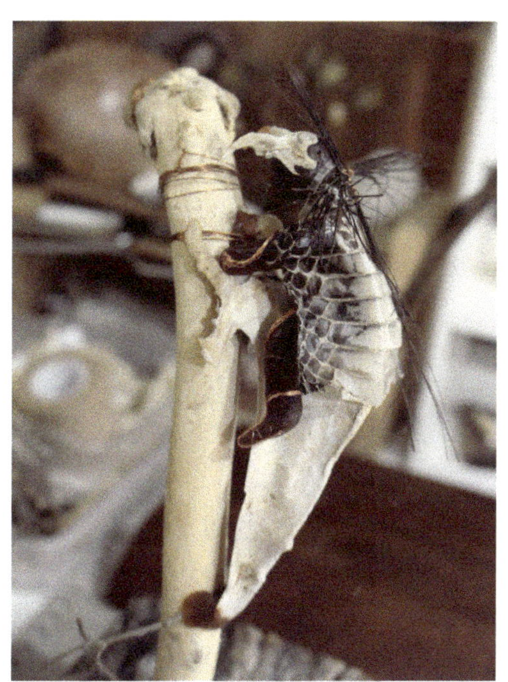

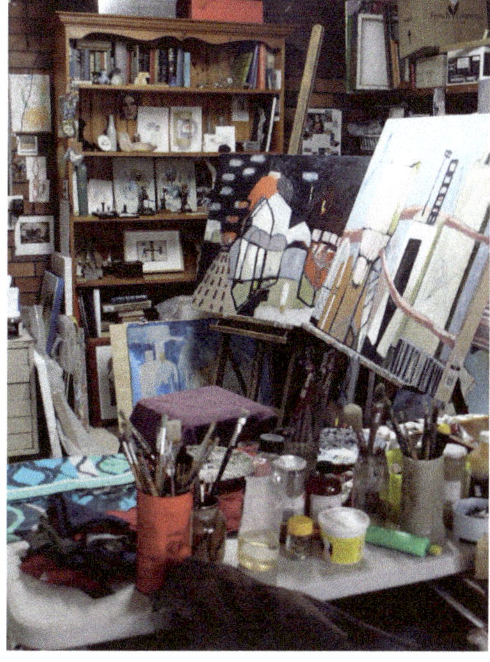

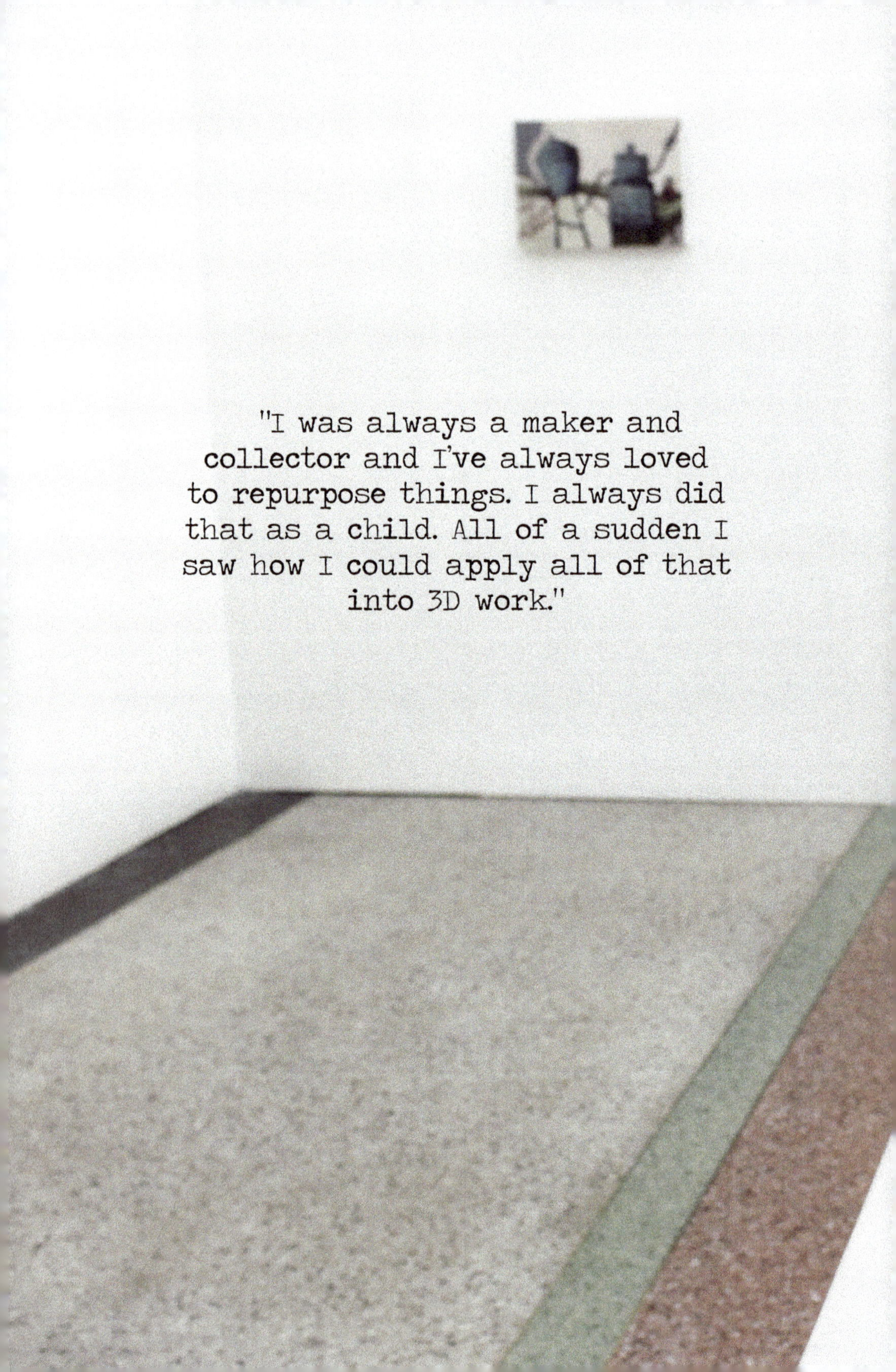

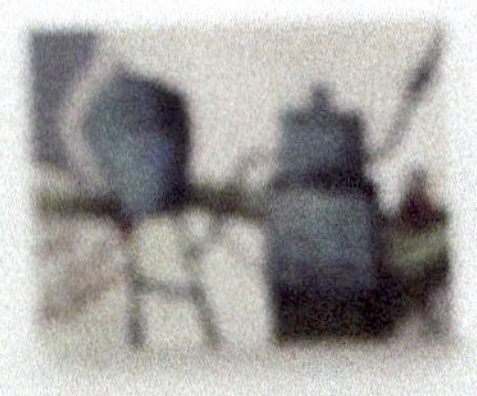

"I was always a maker and collector and I've always loved to repurpose things. I always did that as a child. All of a sudden I saw how I could apply all of that into 3D work."

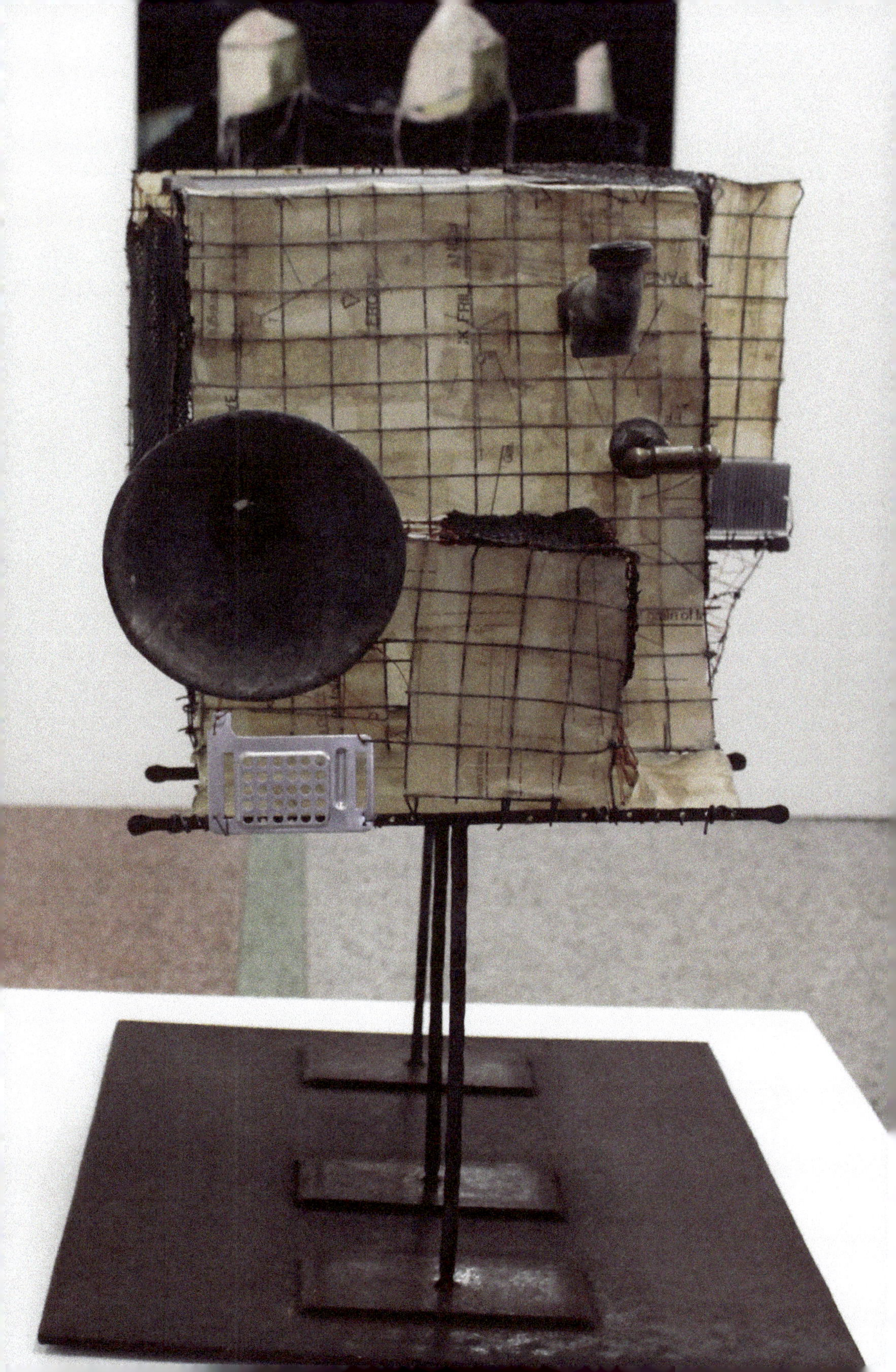

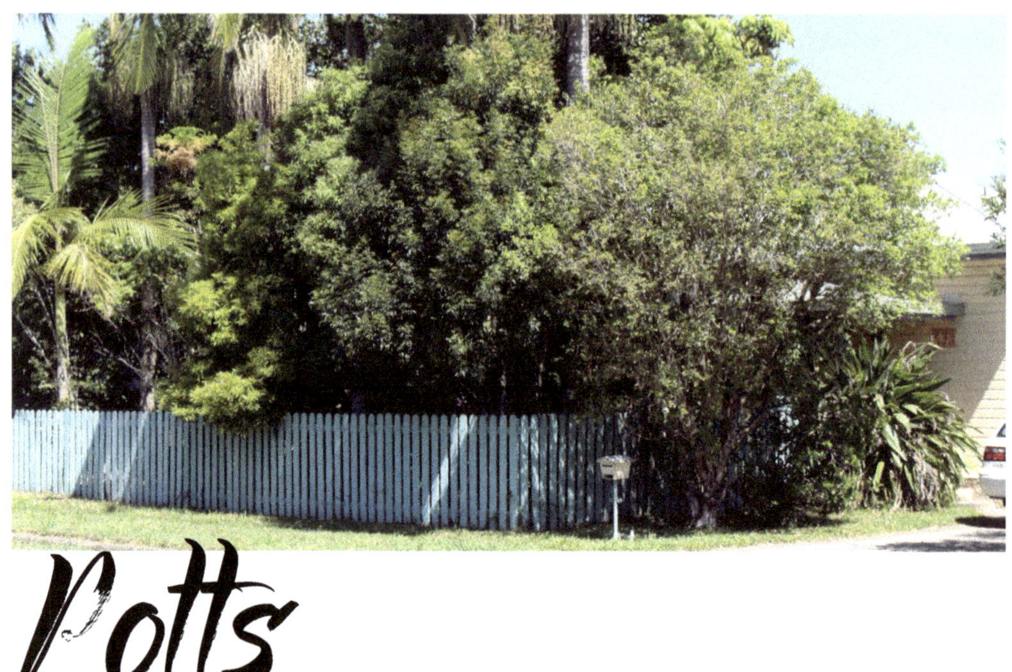

# Potts

## T-shirts and thongs

In the documentary *Step into Liquid*, champion surfer Kelly Slater said, "Once you're a surfer, you're done. You're in. It's like the mob or something. You're not getting out." So what then, of the surfer who can no longer surf? "I'm still there," says Potts.

Mullumbimby artist Potts has been riding waves since a kid. In fact he followed them all the way from the cold waters of Victoria's Surf Coast to the Northern Rivers over 30 years ago. "I had been very ill with pneumonia and I just needed some warmer weather," he says of the move from down south. "I thought I'd end up in far north Queensland, somewhere exotic, but then I realised the surf stops at Magnetic Island."

So Mullumbimby it was, with its affordable housing and ten-minute cruise down to the surf. "It was the lack of traffic lights here that sealed it," Potts laughs. "I ended up buying a house in 'the biggest little town in Australia'."

The property also had the bonus of this massive shed. Potts has decked it out as the ultimate surfy studio, where dusty records and surfing paraphernalia are stacked alongside the art. And underfoot is a softly worn concrete slab, slapped with paint.

Soon after moving here, Potts found himself an integral part of a community of surfers, artists and like-minded people. Everyone knows Potts, on a one-name basis. "If people ask me what my first name is I say, 'just Potts', keep it simple," he says.

"I thought I was going to come here, to this beautiful country, and be inspired to make art, like I was the only person who'd ever done that. And all

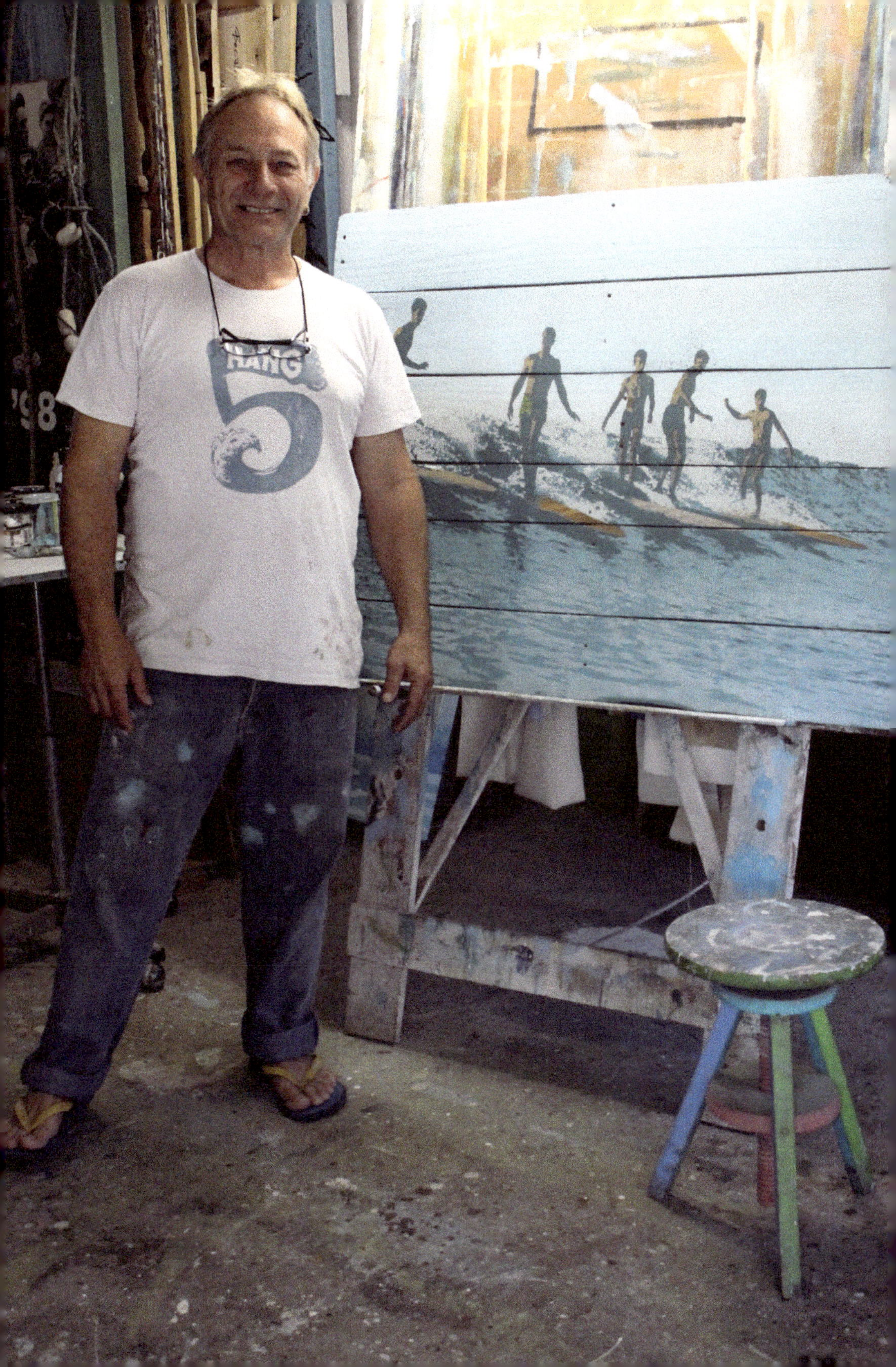
HANG
5

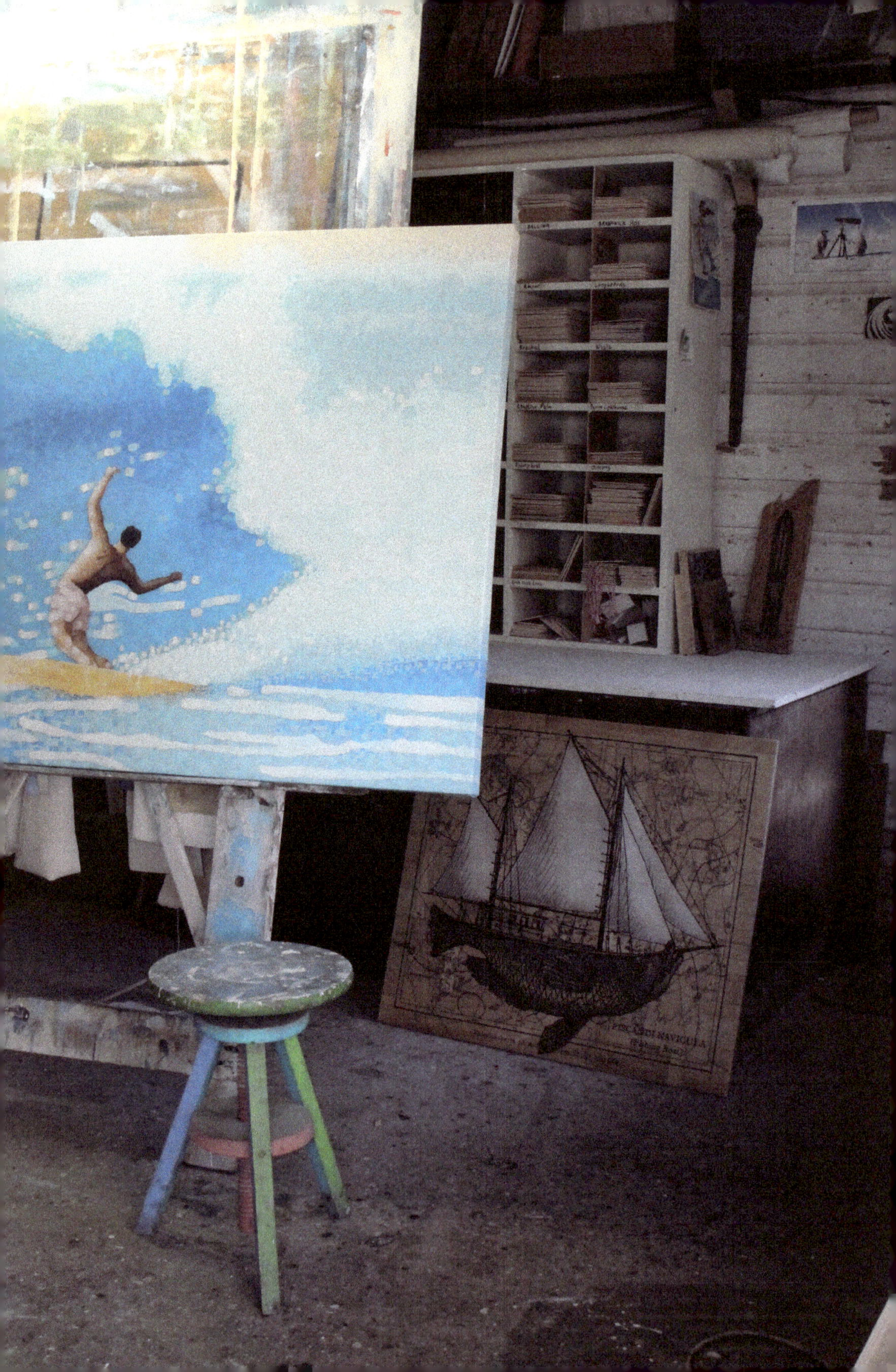

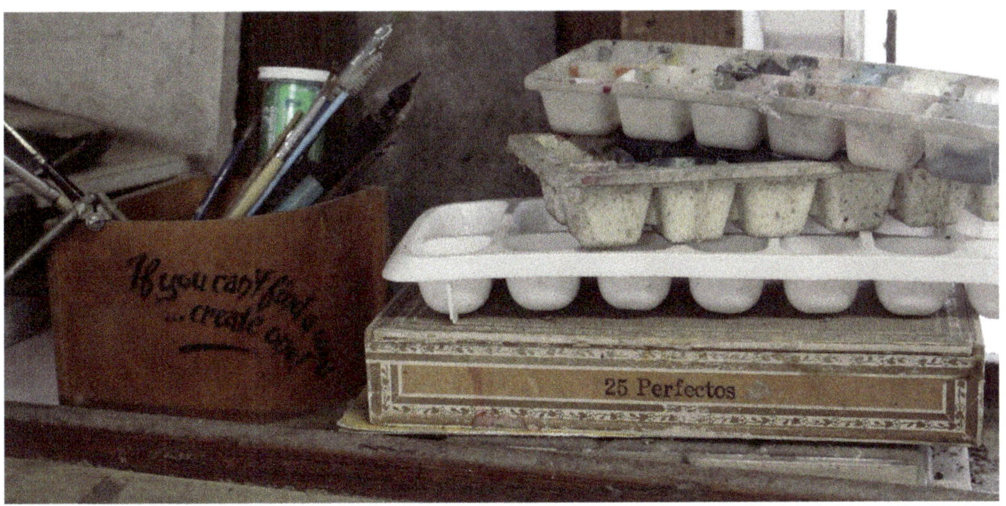


of a sudden I realised that these other artists with the same thought were already here."

Potts has been exhibiting since the early 1990s, all along the coastline of Victoria, New South Wales and Queensland.

His creative life began as a copy boy in an advertising agency, which led to a role as junior artist and then graphic designer. Soon he was freelancing and forging a name for himself in T-shirt design.

"I was left a phone message one day from a guy at Rip Curl who wanted to speak to me about designing some T-shirts," he says. "At that stage they were only manufacturing wetsuits, but wanted to develop and expand into the surf market. They liked what the Americans were doing with surf graphics on T-shirts. I designed a couple of graphics for them with more of an Aussie feel. They loved what I did and so started a ten-year association."

There's a good chance if you wore a Rip Curl Tee in the 80s and 90s, it was a Potts design. The job allowed him to indulge his life-long love of Pop Art, which is still evident in his work.

In the Northern Rivers, Potts got even more serious about his art, alongside freelance work for the likes of Ogilvy & Mather, Rigby Publications, Midori and Ritzenhoff Glass. He completed an Advanced Diploma of Fine Art at Lismore TAFE in 2002 and continued to push the boundaries of style and medium.

"I've always done a lot of illustration and had that love of drawing and painting and silk screen-printing. It was always hovering there," he says. "Recently I started painting landscapes on timber. I wanted to use the natural grain of the timber to represent the texture of tree trunks."

Salvaged wood also makes a great surface to explore surf culture. To finish the work off, Potts takes to them with an electric sander to give the images a worn and weathered feel. Slightly salt whipped.

"My own surfing life came to a standstill two years ago due to injuries," he says. "The knees have gone. I just have to boogie board or body surf now, but I'm still doing it. We're down the beach every day. I'm still there." ■

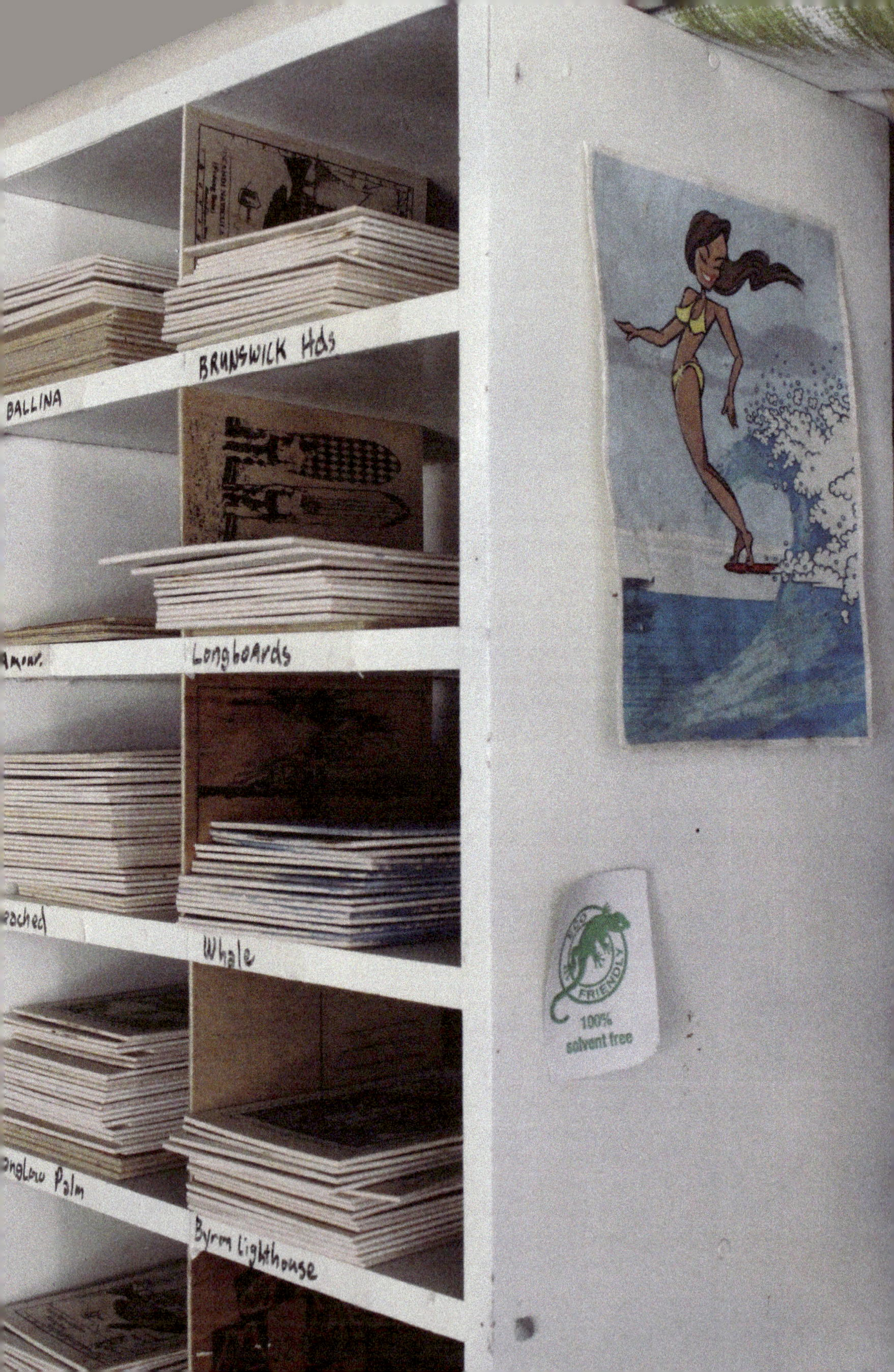
BALLINA
BRUNSWICK Hds
Longboards
Whale
Byron lighthouse
FRIENDLY
100%
solvent free

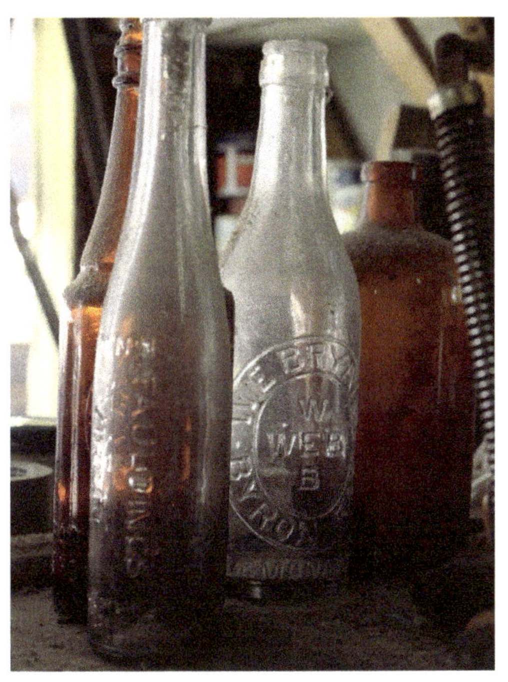

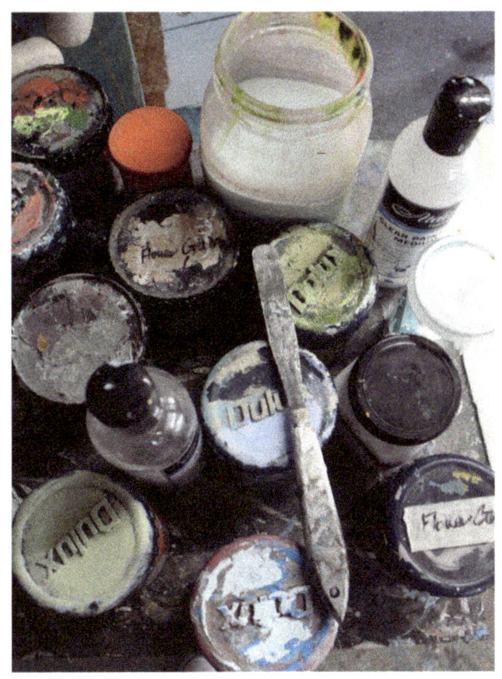

*Potts has decked out the shed as the ultimate surfy studio, with dusty records and surfing paraphernalia.*

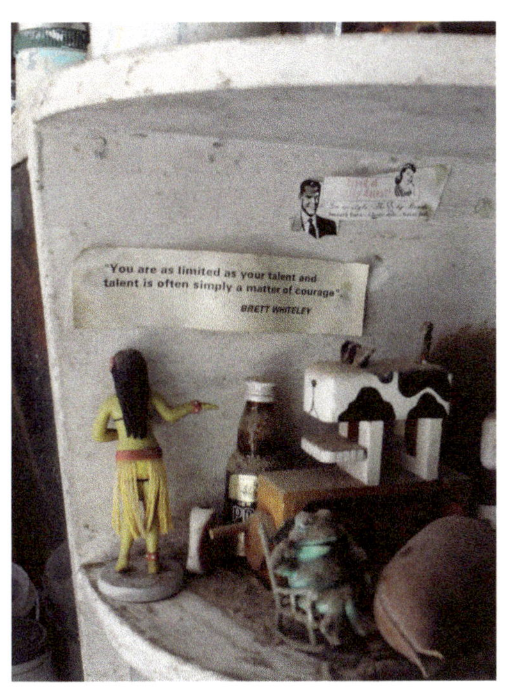


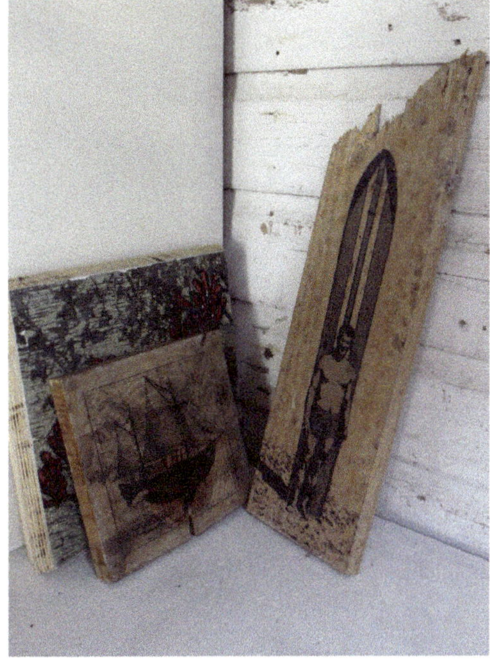

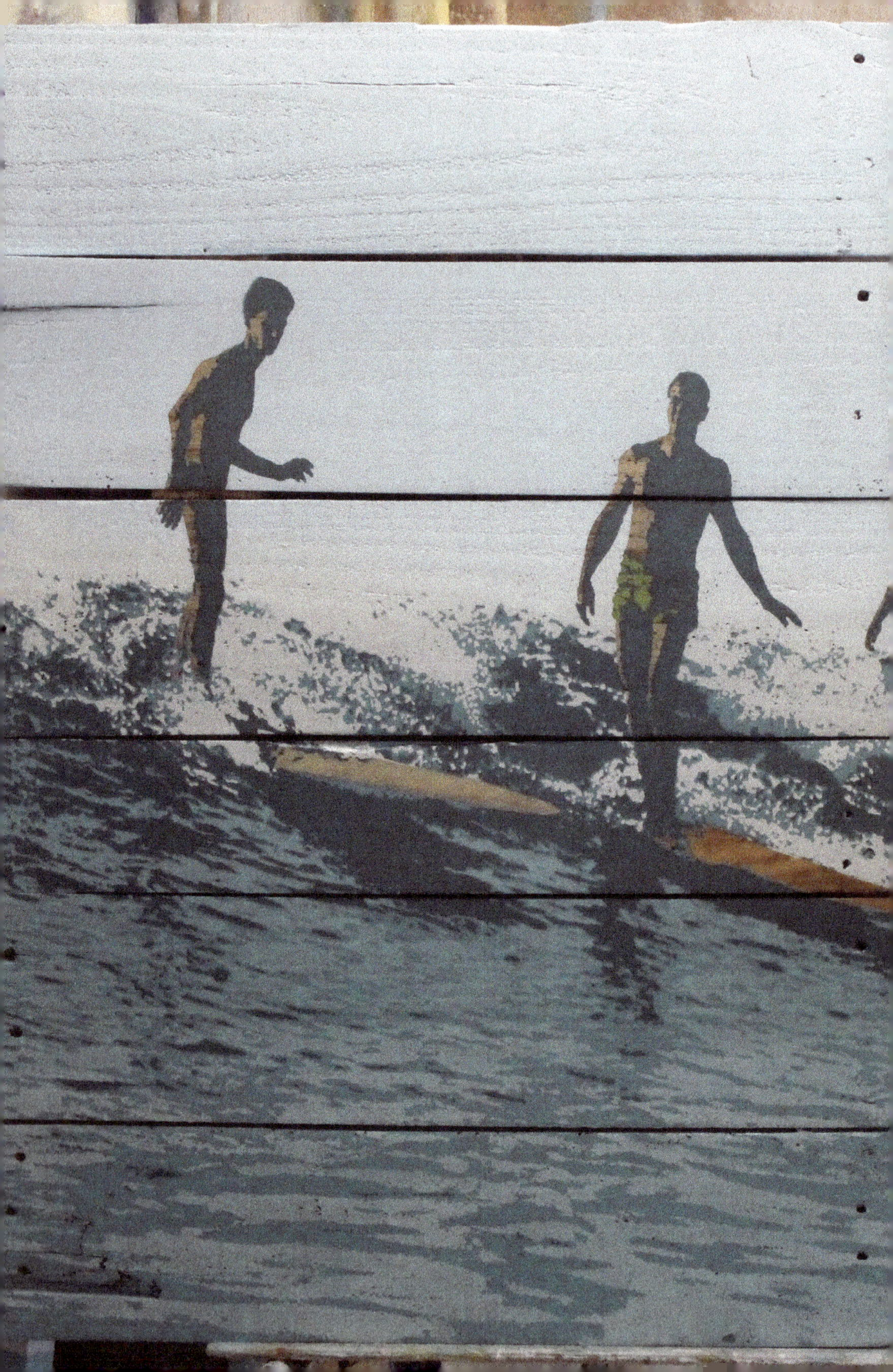

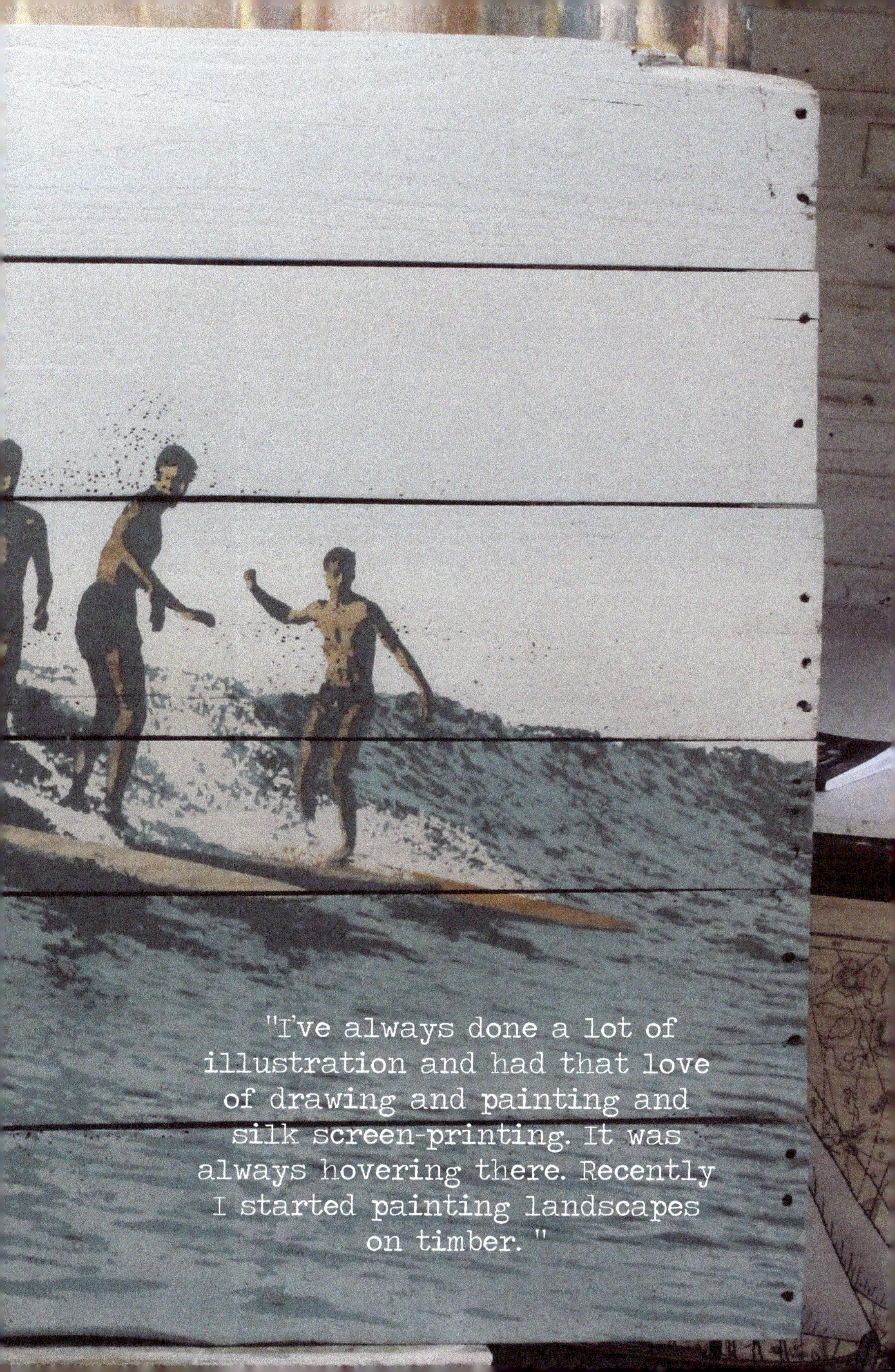

"I've always done a lot of illustration and had that love of drawing and painting and silk screen-printing. It was always hovering there. Recently I started painting landscapes on timber."

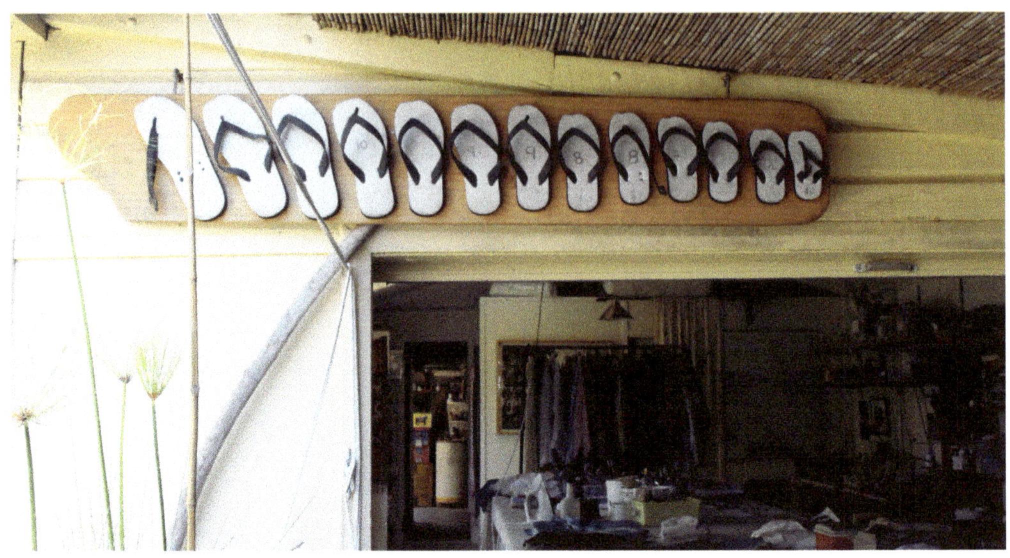

# Anne Leon
## On silken threads

When *Artist Spaces* visits the studio shed of Mullumbimby's Potts (see previous story), it's near-on impossible not to do a double take at the space of Anne Leon; Potts' partner in life, and art. The pair share a love of the coast and creativity. They also share this shed; not to mention the same infectious sense of humour. Exhibit A: the thong display.

While Potts' quarter of the shed is all surfy cool, Annie has adapted her share into a woman's-own domain of silken threads, industrial sewing machines and a continuous production line of screen-printed lovelies.

It was their creative lives that brought them together. "We met by chance through a mutual friend," Annie explains. "He was running an art gallery across the road from my studio and working part time for me. One day Potts walked into my studio looking for him, I walked around the corner dressed in paint-splattered clothes, not unlike the ones he was wearing, and said, 'Who are you?' And the rest is history."

Annie says they have a lot of fun sharing this work space. "I love it, although he's the biggest distraction," she laughs. "I was renting that studio where we met in Byron Bay for 12 years but the expenses were out of control. My landlord just kept putting the rent up, so I moved everything here."

Annie has been a professional textile artist and designer for over 30 years. Her garments and scarves are sold through upmarket boutiques and

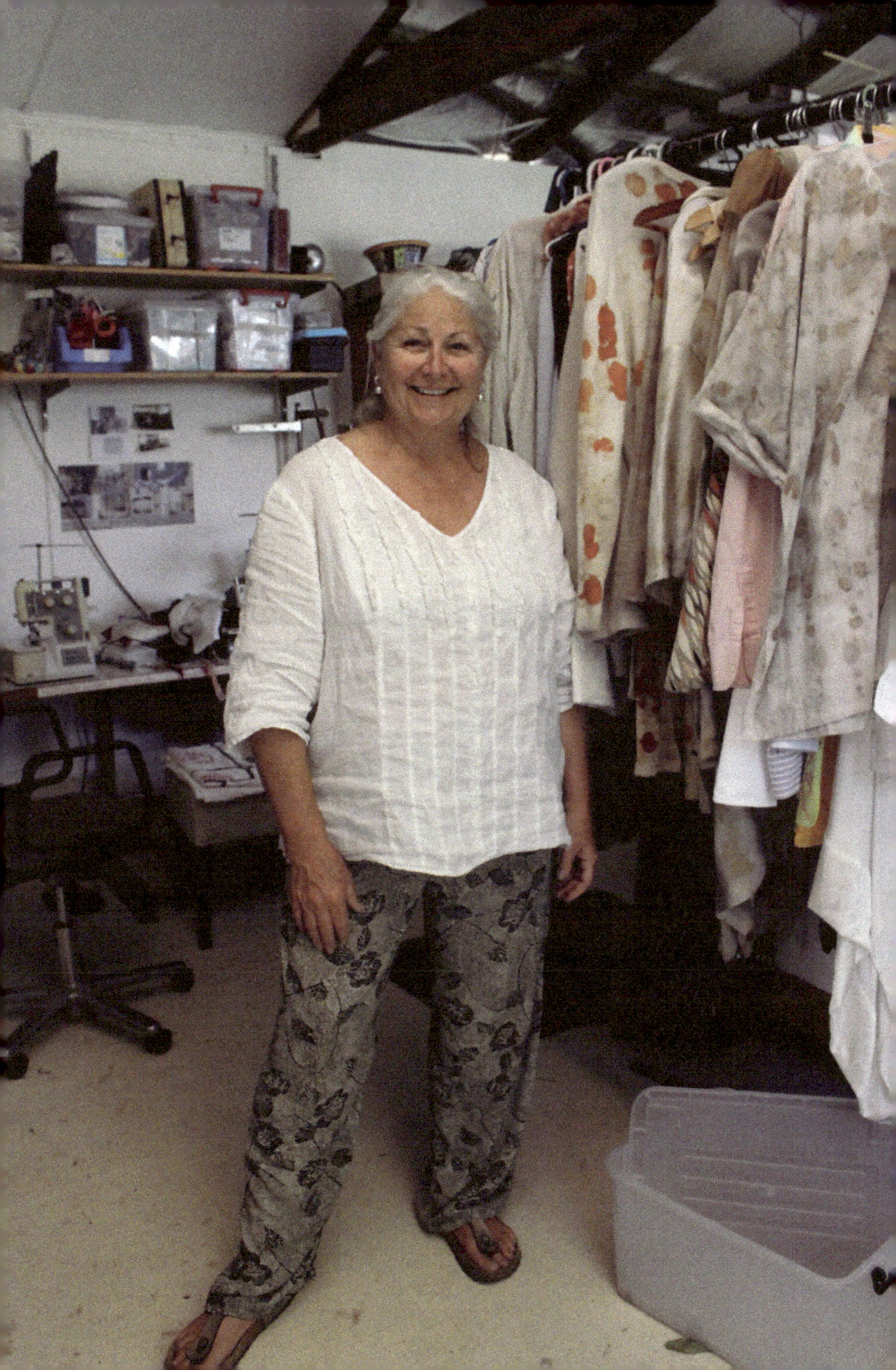

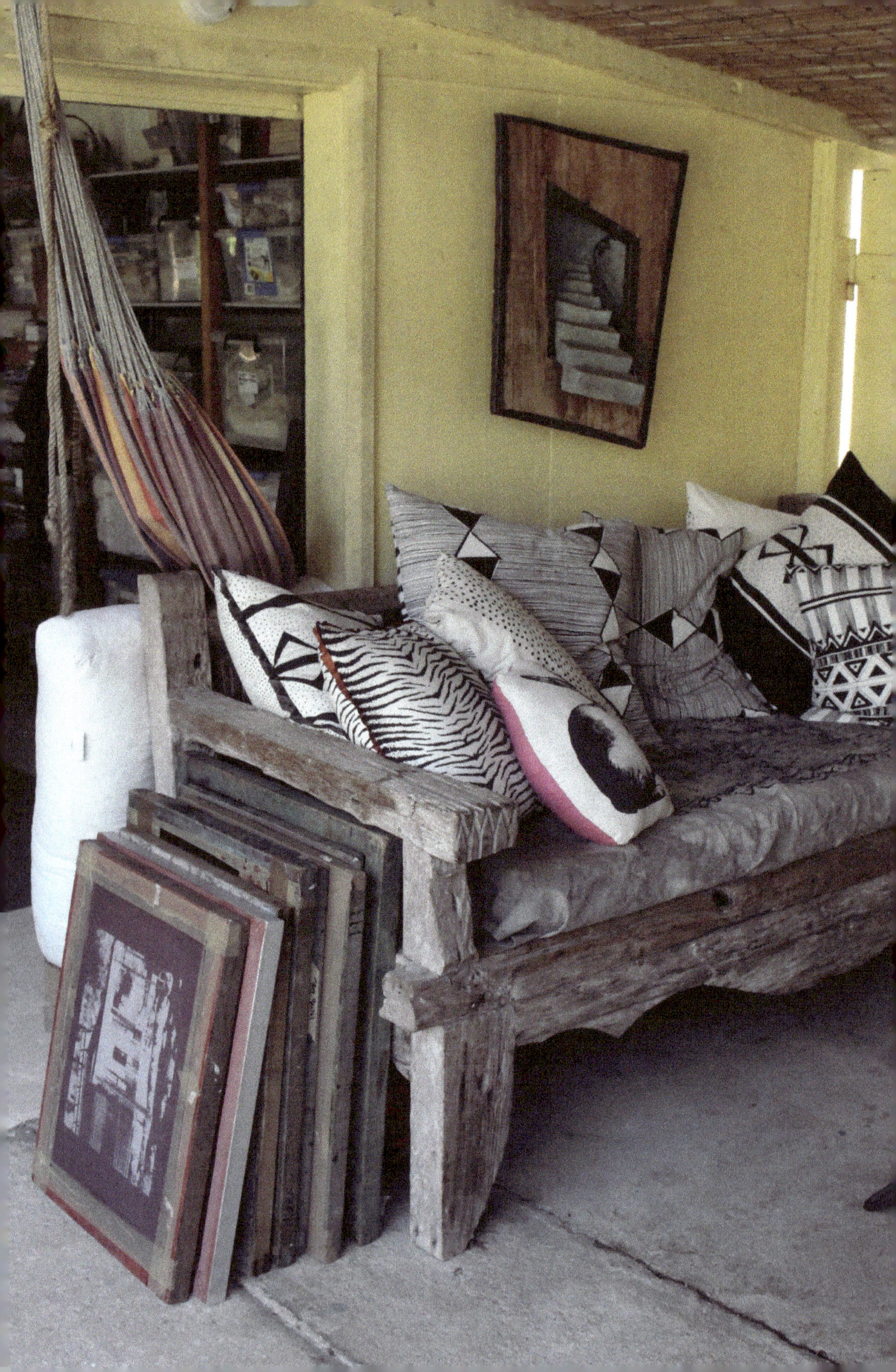

galleries. Imagine clothes as art. She plant-dyes on silk and cotton, hemp and wool, harvesting the natural dyes, shapes and textures of native plants. Annie is forever collecting the likes of casuarina, lichen and eucalyptus leaves, using unique techniques to reveal their secrets. Did you know, the minty green gum leaf reveals in its wake a deep, rusty red? Annie knows.

Like Potts, Annie is an ideas person, always adapting and tweaking and adding to her repertoire in the constant pursuit to make a living from creating. A couple of years ago she began making heirloom scarves using the imprints of flowers and leaves from wedding bouquets.

"The hard part for us is marketing, keeping abreast with social media, and adapting to the demands of a very competitive marketplace so we don't get redundant, or copied," she says. The couple's latest joint project is hand-printed timber postcards, sold in gift shops and visitor centres from Noosa to Melbourne.

Potts explains; "Annie came back from Melbourne with this whimsical little postcard on timber, but it was thin and splitting and digitally printed. We decided to make our own, using sustainable eco practices."

Each 'Postboard' is designed and silk screen-printed in their studio, from renewable plantation timber and solvent-free, water-based inks. The practice combines Potts' graphic design skills and Annie's screen printing expertise.

So, you can view Potts' and Annie's original work in a local gallery, or you can purchase one for $12 and post it to a friend. Cool, hey? ■

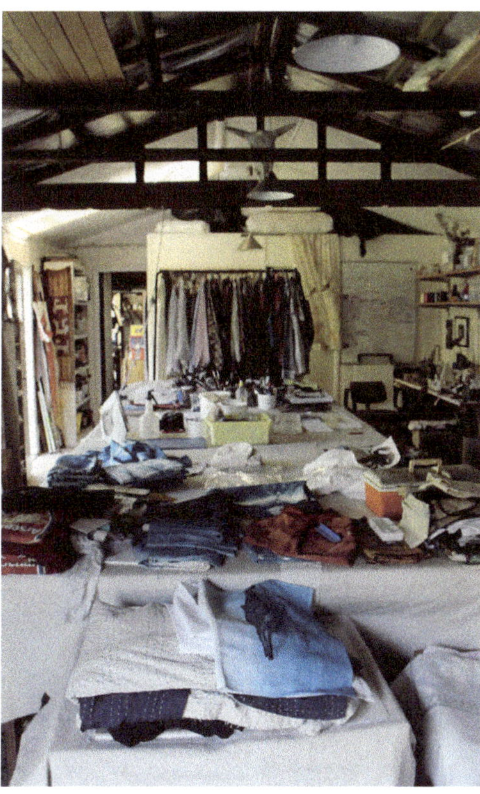

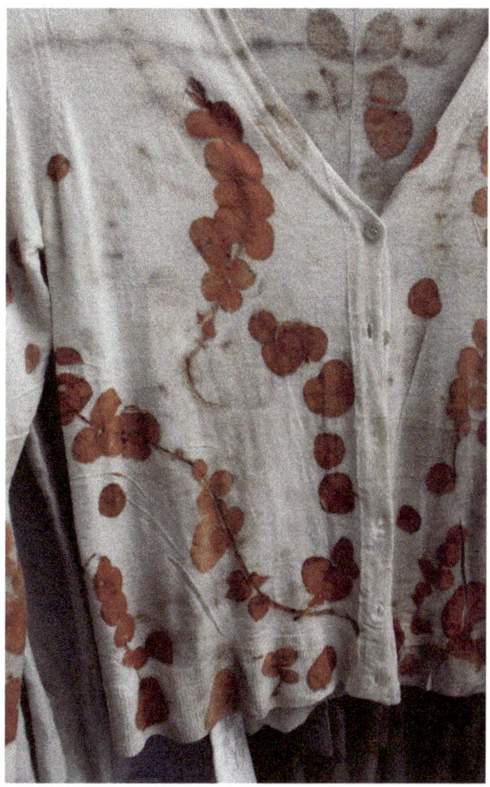

"I am forever collecting the likes of casuarina, lichen and eucalyptus leaves, using unique techniques to reveal their secrets."

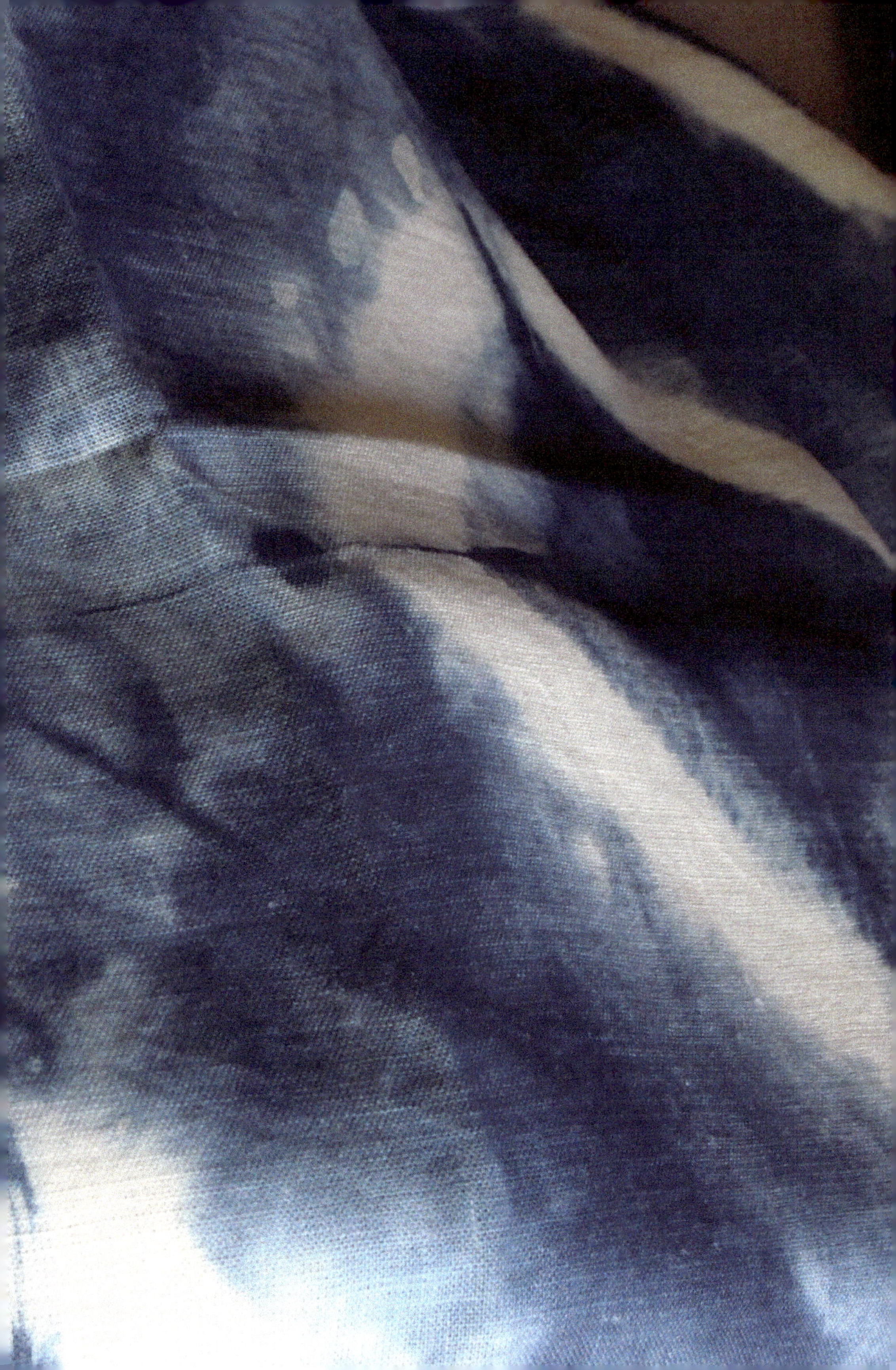

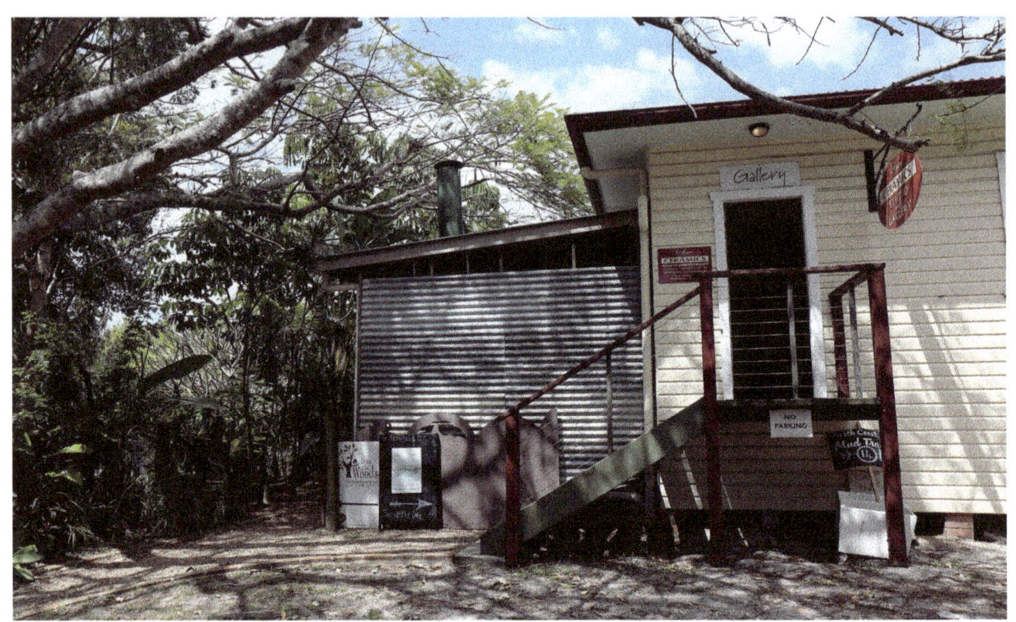


# Lucy Vanstone

## The potter's dream

The gentle, rhythmic whirr of the potter's wheel is music to Lucy Vanstone's ear. She says it takes seven years working full time to master the wheel, much like a musical instrument. If this is the case, Lucy is a virtuoso, and this place is her music hall.

The hall in question is tucked behind St Thomas' Anglican Church in beach-side Brunswick Heads. Here Lucy spends most days making pottery, meeting customers, sometimes giving one-on-one lessons and group workshops, fulfilling her goal to be the unofficial village potter. It's a role the English Lucy had longed to achieve.

"I liked the idea of being in a village setting," Lucy says. "In England there's this tradition of pottery makers in the villages. I think it brings something to a place like Brunswick Heads."

Here, where the Brunswick River meets the sea, all walks gather. Surfers and fishermen and hipsters; the latter flock for the newly-refurbished cool-as Brunswick Picture House across the road from St Thomas'.

Lucy has been in her studio and gallery for ten years. Before that she was working from a caravan in Byron Bay and dreaming of space. "I'd really outgrown the caravan," she says. "I came to Brunswick Heads to look for somewhere that I could teach, because simply making pottery is not an easy thing to make your living out of.

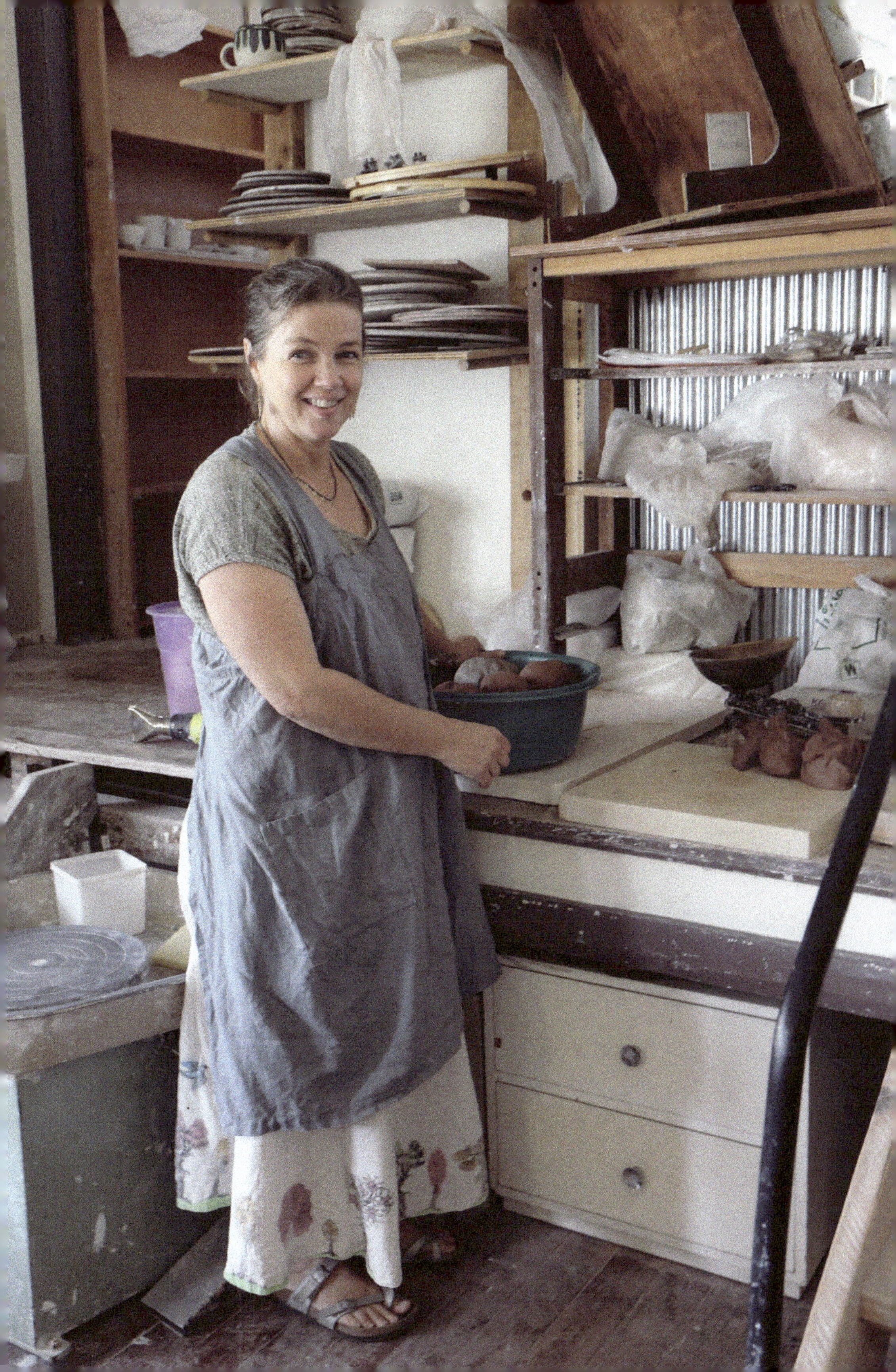

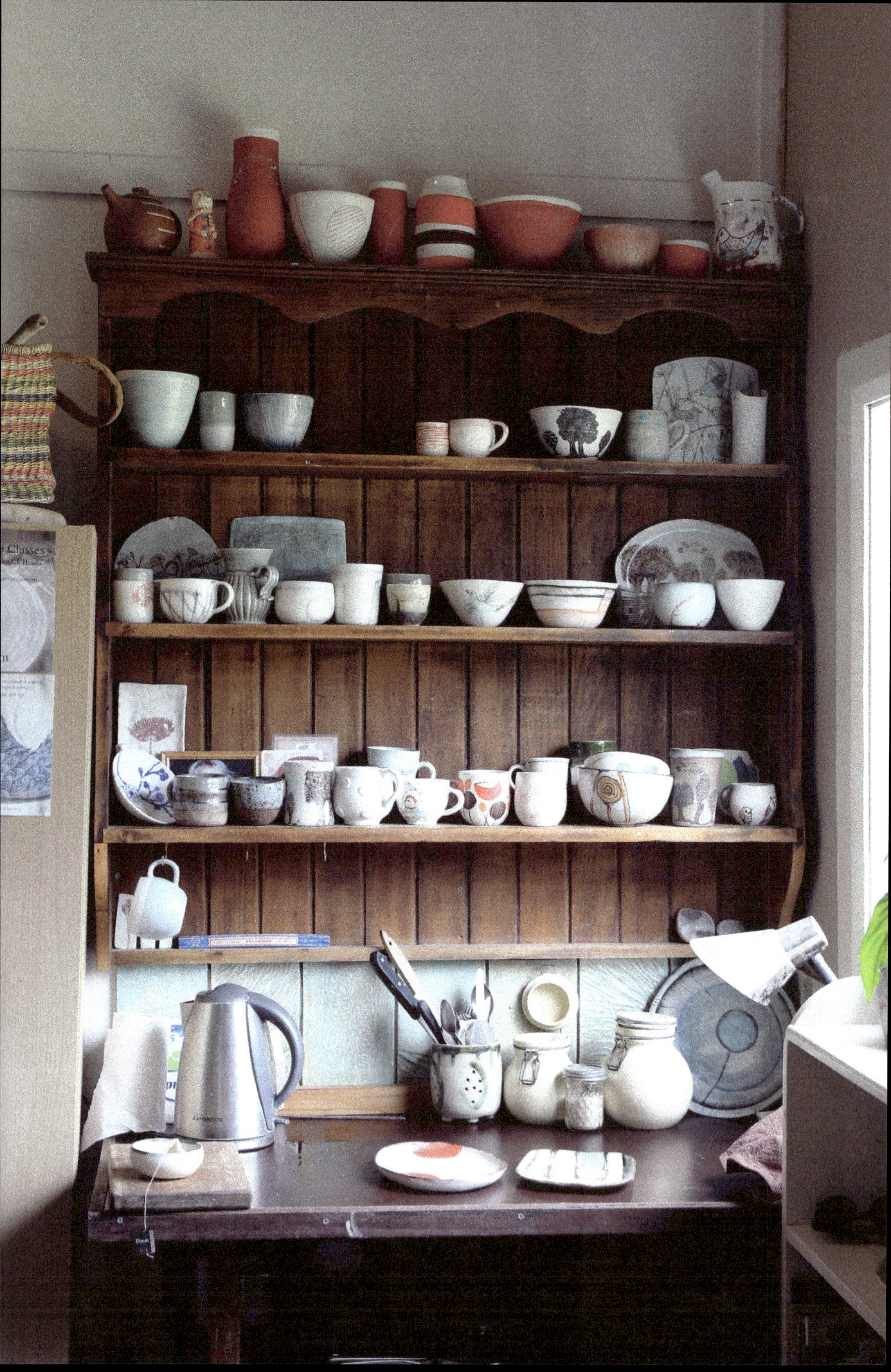

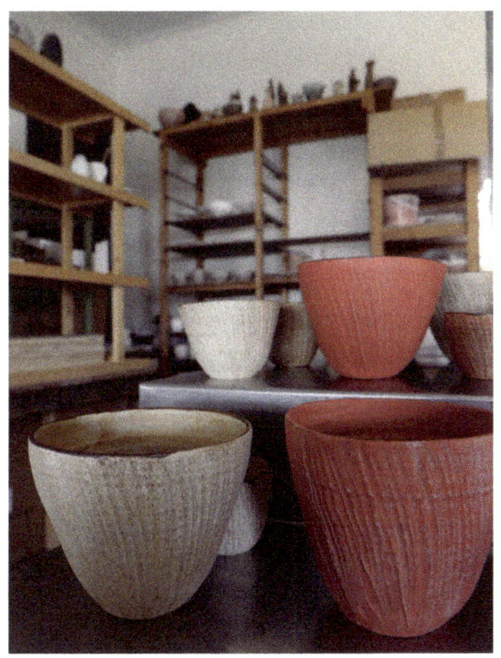

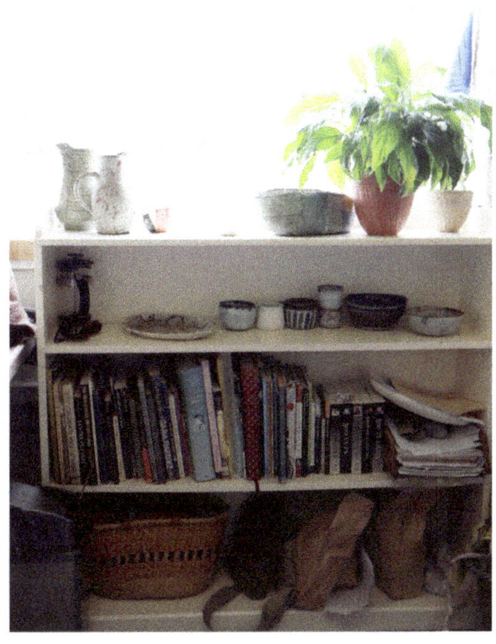

"I asked at the local real estate agents if there was anywhere to rent and they said this hall had just come up. I walked in here and I had goose bumps. It was my dream studio by the beach, and it was a church hall. I've always had a thing for church halls."

Lucy had to meet the hall committee as part of her rental application. She says they were all in their 70s and seemed quite conservative. "I was a single mother and I didn't know how they'd feel about renting the hall to me. I did wear pearls! I find it incredibly difficult to lie, so I told them I was a single mum. They said 'we don't care what you do, as long as you don't run a brothel'."

The hall had previously been a childcare centre and was painted bright green with yellow trim. Luckily Lucy was handy with a paintbrush, too. She built a lean-to for her kilns at the side and put up a partition to sub-let some of the space, and has been happy here ever since. "I'm very attached to the place," she says. "I think I'm more attached to this place than my home. (Home being a couple of timber yurts in the bush, which Lucy and her partner Jon bought one year after she started renting the hall.) "It's the light and the atmosphere here. As soon as I walked in I got a really good feeling about it."

Others do, too. Lucy has inspired many people to try their hand on the wheel. "I could just teach," she says. "I get asked at least five times a week. Pottery is very popular right now, everyone wants to learn. In the last three years it's grown in popularity and I think that's because of people sharing pictures of pottery on Instagram, and because restaurants now buy handmade crockery."

She fully understands the lure, having become captivated by clay in her 20s. "I had begun working for a local potter. I looked after her two kids for a few hours and in exchange she let me use her studio. I got quite obsessed quite quickly. As soon as I got on the wheel I thought 'yes, I want to do this'." The desire was put on hold for a number of years while Lucy ran a café in England, then followed her heart to Australia.

Six-months pregnant, she landed in this region with her then-partner, who knew her well enough to purchase a pottery wheel and place it on their front verandah. There it sat until Lucy received a gentle reminder via a children's book. "I remember reading a story to my daughter about what mother's do. On one page it read 'My mum's a potter'. And I thought, 'I want to be a potter'. I loved the idea of her being around me while I did something creative. I'd always been self-employed, I'd either cooked or made shoes or some sort of creative thing."

Lucy enrolled to study a Diploma of Ceramics at the Lismore TAFE. "I didn't actually get the qualification, I just did what I wanted in the course. I was interested in making practical pottery. The art theory intimidates me actually."

But Lucy's work is art. Each piece a unique representation of her skill and creativity. They range from rustic stoneware to fine porcelain. From earthy tones to watermelon reds. "I experiment constantly," she says. "I'm unusual in a way in that I have lots of different styles and I work with a lot of different clays and porcelain. Sometimes I go back to things I've done years ago. I don't think I would ever get bored doing pottery, and the wheel is still my favourite part of the whole process. I don't need to think about it, so it's quite a meditative space to be in."

Making pottery her livelihood has also called on Lucy's creativity. Since she's been in this hall, the rent has gone up by 80 per cent, in line with Brunswick Head's growing popularity. Lucy says it forces her to constantly adjust her business model, consider her prices, to add an extra workshop to her monthly schedule every now and then.

"It hasn't been the easiest thing to make a living out of," she says. "Sometimes I think I probably should put my prices up, but I really like the fact that people can come in here and afford to buy something that they can then use every day. If someone spends $30 on a cup, I know they're going to use it."

Lucy places a fist-sized lump of dark clay on the wheel and gently presses her foot on the pedal. "I talk a lot to people about what drives them," she says. "For years, throughout my late 20s and 30s, I really wanted to find something that I was passionate about. I'd wake up thinking, 'what is it? What am I going to do?' And I found it. I feel quite lucky that I found it."

Lucky, too, that she found this place, with its lovely light, lofty ceiling and worn timber floorboards. The hall's 95-year-old neighbour remembers when this place was built. Those timber boards were repurposed from the town's memorial hall. The dance hall. They'd seen some rhythm all right. ■

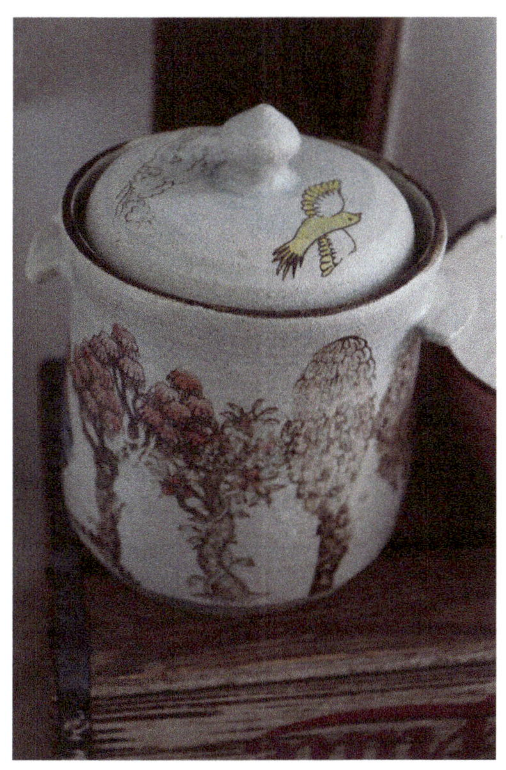

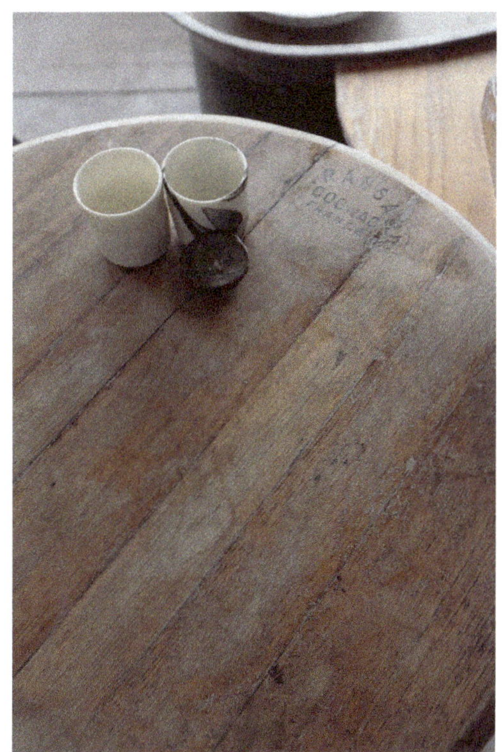

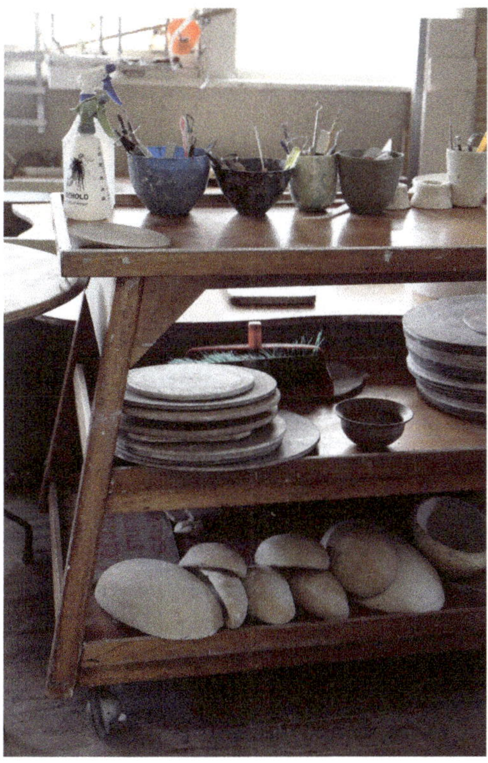

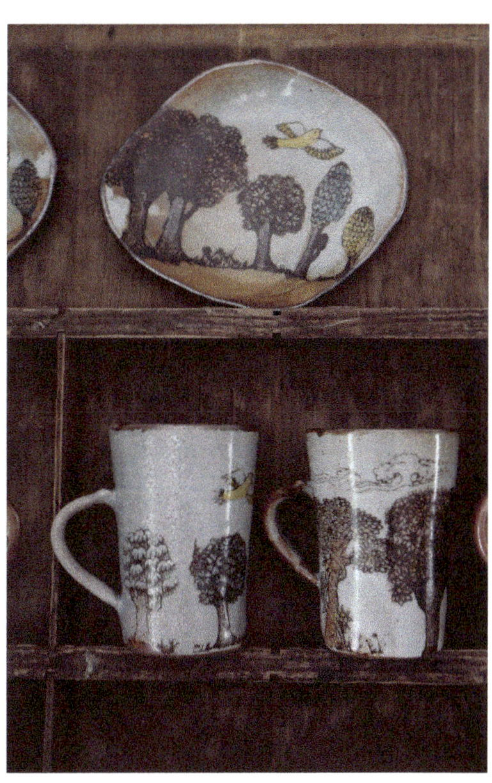

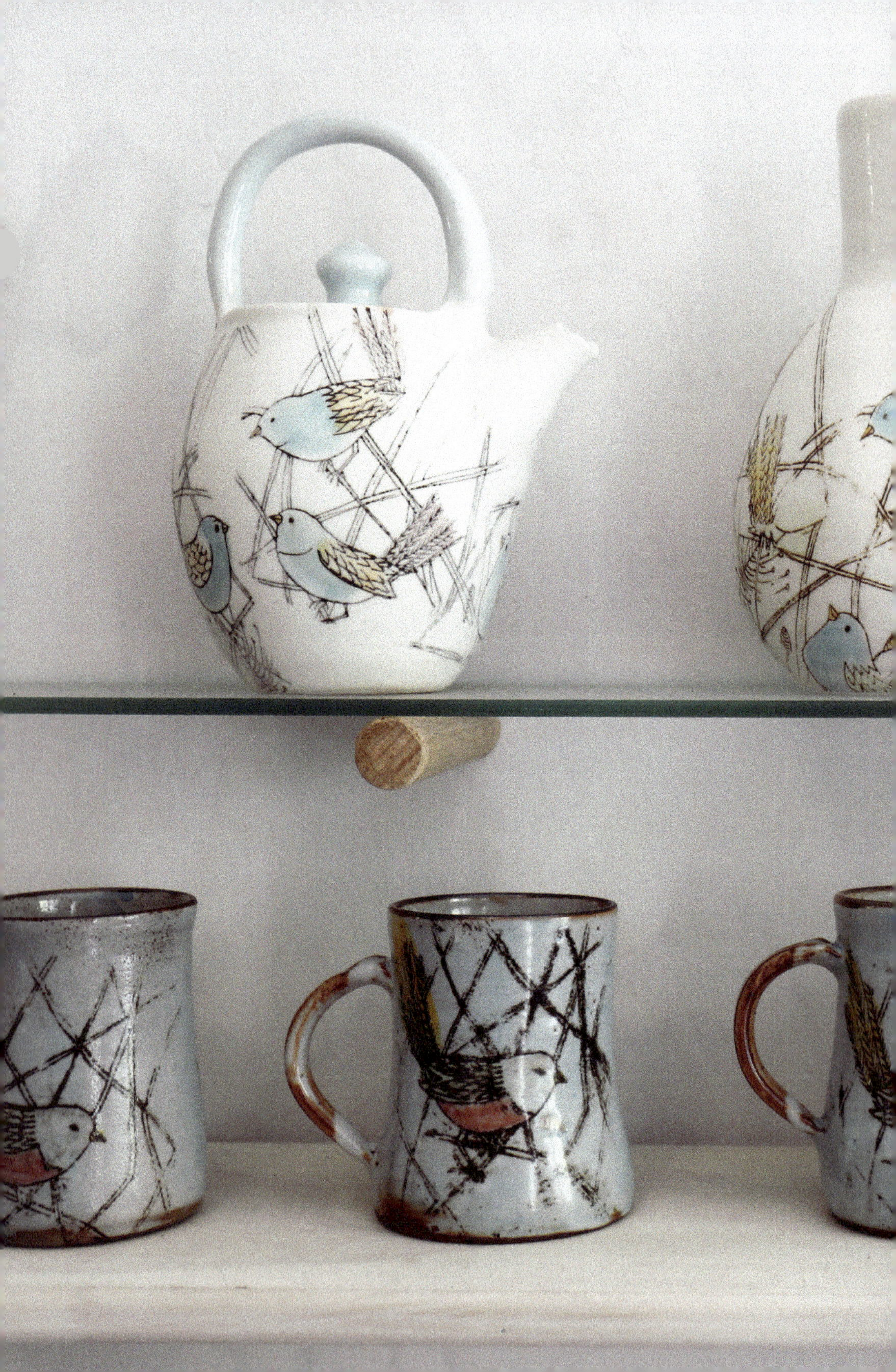

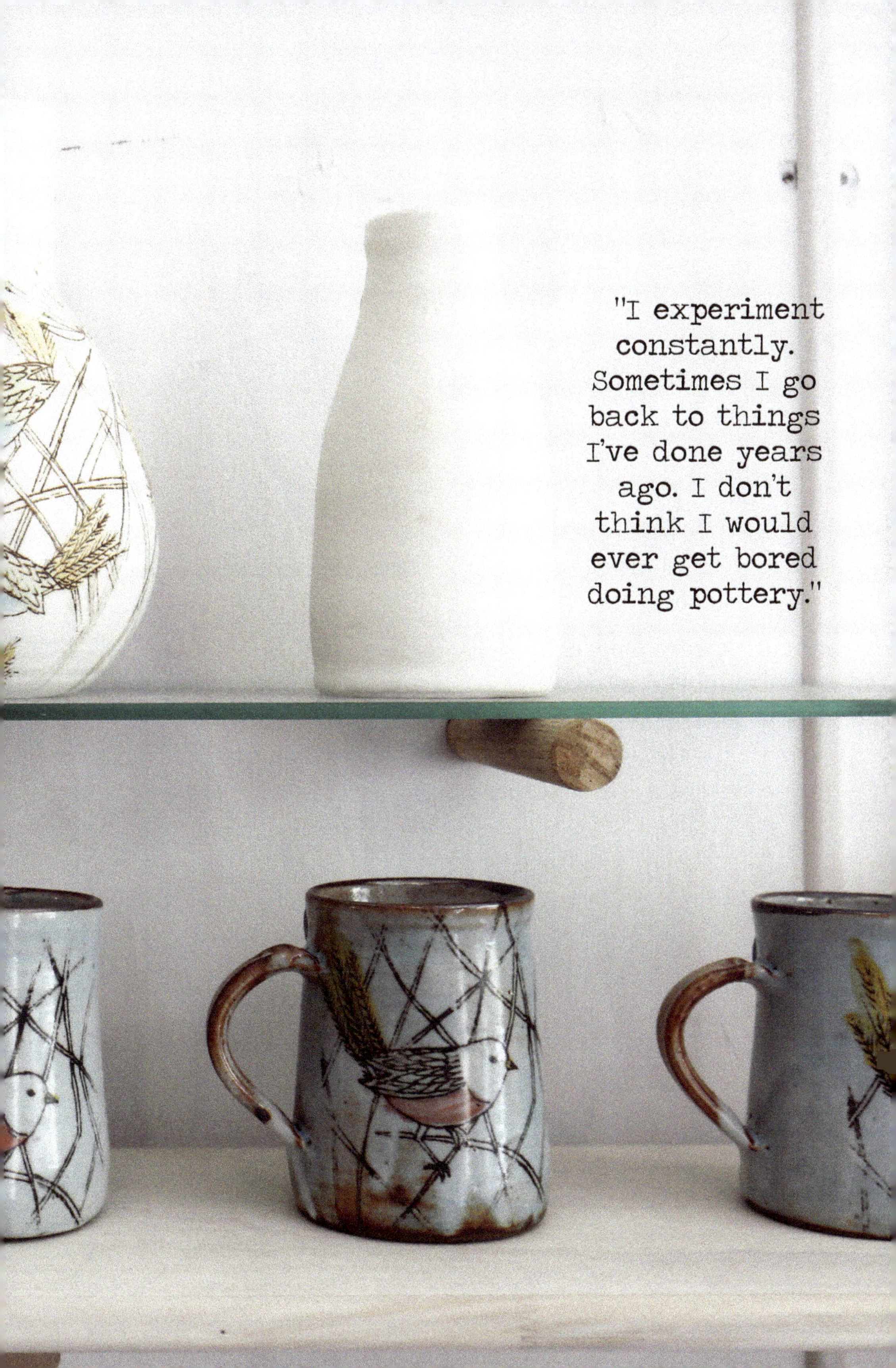
"I experiment constantly. Sometimes I go back to things I've done years ago. I don't think I would ever get bored doing pottery."

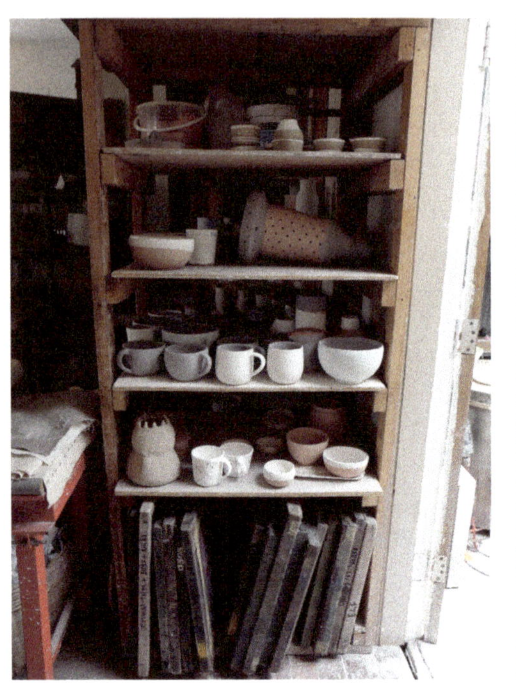

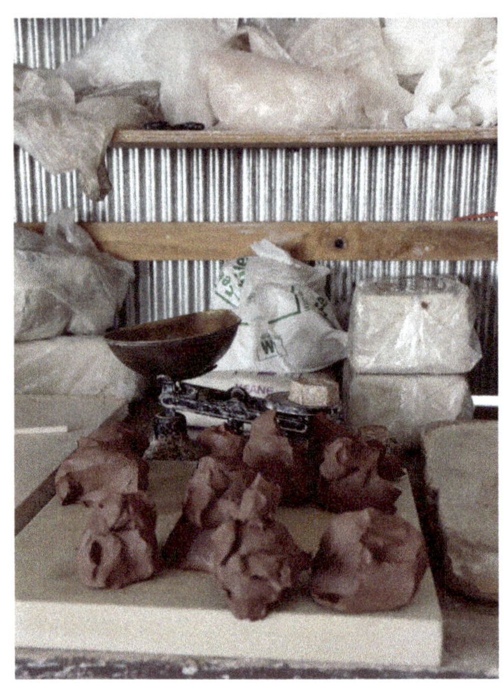

*Lucy built a lean-to for her kilns at the side and has been happy here ever since.*

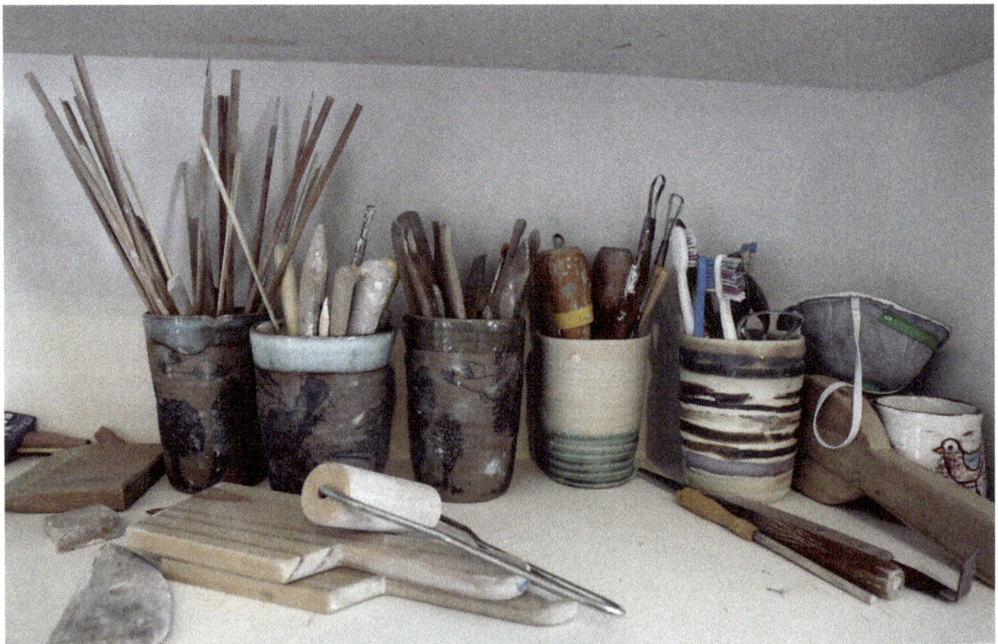

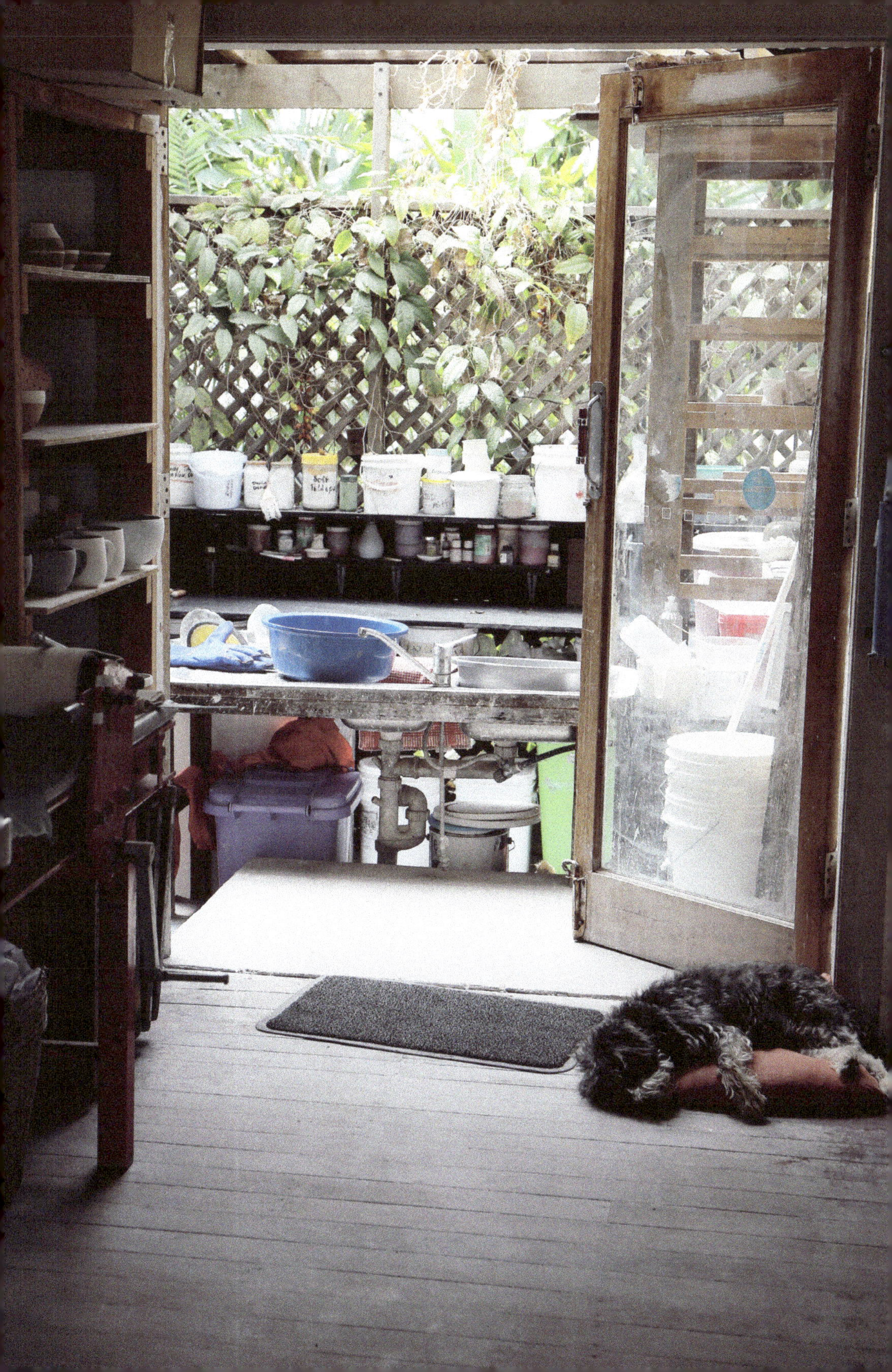

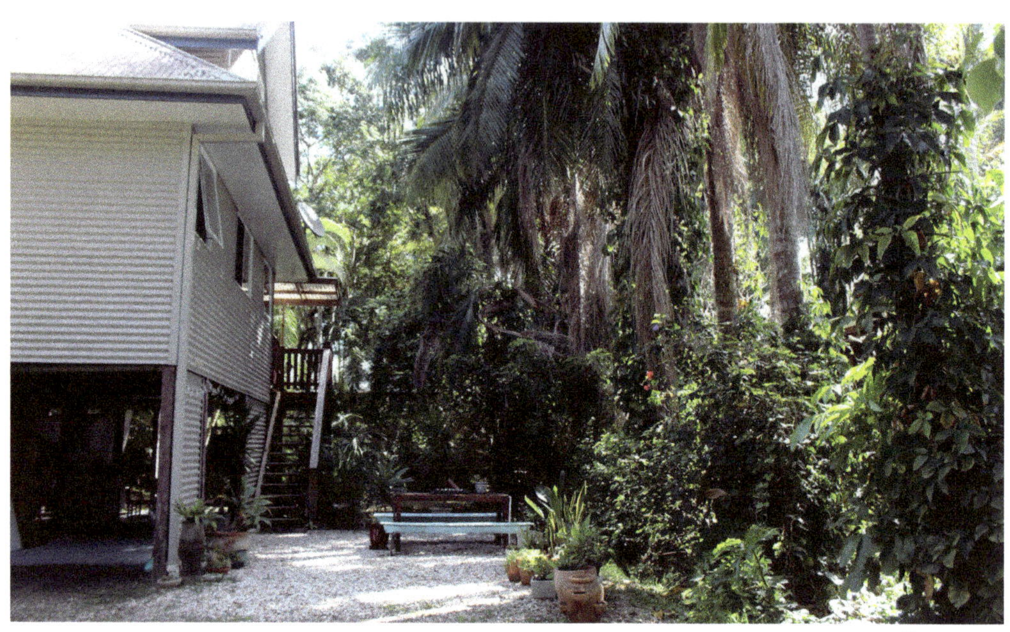

# Casey Arnaud

## Life's just golden

Casey Arnaud, of South Golden Beach, is on the cusp of her first exhibition. Her third incarnation of a creative life. "I like to say I'm a creative rather than an artist," she says. "I feel like there's a real stigma for some people when they ask, 'what do you do?'"

Anyone who visits Casey's home need not ask. This is a creative place. A light and lofty zincalume tree house that filters breeze and sun and ocean sounds. An interiors magazine would need to coin a new phrase for this place. Earthy boho would do it. There's plenty of quirk and collected treasures lovingly kept, from life and ocean's bounty.

Here Casey lives with her two daughters, surrounded by vines and palms and the easy-going South Golden locals. "It's a really close community and I love that," she says. "It's flat and the streets are quiet so the kids can ride their bikes and walk everywhere. I have found my tribe here and that makes for a great home."

It begs the question, what sets the scene for the character of a place? Is it the environment, or the people? Casey says this area changed when the people did. It's built on a flood zone, hence the high-up houses, and was originally called Black Snake Swamp.

"I've been told it used to be quite a seedy area. There'd often be drug hauls left on the beach. It was very hippy and quite raw. Eventually it

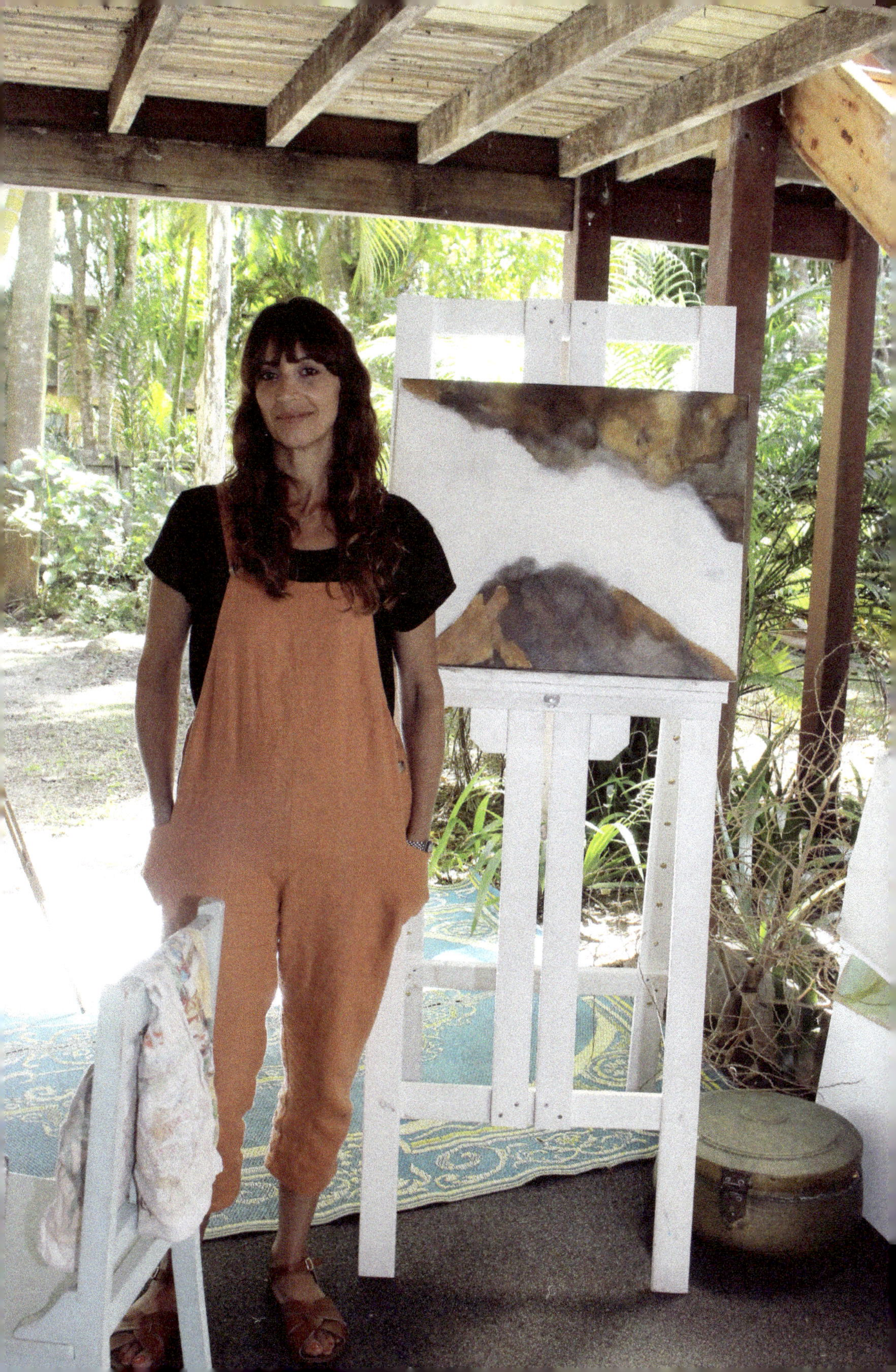

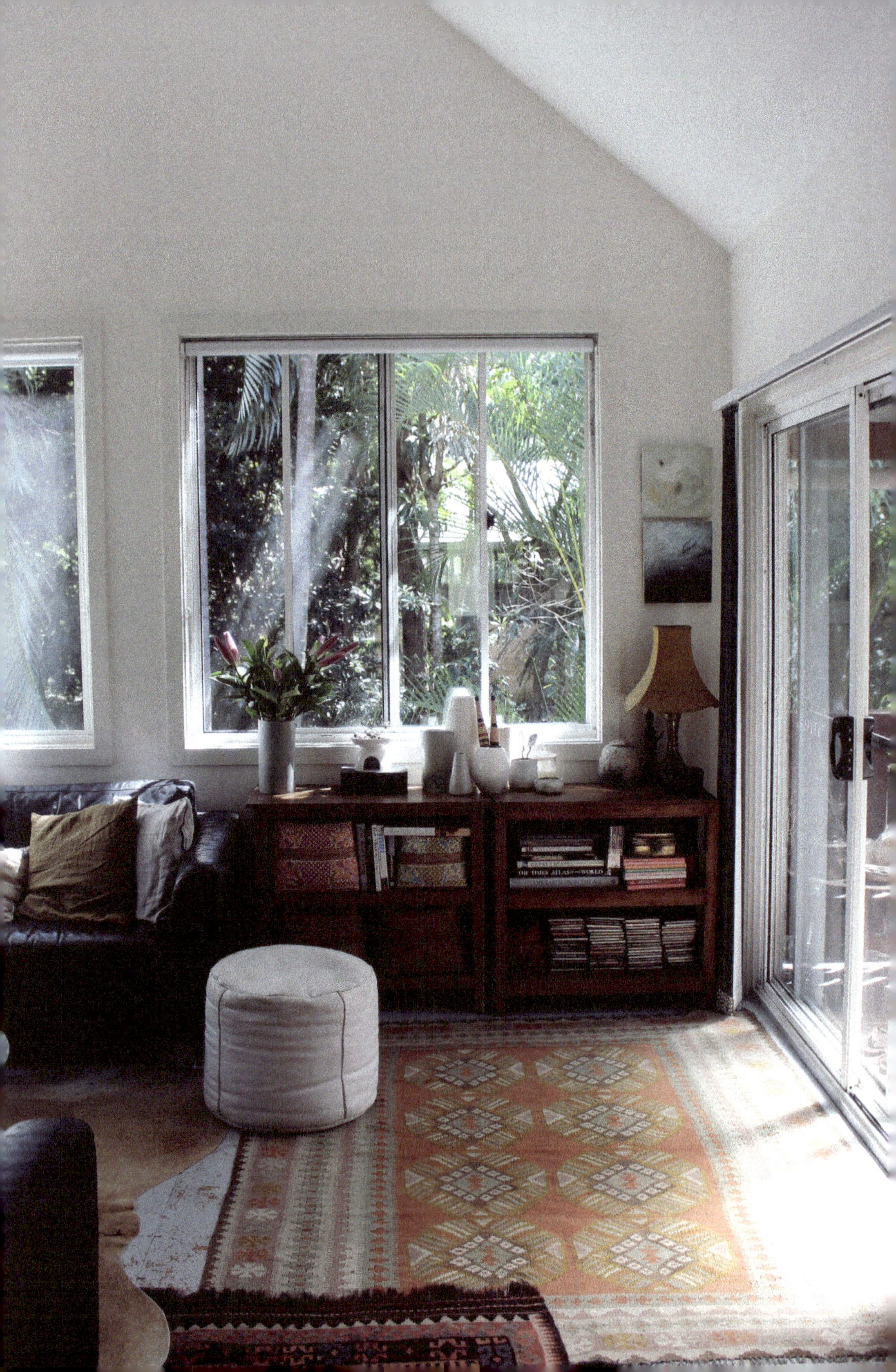

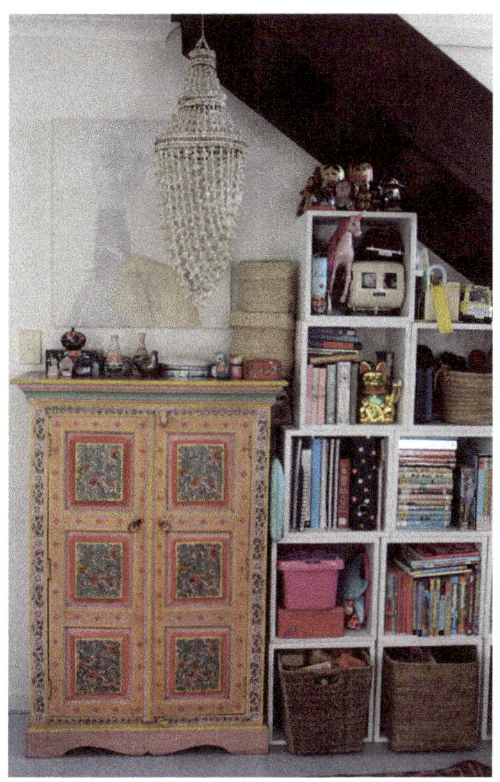

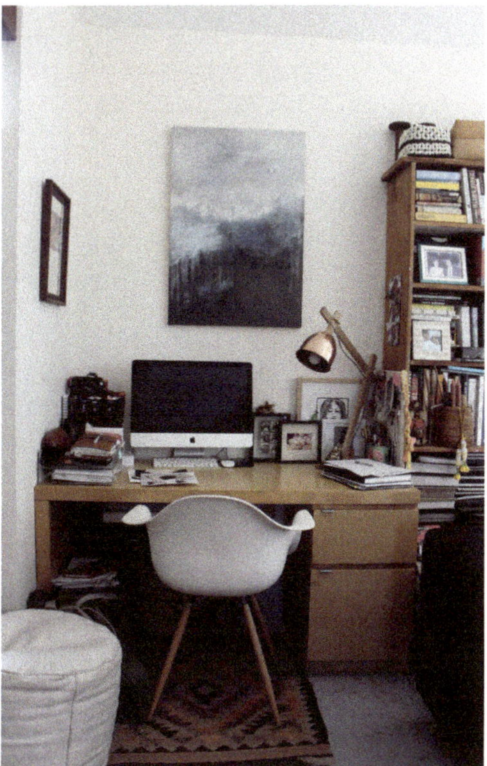

changed when the high prices in Byron Bay pushed people out here. It's seen a lot of changes."

So has Casey! Three big ones, remember. At 22 Casey scored herself a $3000 young entrepreneur business grant, which she turned into a highly-successful cosmetics company called *Arnaud*. "I produced upmarket gift products with an aromatherapy base, which I sold nationally and internationally, predominantly in the US and UK," she says.

"After ten years I sold the business to a US cosmetics company. It was a good decision at the time but it was like letting my baby go. I'd just had my first child and it was hard, juggling the business with being a parent.

"Even back then I didn't really know where my place was. Financially I wish I was drawn to a full-time job but I've never been like that. I've always had the desire to work for myself and be creative."

Soon enough came business number two. Travels throughout Asia inspired Casey to source and import ethically-made, Fair Trade toys, games and clothing from the likes of Indonesia, India and Burma. She traded online under the name Little Gypsies. Little did she know she was about to become one herself.

When Casey's 15-year relationship ended, she moved to the Byron Shire, after 24 years in Sydney. From a semi in Bondi she landed in a little Queenslander. "We used to holiday up here and come to visit friends. There's a certain energy here that's just beautiful," she says.

"I did get a little bit lonely at first. Bondi is such a busy hub that when I first came here I felt like I'd moved to a retirement village. It's taken seven years but now it feels like home. The frenetic pace of Sydney doesn't suit me anymore." She's referring to the overwhelming stimulation of traffic, shopping centres and constant over-consumption.

At one stage, in the pursuit to save some cash to buy a home, Casey moved herself and her girls into a 1960s caravan on the bank of the Brunswick River. It was only for a few months, but it made an impact. "My eldest daughter didn't think that was cool," she laughs. "But there was a moment when she said, 'this is pretty special mum'. I have this memory of cooking dinner, with music playing, the girls huddled around the table playing a game and thinking, 'I'll look back and remember this as one of the best times of my life'." By that stage Casey had embarked on making art. She talks of printmaking at the tiny caravan dinette table.

It's only been in the last three years that Casey has seriously confronted canvas, although she's been drawn to art since her teens. "I applied for art school when I finished high school at 17. I didn't have a portfolio so I used my sister's artwork. It was a drawing of an onion, among a few other pieces. I didn't get in," she says, laughing at the realisation it was her sibling that didn't pass judgement. Judgement. That perceived condition inflicted by others has been Casey's biggest hurdle.

It's taken three years of learning and connecting with like-minded locals to find her delicate, yet confident brushstrokes. Casey began by enrolling in a TAFE course three years ago. "It was very hard at first," she says. "I'd go to class and cry on the way home, because I had these overwhelming feelings of inadequacy. I couldn't show my work to anyone. It was that feeling of opening myself up to judgement. Everyone else in the course had experience. I'd only done one painting since high school.

"I was scared of being judged and of letting go of control. Art when it's controlled doesn't seem to look natural. When you let go, that's when it feels and looks natural to me." She says the hardest thing has actually been to let go of the judgement she placed on herself.

After TAFE, Casey progressed to the Byron School of Art. The show she is preparing for is the result of two years of dedicated training. Of expanding her mediums, as well as her mind. Studying art has helped her find peace and purpose in this place. "Everything has slowed down a bit," she says. "My priorities are more in balance and I seem to have a better grasp on the work, family, pleasure and creative juggling act. Yet I still have the strong drive in me and love to surround myself with people that inspire me and push me that bit further."

There's no pressure, however, in the cool of Casey's open-air studio, under the house. Here she has thrown down rugs, placed an easel and a table of paints and brushes. Here the fat roots of the garden palms push their way up from the earth. And so every aspect of life is grounded; motherhood, nature, creativity, home. ■

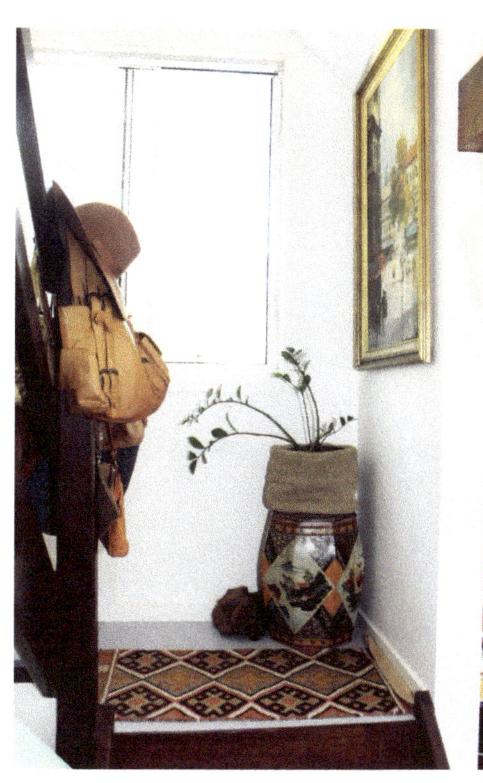

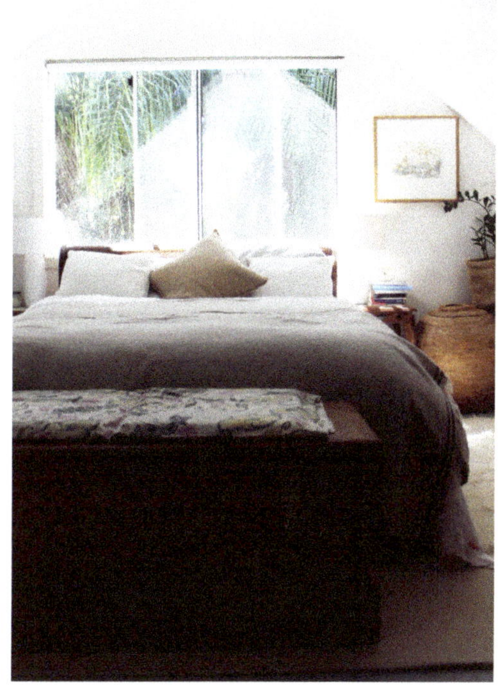

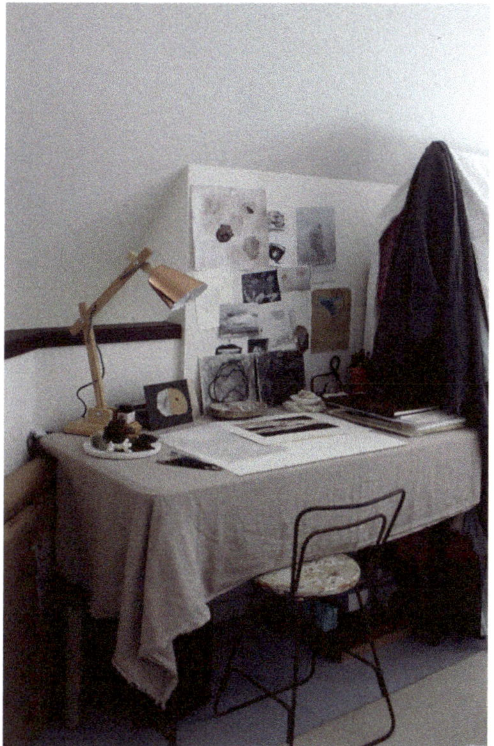

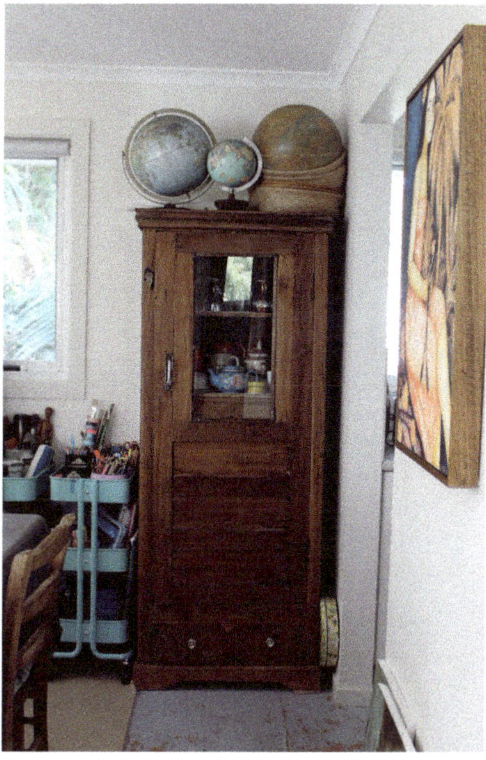

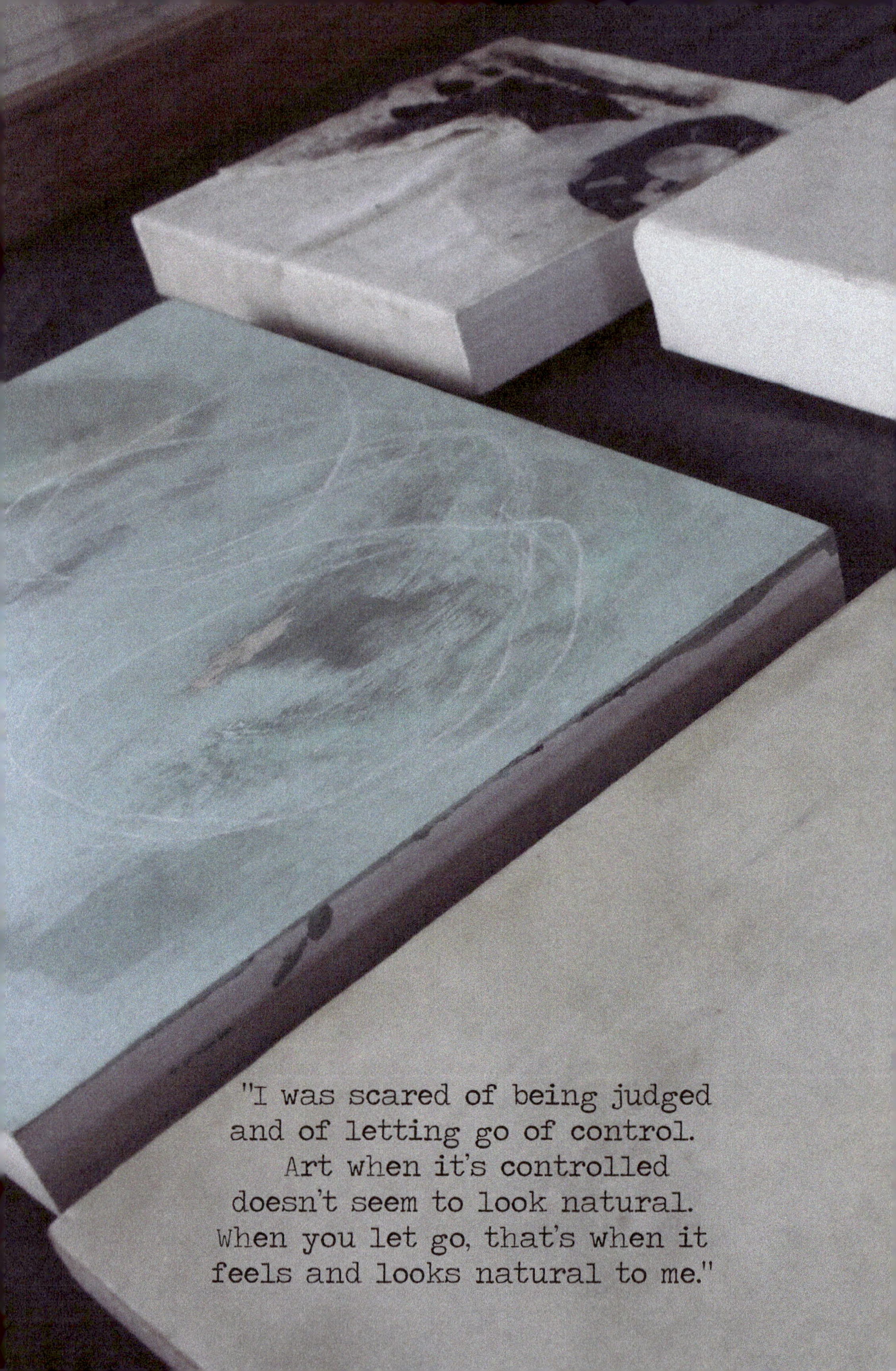
"I was scared of being judged
and of letting go of control.
Art when it's controlled
doesn't seem to look natural.
When you let go, that's when it
feels and looks natural to me."

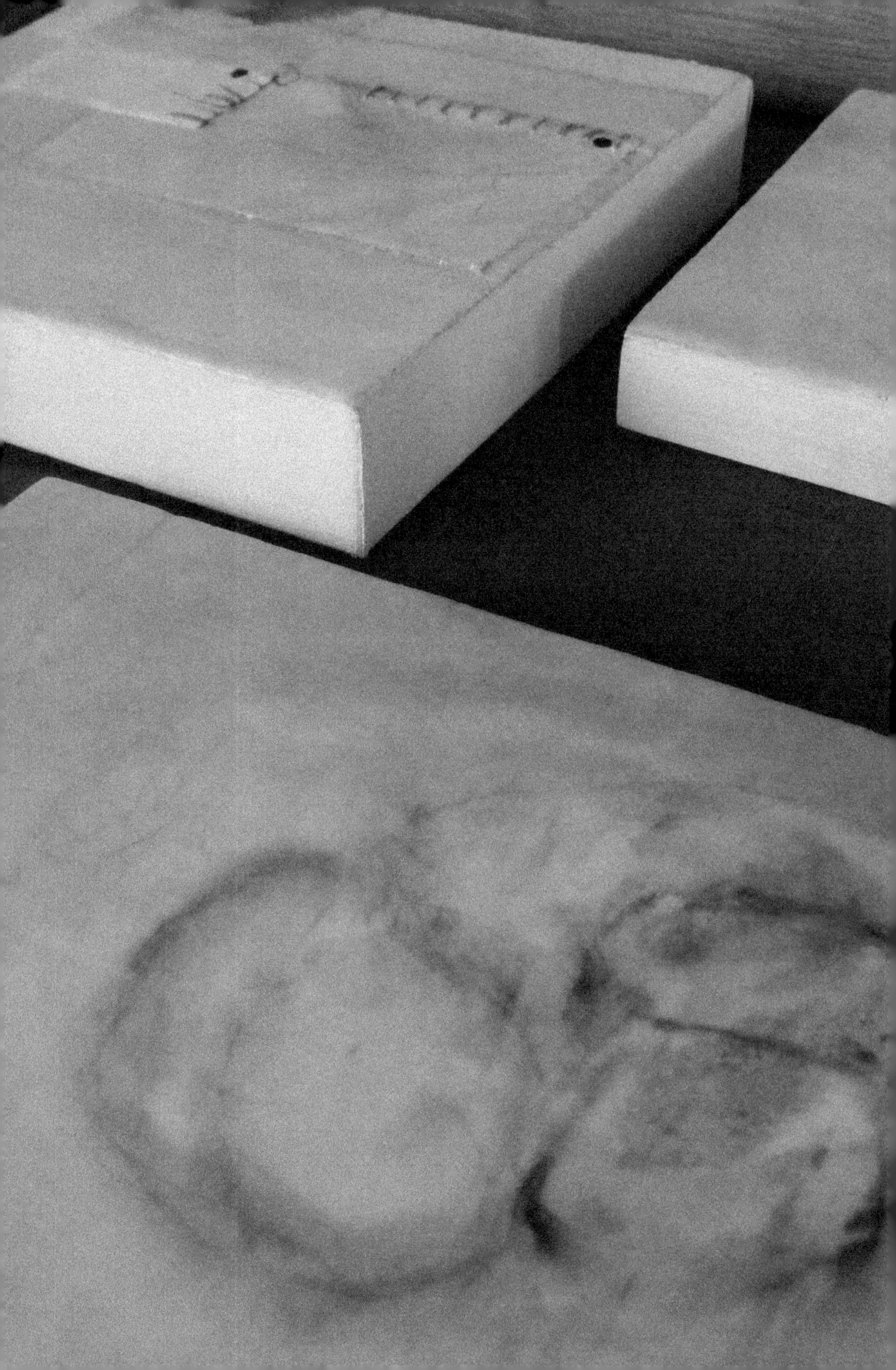

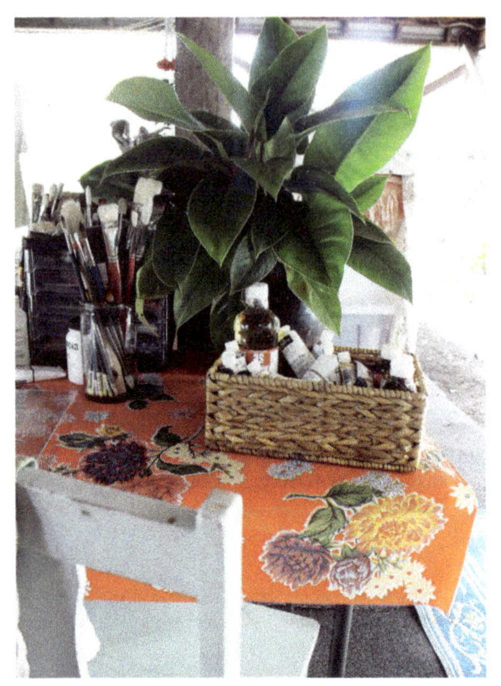

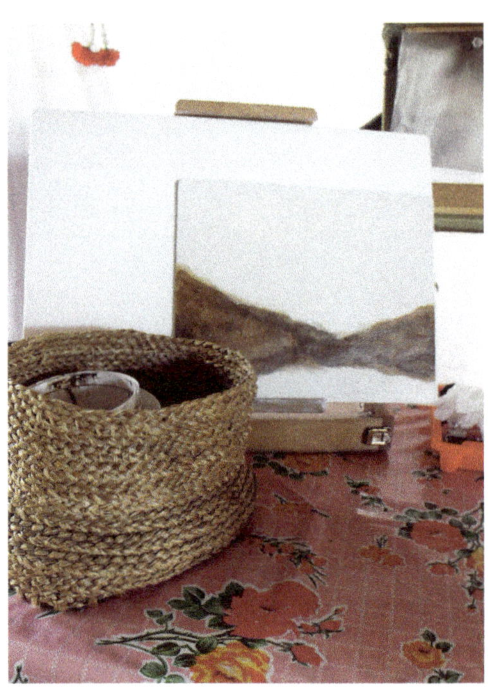

This is a creative place. A light and lofty zincalume tree house that filters breeze and sun and ocean sounds.

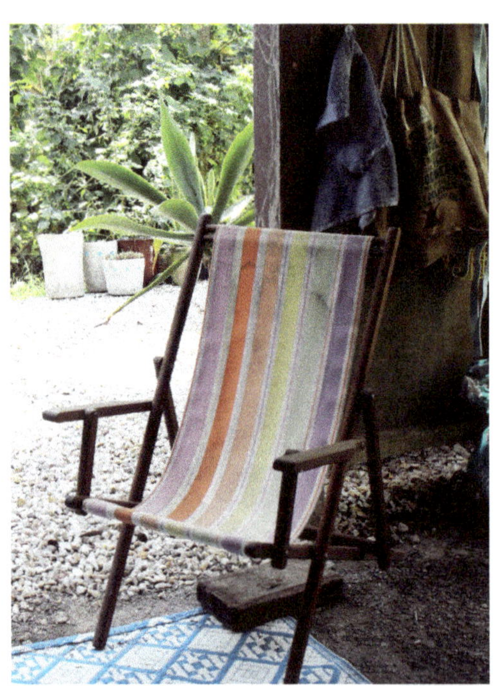

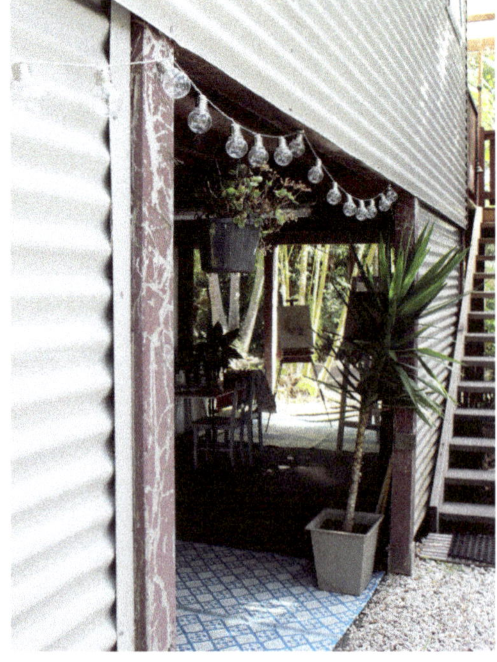

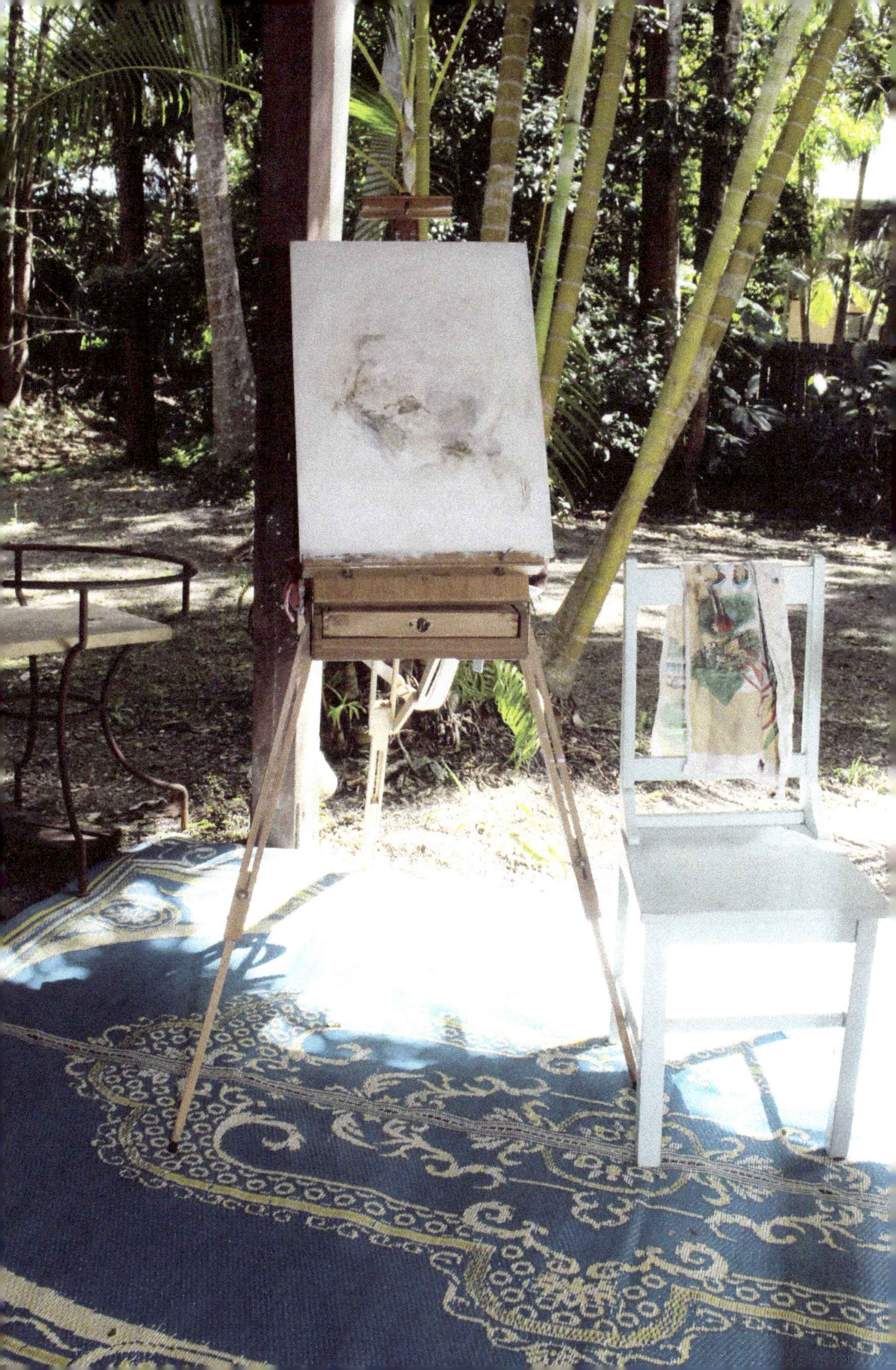

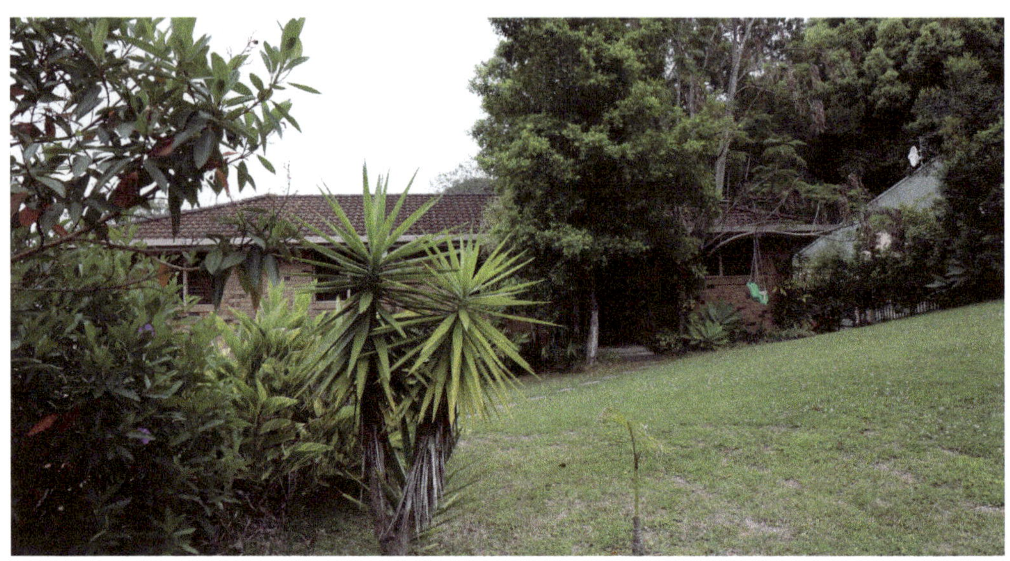

# James McMillan

## Surf's always up

Throw away the clocks. Forget time. James McMillan lives by the tides. It's beautiful to find someone like this, at a time when most people are more in tune with their mobile phone ring tone than the push and pull of natural forces.

*Artist Spaces* arrives at James' Byron Bay home to find a sign on the door that says 'Gone Surfing'. All else happens in good time, but the tide comes first. "Because this is the most easterly point in Australia there's always waves hitting one of the beaches," James says. "This morning it was at Wategos, so my wife and I took out the logs (old style longboards). You can surf every day around here.

"Everyone you deal with around here is working at a very different pace. Things are just a bit slower. Don't get me wrong, stuff gets done, and there's quite a solid surf and arts industry, but if things get delayed it's not a big deal. This is the main reason I'm able to surf and work as an artist, because there is a space for that up here, and it's accepted. You can forge a path and make a living from these kind of pursuits if you're willing to work hard when you're onshore and put your mind to it."

Apart from being an artist, James is also a published author and photographer, and creative director of the Byron Bay Surf Festival. His other passion is kids, and seeing them thrive and grow, both his own three boys, and the ones he has mentored through his youth charity *Wings*. James founded *Wings* in 2002 after he hitchhiked across Australia with his surfboard, sans money or food, to raise dollars for a youth centre in

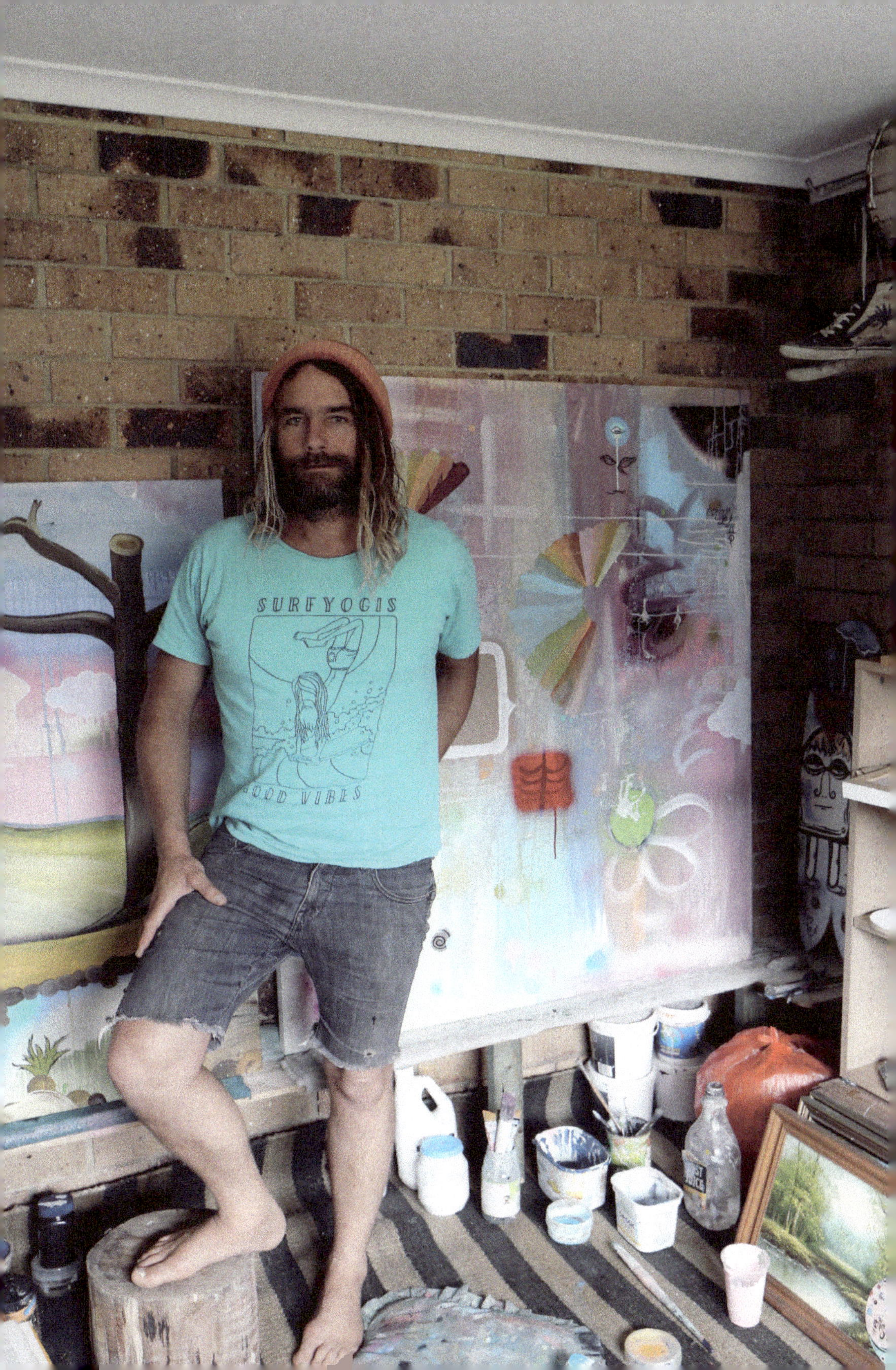
SURFYOGIS

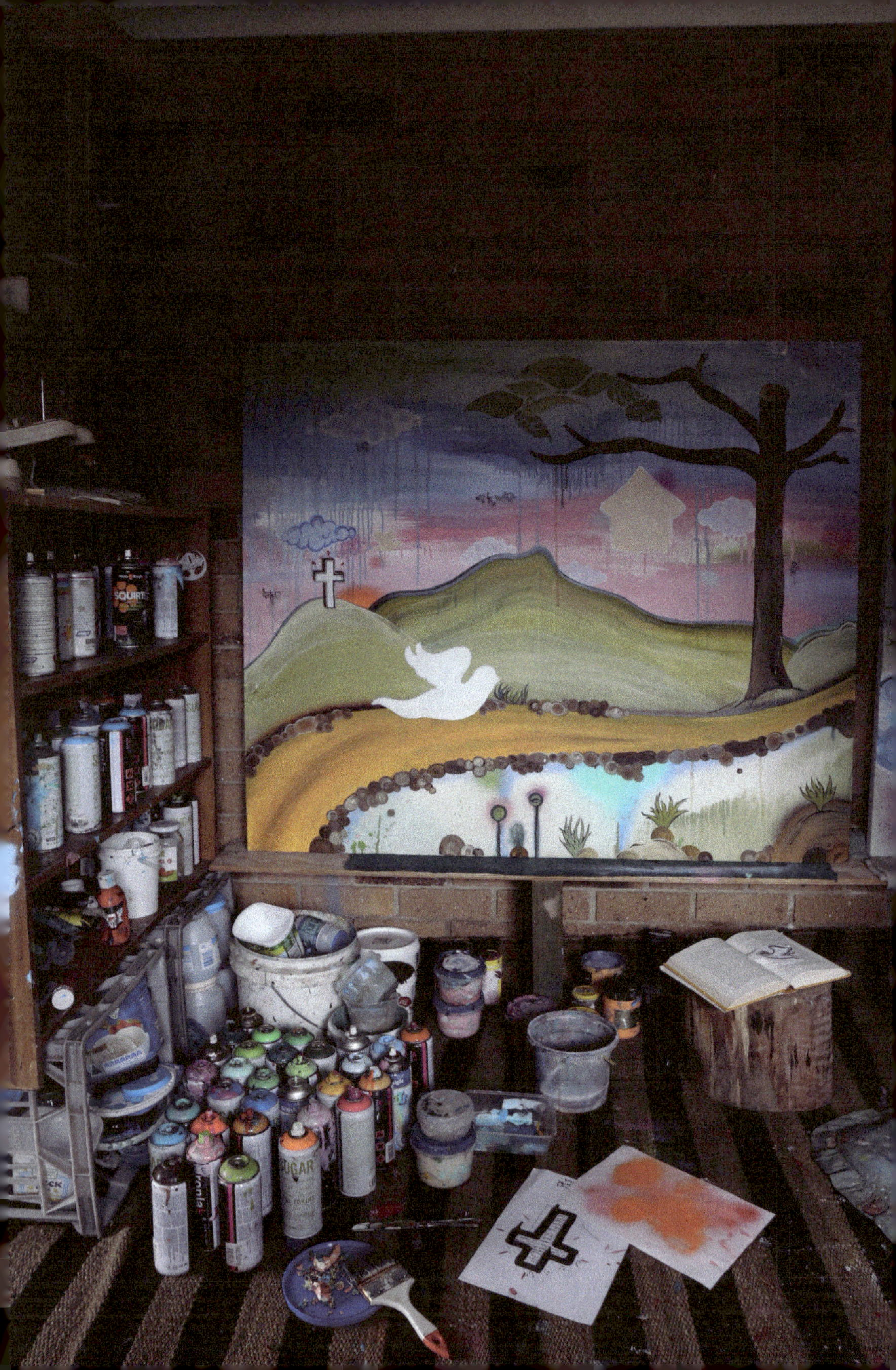

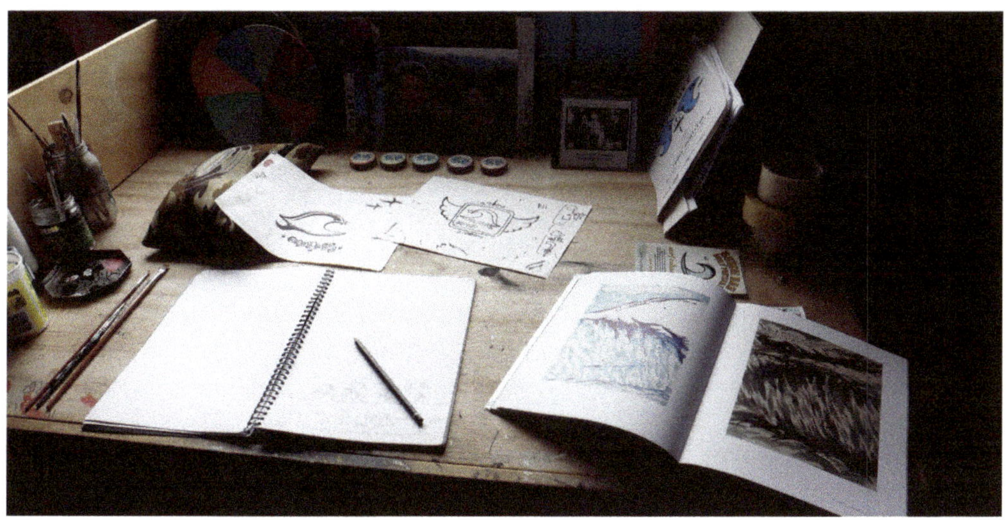

Uluwatu, Bali. "I raised enough money to build them a large skateboard ramp and purchase a few new computers," he says.

"I really believe in the lifestyle that comes through genuinely pursuing surfing and art, and they have both served me well in life in lots of different ways. They have put food on the table for my family and helped me grow as a person. They are also quite spiritual in their essence, especially if you're already bent that way. They make you lean even further. I want to promote those pursuits to kids."

James grew up in the beach-side Sydney suburb of Cronulla. He started making art as a teenager, influenced by his father and sister who both painted. He later landed in this leafy street after a two-year pit stop on Mount Jerusalem beyond Mullumbimby.

Most people who migrate to the Northern Rivers do so for the lifestyle. James came with a higher purpose. He was on a mission to find Australia's foremost expert in surfboard design, George Greenough. "Basically George is the most important man alive in surfing today," James says. "The rest have passed away. He's the go-to guy for anyone looking at surfboard design." James was in search of George's story for his book, *Blue Yonder*; a collection of surf-related articles and photographs published in 2005.

"The book was a huge part of everything," he says. "I was up here doing the book and researching, and I kind of fell in love with the place."

Before that James had been travelling and competing in surf and snowboarding competitions, and writing about the elite athletes around him for magazines. "As my writing evolved I began submitting bigger pieces but the magazines didn't want to print long stories, they wanted short punchy hits, so I quit writing for them and naively started gathering stories and images for a book. Then through a series of profound events I was lucky enough to get published and *Blue Yonder* was a best-seller. That publishing deal meant I could actually afford to buy this house."

Before his move to the 'burbs, James holed himself up on the mountain while he wrote, painted and found his place in this community.

"I got here and I wanted a live-in studio space," he says. "On weekends in Sydney I used to go hang out at Brett Whiteley's studio in Surry Hills. It was just a studio with a bed in the corner and that's what I wanted. When I got here, I went for a drive and found this cottage in the mountains. It was all timber and glass and it was $100 a week. I could see the ocean, and I could paint and create with no one bothering me.

"Some weeks I'd spend three or four days straight up there, then come down to Byron and teach people how to surf, and I'd stay on a friend's couch before returning to the mountain. After two years I felt I was getting a bit too detached from society... thought I probably needed to get back to the people for a little while, and after a short stint in Skinners Shoot I ended up here. It was a good move."

Becoming a home owner allowed space for James' growing family, and for friends to visit. The backyard slopes down to a permanent camp site for such times and a retro caravan-cum-spare-room.

James' studio is in the garage below the house. He's been making art in garages since he was a kid.

"All our living and family stuff happens upstairs and it feels good knowing that I've always got this space to come down to and create," he says. "It's much bigger than what I first started with which was about as big as a small bathroom. And I love that it's a garage because it has a kind of industrial feel and I don't care if I spill paint anywhere or whatever. I'll usually put on some music and close the door for as many hours as I can before someone in the family starts searching for me, which is probably why you'll find me down here around the midnight hours when there's no chance of interruption."

He says it took him a few years to work out his own style through studies of surrealism and the modern contemporary art that he related to in the surf and skateboard cultures.

"It took me a long time to accept that I was an artist. When I did that, it brought freedom." Letting go of all expectations allowed James to forge his signature style of brightly-coloured layered acrylics, ink and spray paint, and the regular appearance of Waterbird.

"Waterbird came about from a need of mine to add life to my paintings," James says. "I didn't want to create a character that was a mirror of the human form. Realistic art kind of bores me. I see it everywhere every day. That's life and I can capture that with photos. My art is about a slightly different reality. A little bit bent. The new stuff I have been working on for my god/surf collection is a little more literal than in the past and it's kind of illustrative in a way too I guess. Some of the works are on canvas, others on resin-coated timber, with a surf-board finish."

Many people have asked James how he achieves such a smooth resin finish. "I tell them it's hard and to go and start playing with it and come back and exchange notes with me in a few months," he laughs. "I'm enjoying working with the resin because it has that connection to surfing. I really believe in the positive lifestyle of surfing and art." ■

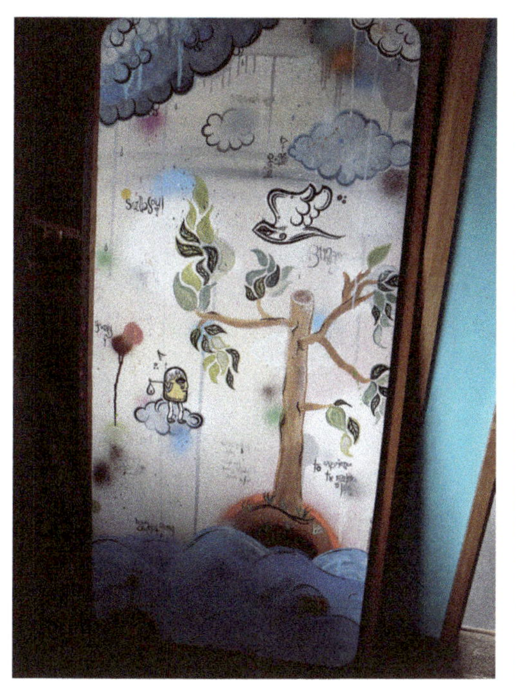
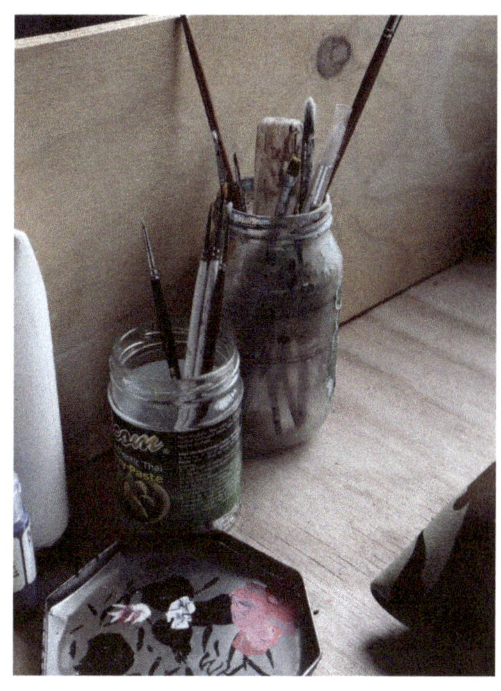

*James' studio is in the garage below the house. He's been making art in garages since he was a kid.*

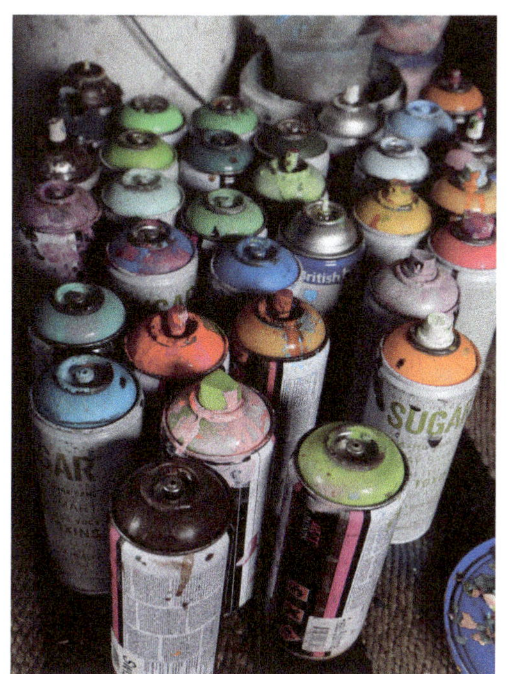
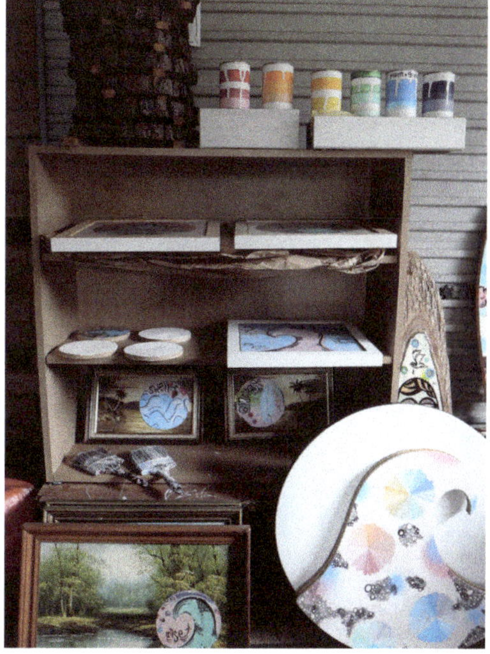

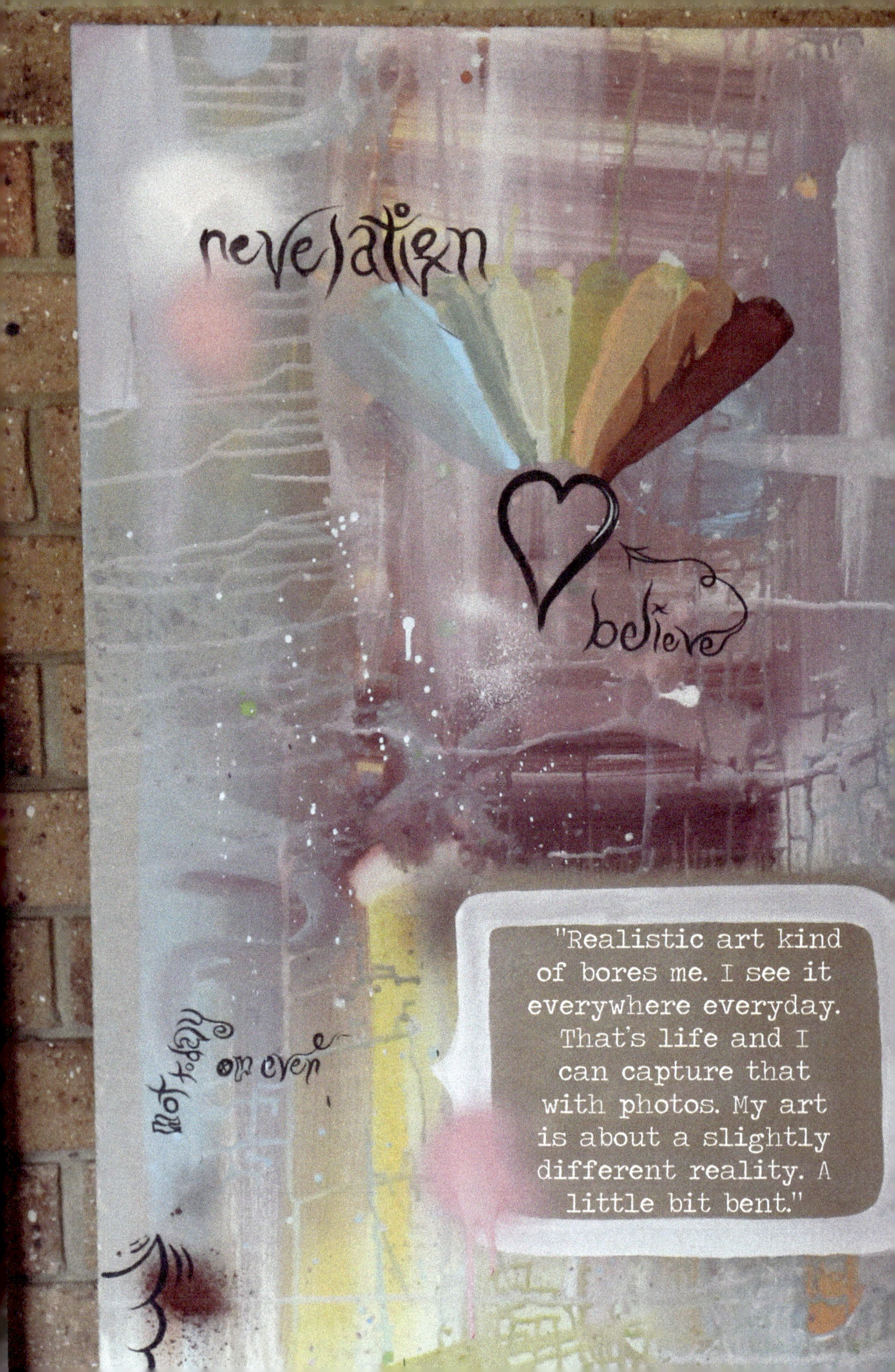

"Realistic art kind of bores me. I see it everywhere everyday. That's life and I can capture that with photos. My art is about a slightly different reality. A little bit bent."

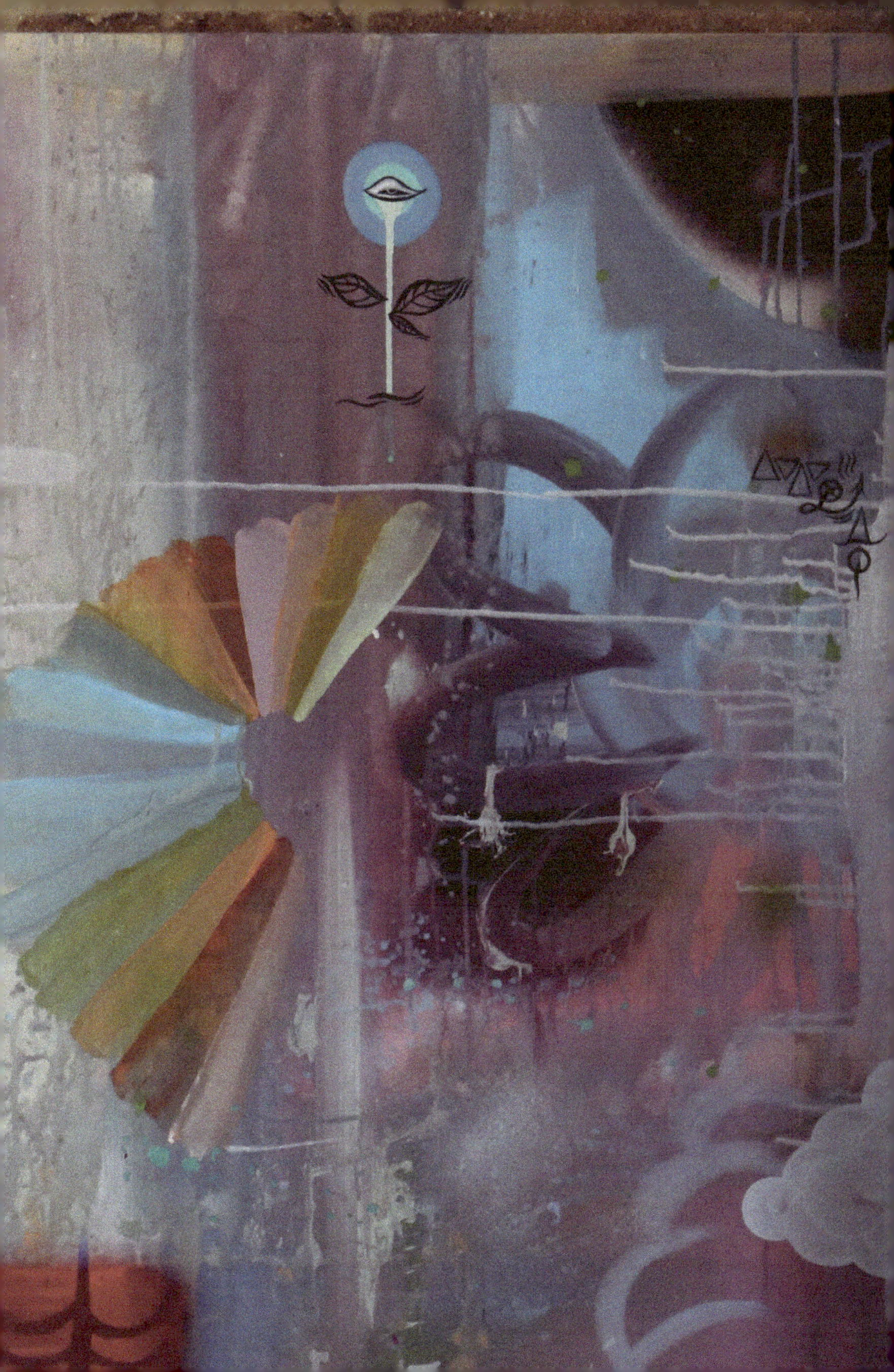

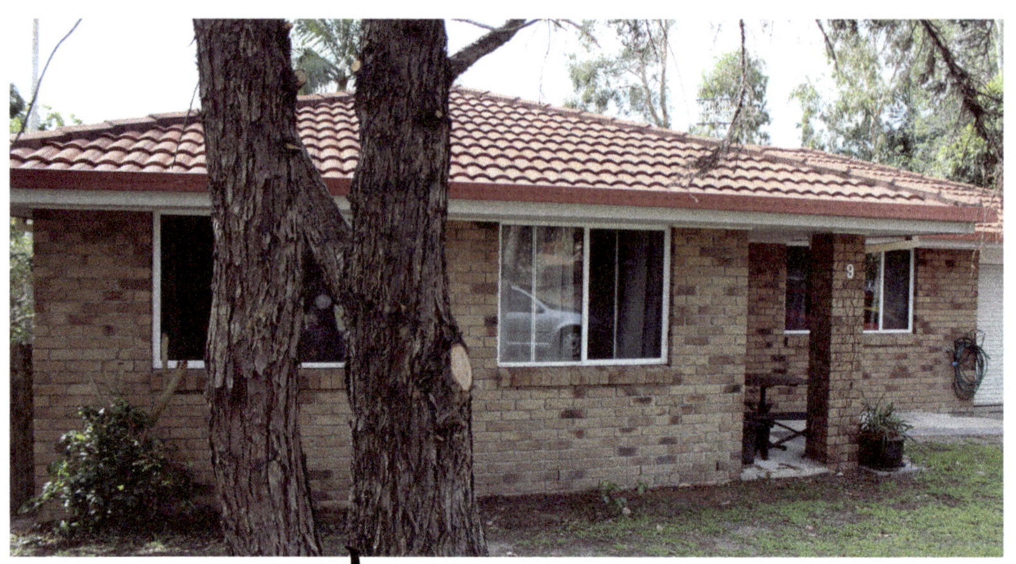

# Timothy Ives

## Carving a life

If anyone knows the lure of the Byron Shire it's Timothy Ives. The Aboriginal elder has lived in his suburban Suffolk Park home for 18 years, although he has been in the region most of his life, and his ancestors date back many thousands of years here. He has a laugh to himself when he hears people talk about 'discovering' the region, and joining its melting pot of residents.

"Byron Bay is also a mecca for Aboriginal people," Timothy says. "They called it Cavanbah, which means 'meeting place'. The seven clans of this region, the Bundjalung Nation, would come here every year for corroborees and the elders would have discussions about things like borders and marriages. It was almost neutral ground. They just adored it."

The shire contains a wealth of Aboriginal cultural sites, including middens, stone arrangements, rock shelters and tool-making sites. And many Aboriginal words are used daily as place names like Mullumbimby and Billinudgel. Timothy says there is also a strong community of his countrymen and women here. "We still get together and we have NAIDOC (National Aborigines and Islanders Day Observance Committee) Week events and exhibitions and language meetings," he says.

The local artist is an important part of these celebrations and in 2016 was named local NAIDOC Elder of the Year. "That was a real honour," he says. "You don't think about it, that you're helping people. You just set an example of no drink or drugs and you just look after yourself."

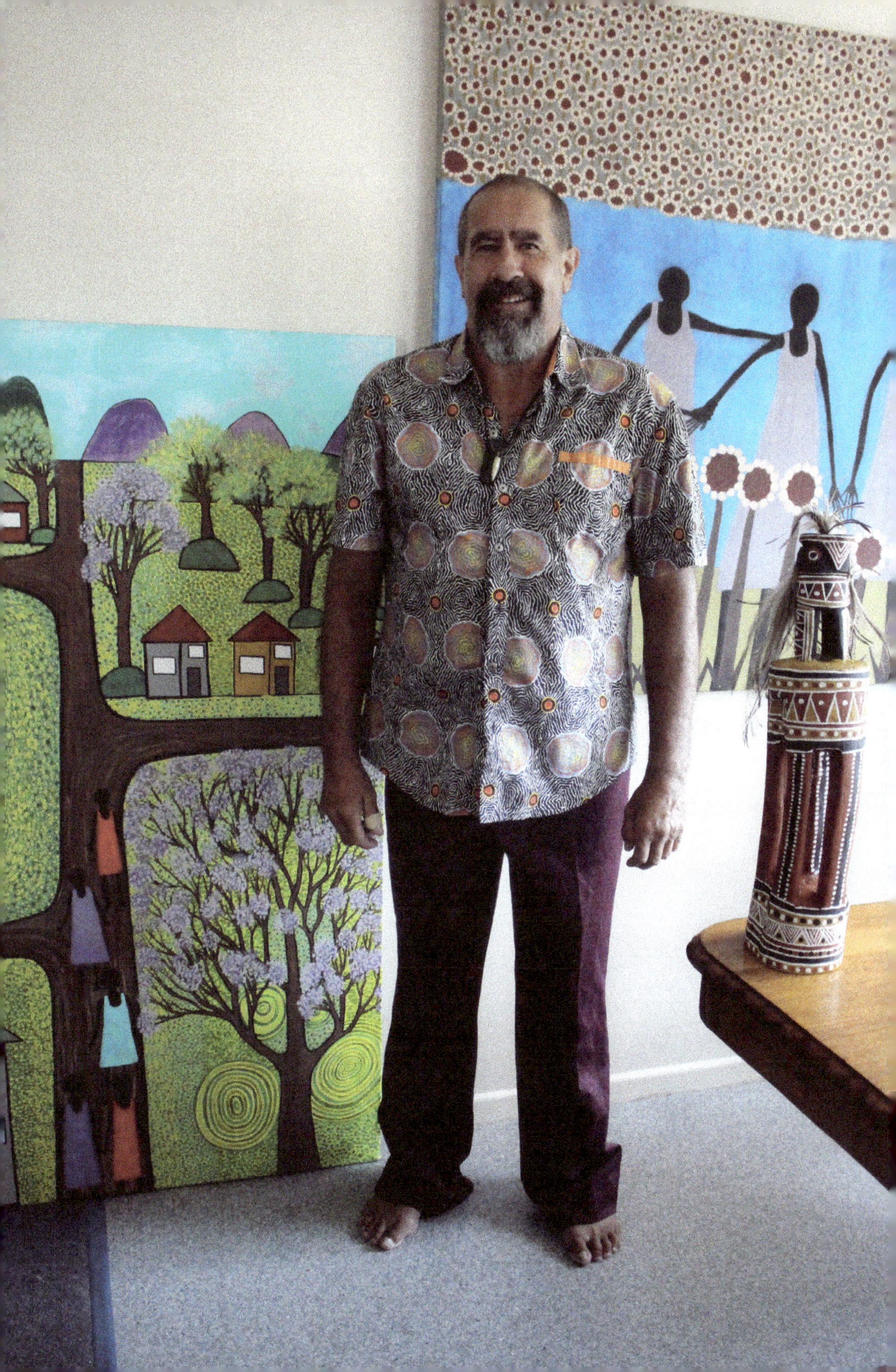

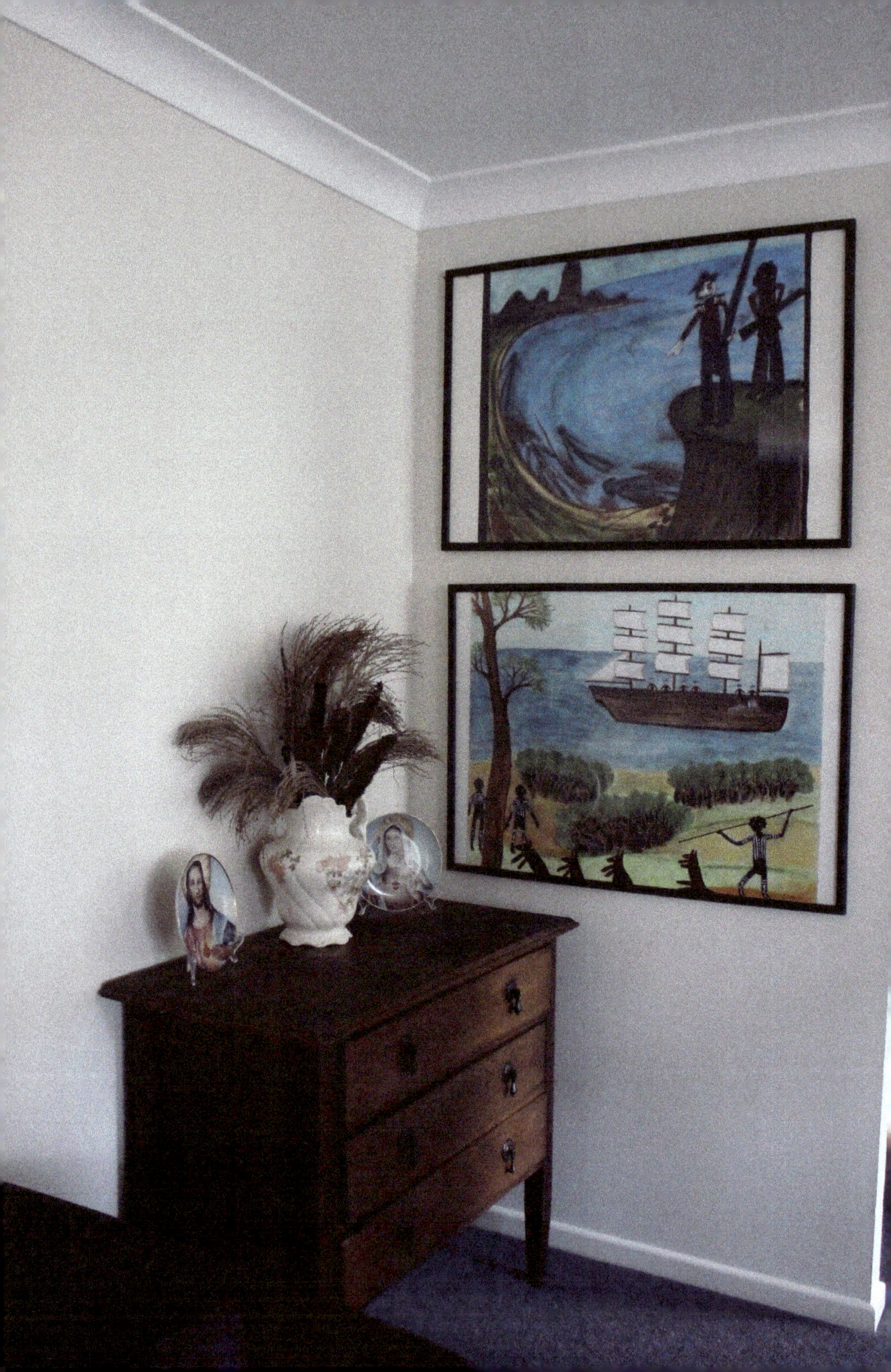

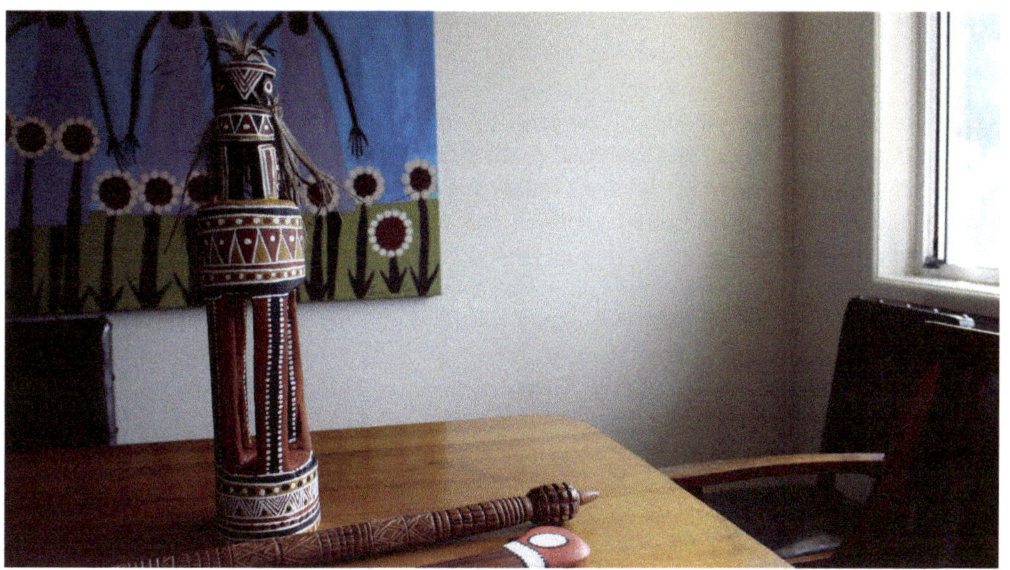

Timothy was also recognised for the work he does with young Indigenous locals, passing on the traditional language, arts and crafts. Telling his stories. "By teaching the young fellas things like how to make a shield and spear, I'm keeping alive the old traditions and handicrafts that were actually needed in those days for survival."

They're skills that have helped Timothy to not only survive, but thrive as an artist. He has earnt a living from his art since 1984, after the Byron Bay meatworks closed. He'd worked there since the aged of 17.

"When the meatworks shut down here the whole town was out of work," he says. "It was only a very small town then, Byron Bay. There were no jobs and if a job did come up, someone else who'd worked at the meatworks would snap it up." Timothy reckons 400 people were left unemployed.

"I was living on a farm at Mullumbimby at the time. I had nothing to do so I'd just go and explore the farm, and pick up bits of driftwood from the creeks." He started noticing the shapes of native animals in the timber, which he'd tempt to life with sandpaper and knife.

"I ended up with a box of little carvings and someone said to me, 'you could sell those'. I took them into an art gallery and the owner jumped at them. That was my first sale." That same day he met a jeweller who gave him some good advice. "He said, whatever you do, don't sell on consignment. If you make something, sell it. Those were wise words and I've never sold on consignment since." The principle helped Timothy make art his livelihood.

Over the ensuing years Timothy built up his tool collection and developed his craft, and has since sold thousands of pocket-sized carvings. "I learnt how to make traditional handicrafts from a friend who lived in Cape York. He taught me how to make spears and boomerangs and apart from that I taught myself." The pursuit for knowledge took him around the world to meet other Indigenous peoples. "I've wood carved with Maori, American Indian,

Hawaiian and Easter Island carvers. Every culture has its own style, like a lot of the Maori's work represents the river monsters and sea monsters."

Timothy's work represents stories. Some from thousands of years past to explain the natural way of the world. "I think about the stories when I'm making things; how the river was made, how the mountain was made, I'm always thinking of that," he says. Other, more recent tales are harder to hear. When Timothy started painting, he found a way to express some of the dark past of the region.

One artwork on his living room wall depicts the 1800s massacre at nearby Broken Head. "Military police rounded up and chased the Indigenous people down to the end of the beach to the headland and slaughtered them. They had been made to dig their own graves, were shot and pushed in. Some people got away and the story was passed on."

Another work shows Indigenous people at a local mission, the windows of their little homogenous houses lit up like candles in cans, to ward away bad spirits. "Everything is a story," Timothy says.

The elder's actions and examples are helping write a new chapter for Indigenous people here. He is helping keep his culture alive and strong, and says a large part of that lies in language. "We're making steps, just in recent times the government has allocated money to help us pass on the language," he says. And just as this area was shared among many clans, now its language is too. One Indigenous group in Victoria adopted the Bundjalung Nation language after losing its own.

Timothy says he's just about ready to retire from making art, but there's a freshly-carved sculpture on the kitchen table that's been made in his garage workshop. Just because. It seems those beautiful, palm-worn carving tools may be in use for some time yet. ■

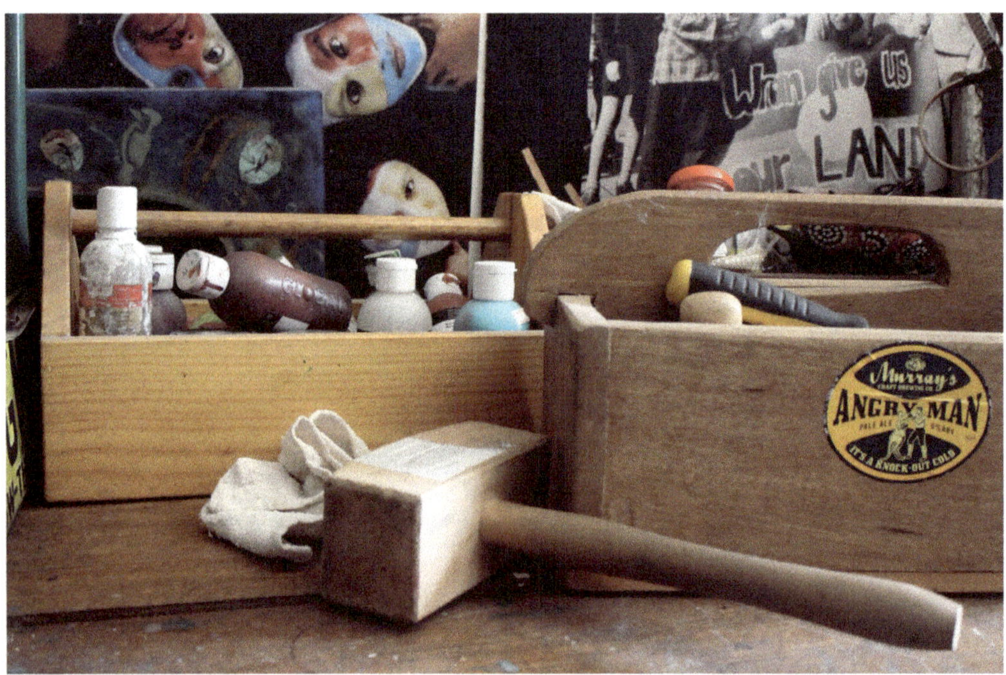

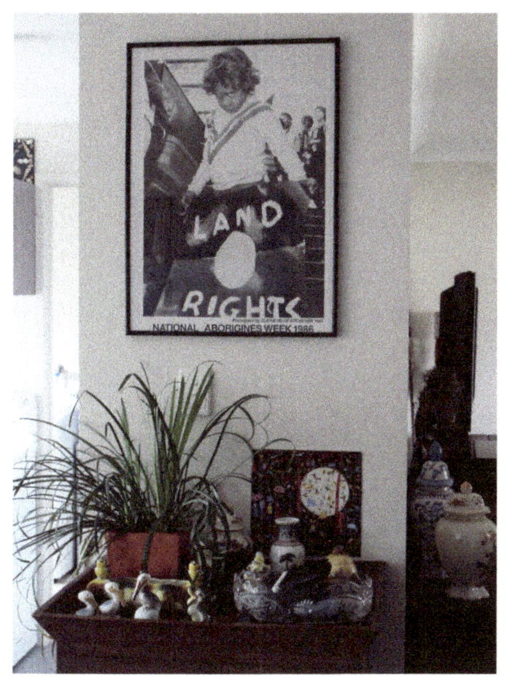


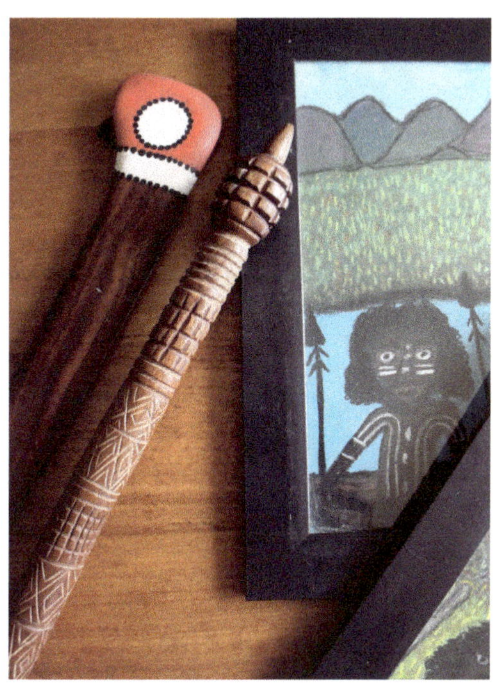

Timothy's just about ready to retire from making art, but there's a freshly carved sculpture on the kitchen table.

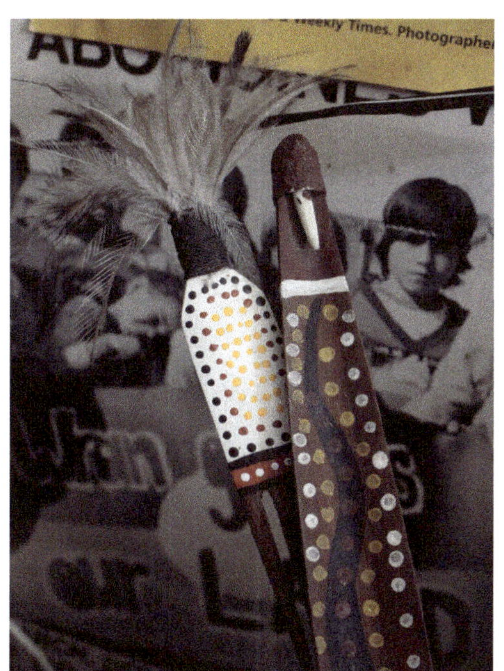


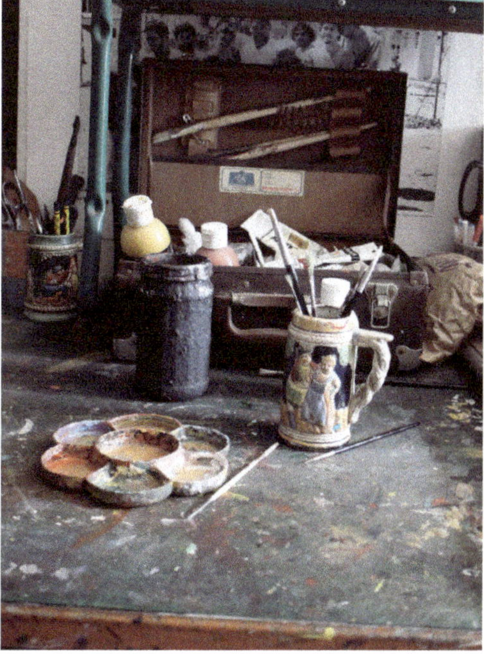

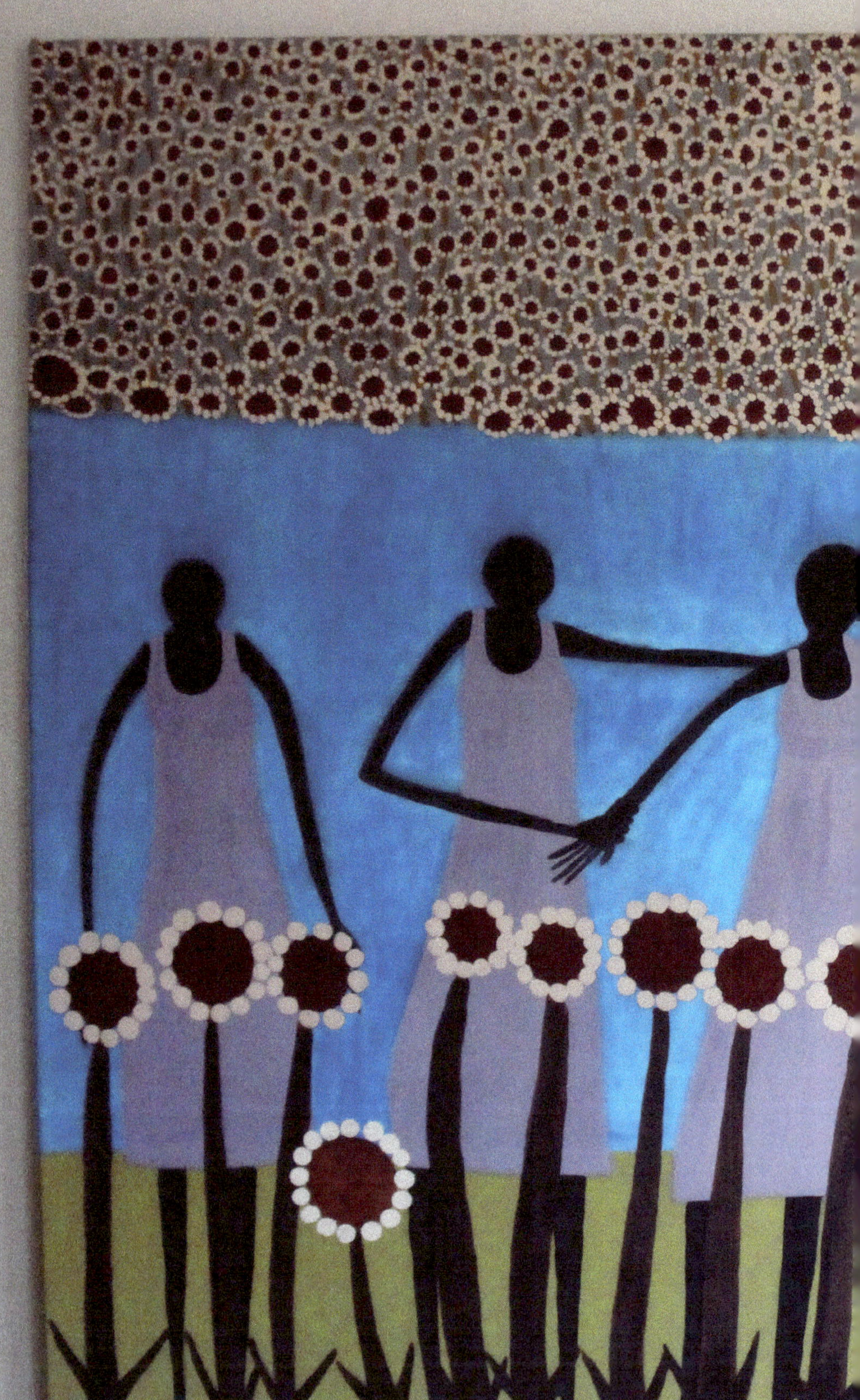

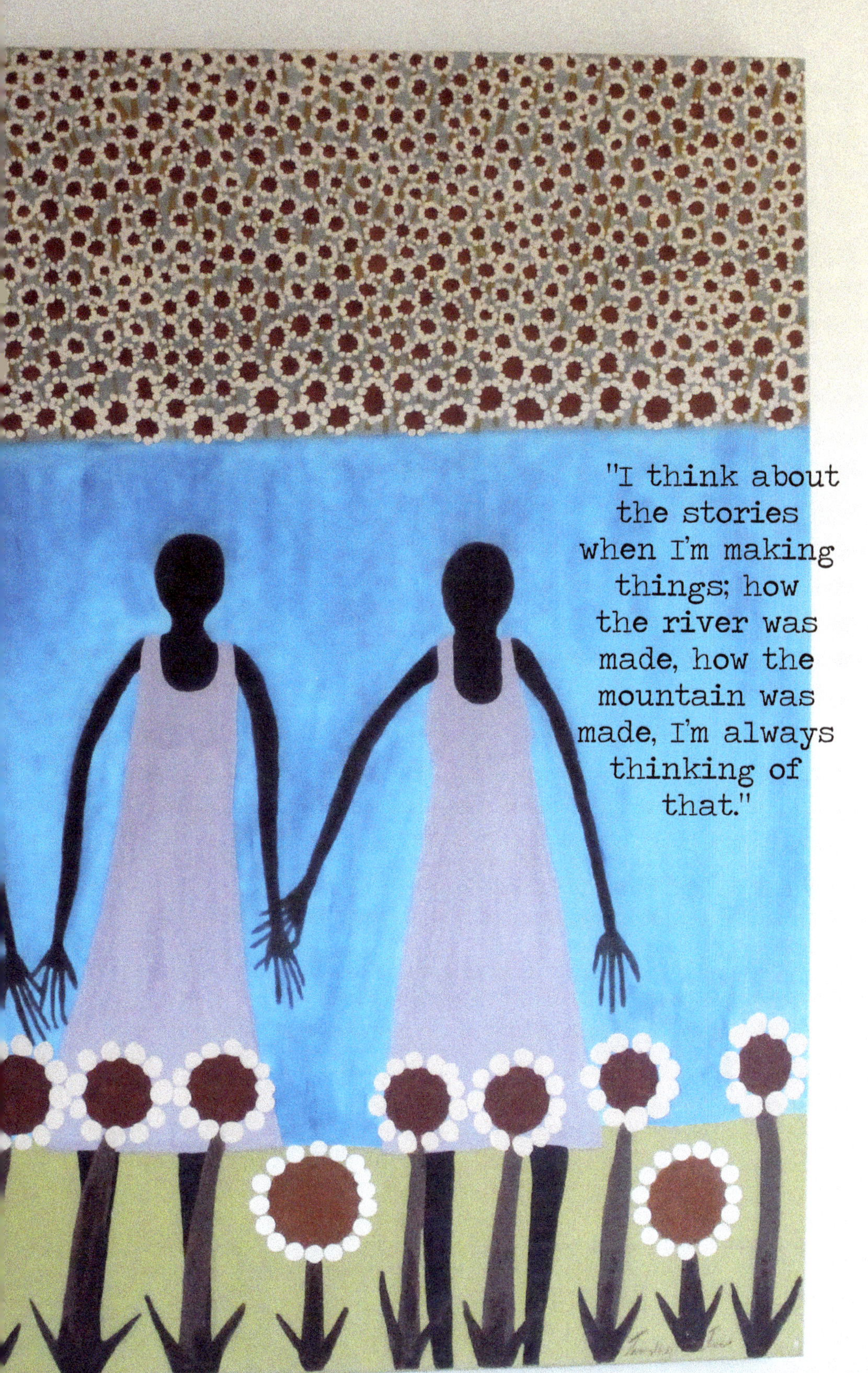

"I think about the stories when I'm making things; how the river was made, how the mountain was made, I'm always thinking of that."

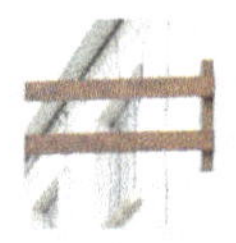

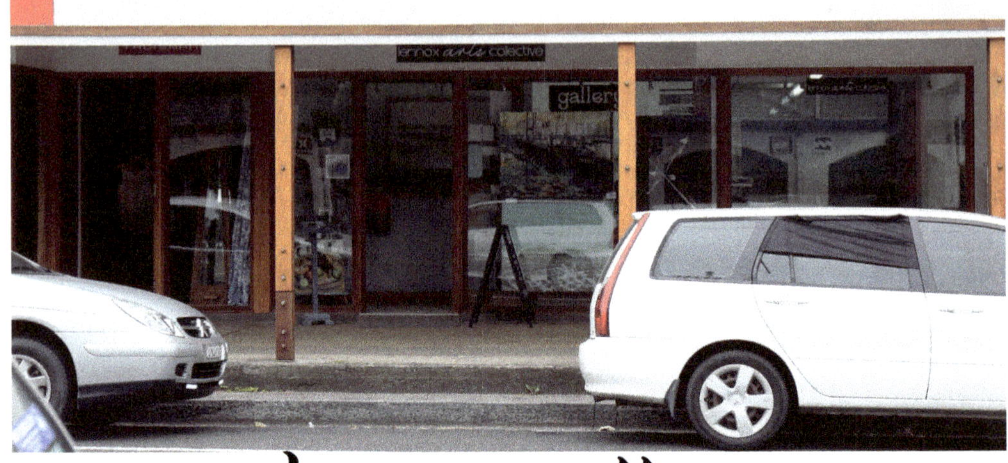


# Mark Waller

## Sunsets and shorelines

Mark Waller is paint-splattered and full of stories. Calm and wild at once. He is the colours and moods of the ocean beyond. "I adore this place. I really do. It's hard to know where I end and it starts," he says.

Mark is standing at the window of his second-floor studio in the Lennox Arts Collective. He's got a view down the opposite street and straight out to the ocean. The sky is dove-grey. On a day like this it's hard to see where it ends and the water begins.

"That view is responsible for quite a few paintings not being finished," Mark laughs. In case of good surf, he keeps a collection of boards at this gallery and studio space he shares with six other Lennox Head artists. They opened this business in the main drag in 2015, but Mark has been a fixture here for all his life.

"I grew up in Lennox Head," he says, adding he's been painting since his mid-teens. "My father jokes, was I staying on the beach to paint, or painting to stay on the beach? Either way's fine with me. The end results are the same."

Mark has been a full-time artist since the age of 25. He paints the ocean, its birdlife, its sunsets, and the iconic pandanus trees that border the beaches. "They've got these wonderfully distorted trunks and bizarre,

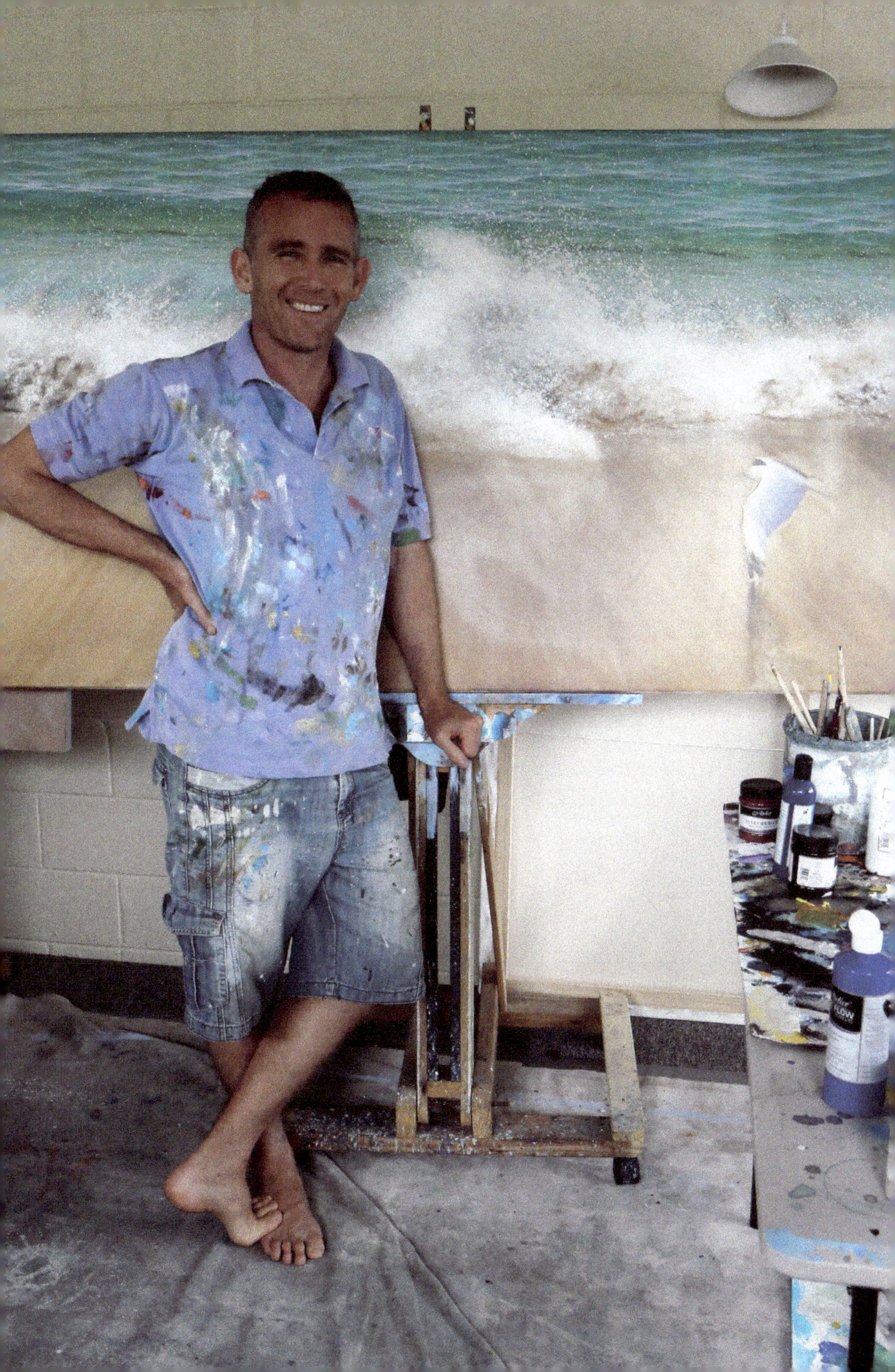

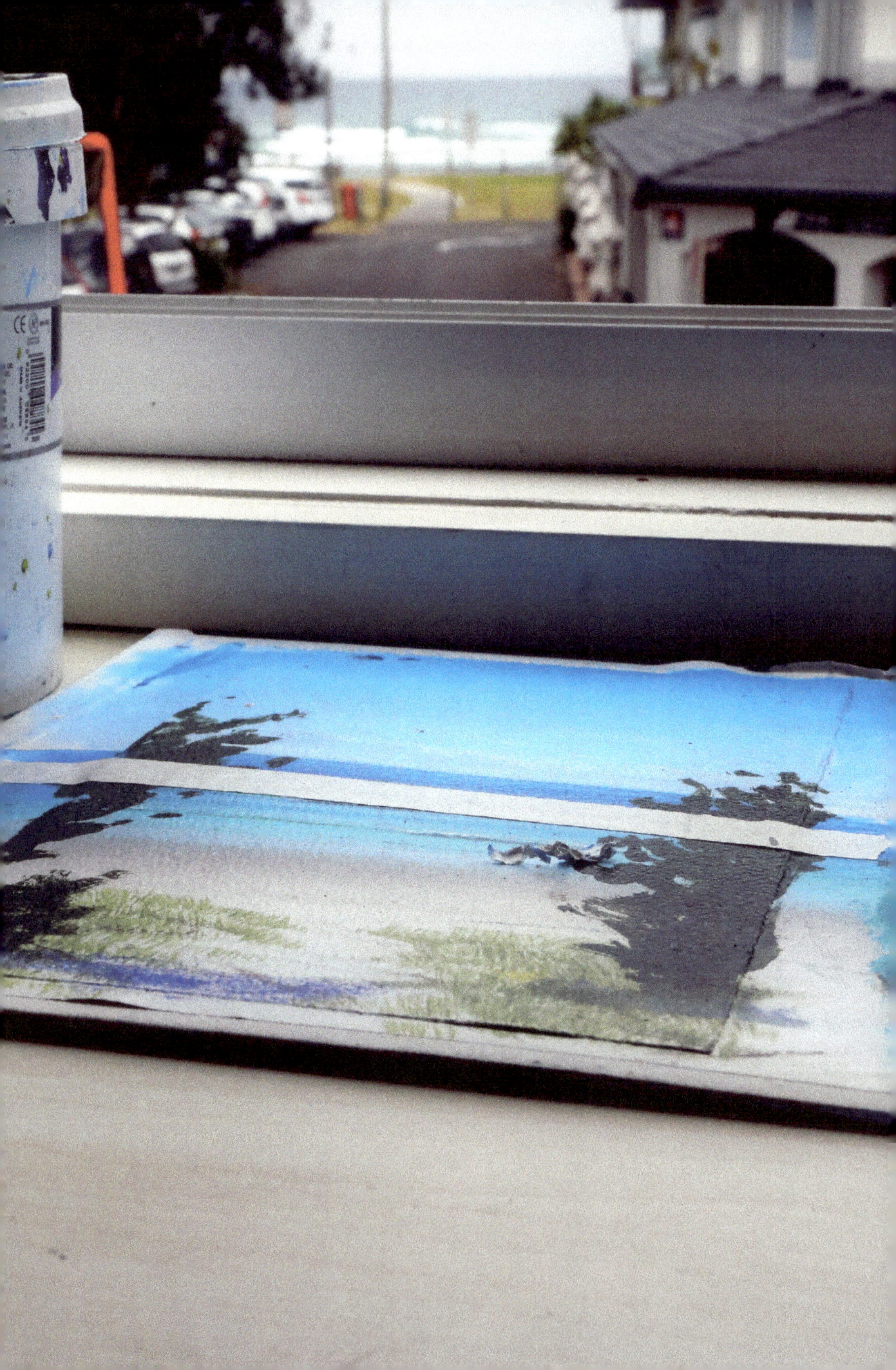

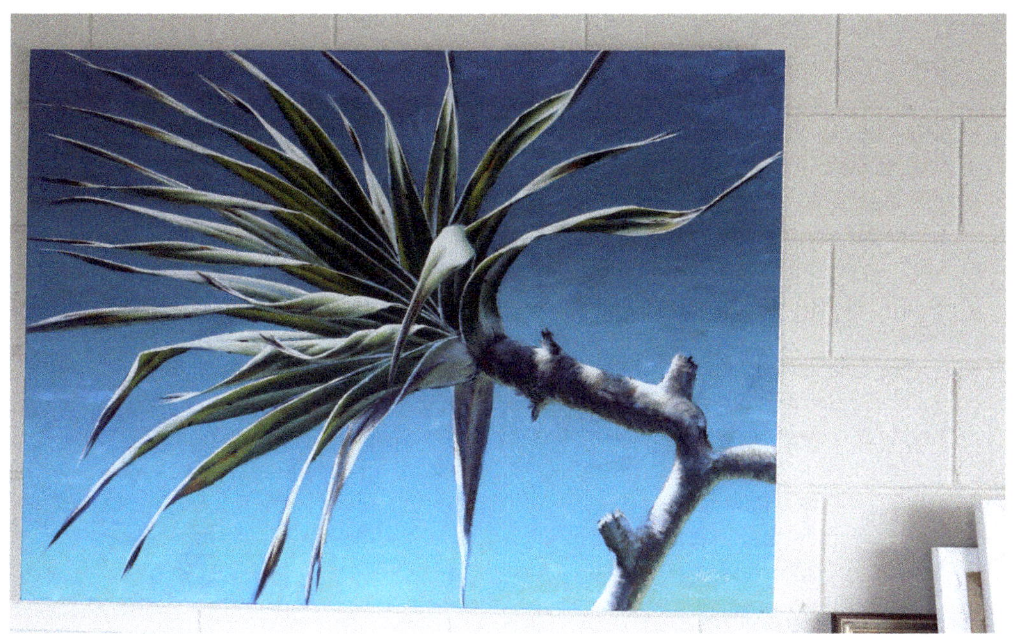

twisted leaves that hang over each other, and behind that, there's the turquoise sea and blue sky peeking through," he says. "As far as depth of field goes, they are every artist's dream.

"Every major experience of my life has happened under a pandanus tree. Getting my heart broken, hanging out in the rain, getting drunk, being hung over... that's why they feature so heavily in my paintings. I've pretty much had all my life experiences under them."

And the experiences keep coming. As he speaks, Mark is still making sense of life's greatest. In early 2016, he was in Western Australia and preparing to host a string of workshops to coincide with an exhibition when he collapsed and found himself in hospital having brain surgery. "I gone and caught me a dose of cancer," he says. "I walked out of hospital four days after the surgery, and six days later I painted. I roughed this in, just to see what was there and what wasn't." He refers to a large canvas of a gentle shoreline and citrus sunset. When that painting emerged, he says he cried like a baby.

"I realised my hands weren't quite right but that was something that would come back. But it's the questions. People always ask, when is a painting finished? I never knew the answer to that before, but now I do. The answer is when the questions are finished." He means the roll of queries that solve a painting's puzzles, such as what time is it in this work? Where is the sun? Where is the wind coming from?

Mark says having cancer, and the near-death experience that came with its discovery, has answered many more questions for him. The sort that others spend their whole lives grappling with. "Someone asked me what happened, where I'd been," he says. "I said I was grabbed by the forearms and dragged through the cosmos until I met the source." He emerged with a profound gratitude for life and an even deeper passion for his art.

"I love it even more," he says. "This has probably been one of the greatest things that has ever happened to me, in a weird kind of way. A lot of people spend a lot of time in the world missing out on magic. We spend most of our life numb to it and unfortunately we miss out on the things that give us joy. As an artist, I already knew this inherently. The thing that's different now is I'm living with purpose and intent."

Mark says one of the biggest lessons has been to just chill out and enjoy life. "In my opinion, there's only two things we really need to do – the first is to play and the second is to be kind to each other. The rest is fluff and mirrors."

He says playing is acknowledging being in the world. It could take the form of dancing, gardening, surfing or painting. "Kids know how to play," he says. "But over time we forget. We take everything way too seriously..."

Mark nods to the busy shopping strip below. "When I was a kid, none of this was here." Lennox Head, south of Byron Bay, has not escaped the slick hand of city-style retail. Mark has known it as a different place, back when he was a "long-haired rat hanging out at the milk bar".

"We'd surf until we couldn't move our arms anymore, then we'd sit and play the pinnies and if we could manage it, then have another surf, or go swimming or spear fishing. Or we'd tow each other up and down the sand on an old car bonnet. My mum said she didn't expect me to live to 30.

"Everything was very raw. It was dumb boys' crap. Then girls turned up and we'd do even more stupid things to try and impress them. I really do feel sad for kids these days that they can't have those experiences.

"I see this place becoming commodified. Because of that, some of its soul is being lost and some of what's beautiful about this area is being missed."

You need only pay attention to Mark's paintings to see what's beautiful. Despite a date with the local oncology ward for treatment each three weeks, he continues to add new work to the gallery walls here. They're a slightly new style of work, too. "There's a subtlety in my hand that's not there anymore. But I'm okay with that. I like it," he says. "Right now, I need help to find my way home, but I can still tell you what colour a pandanus tree is." ■

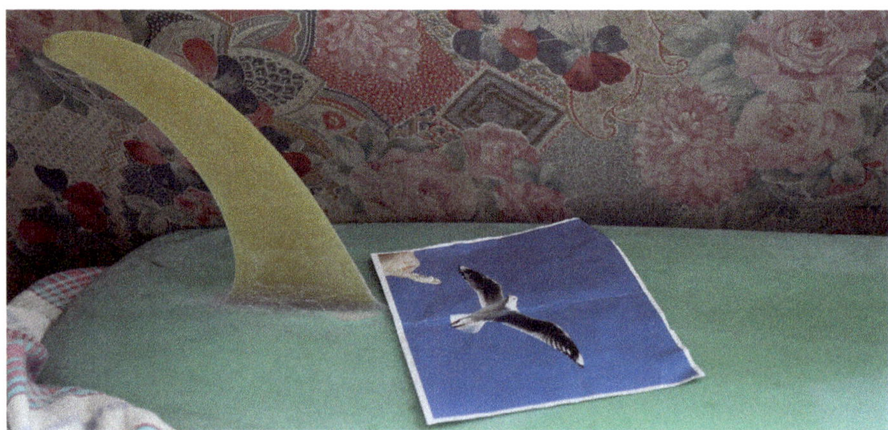

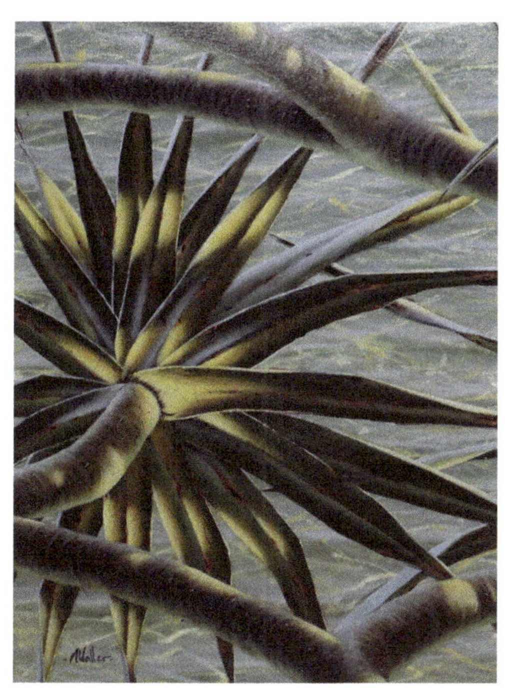

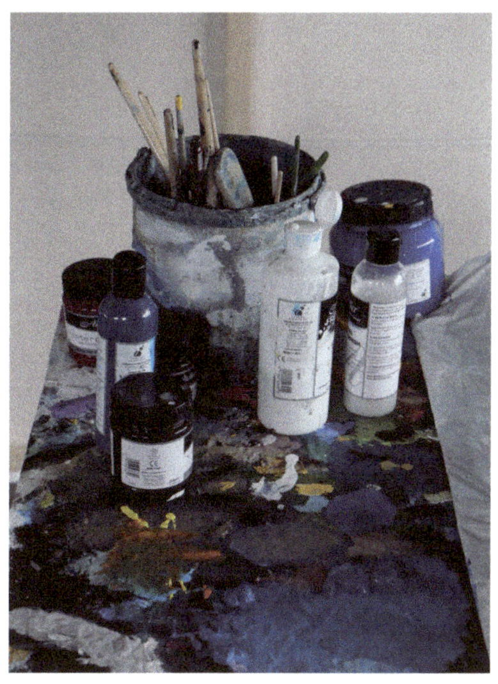

In case of good surf, Mark keeps a collection of boards at this gallery and studio space.

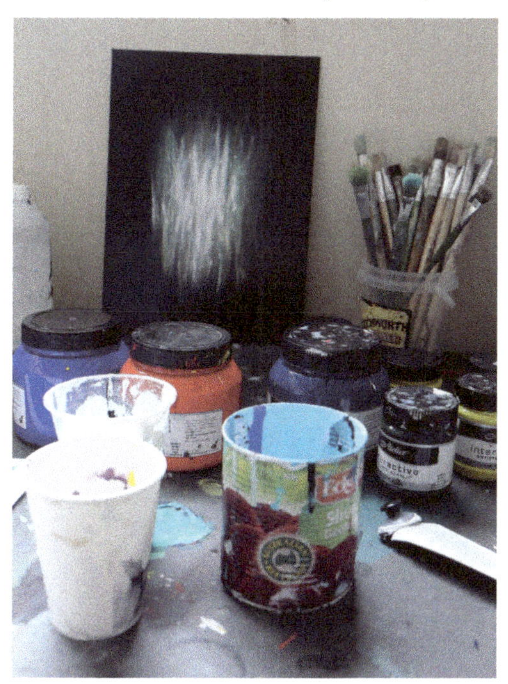

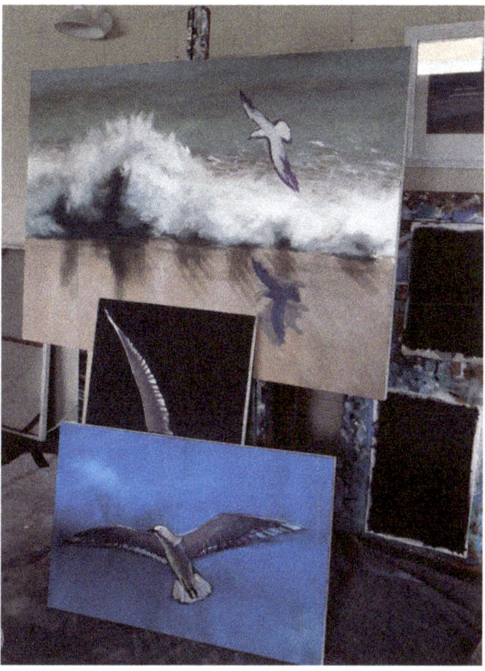

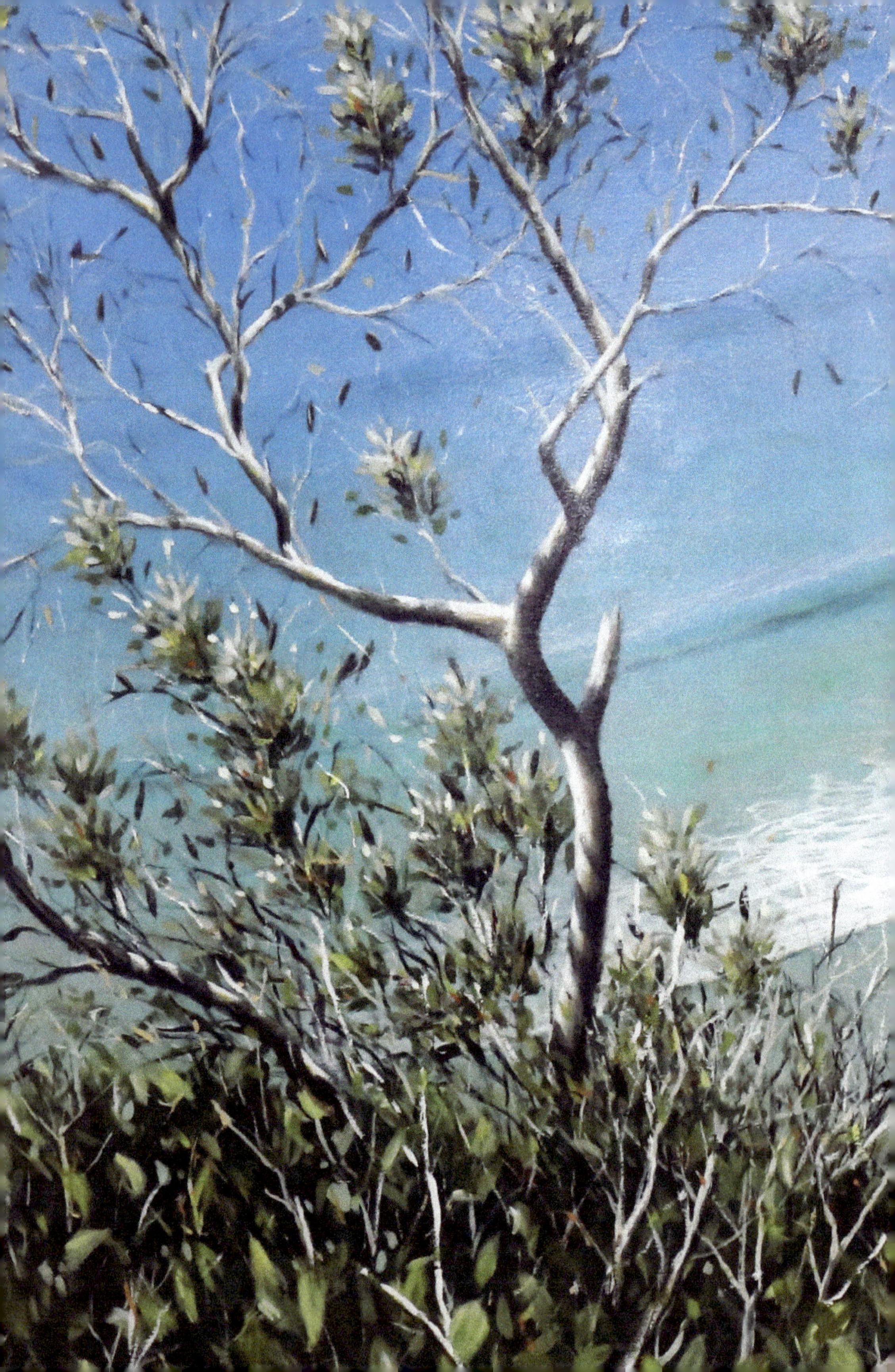

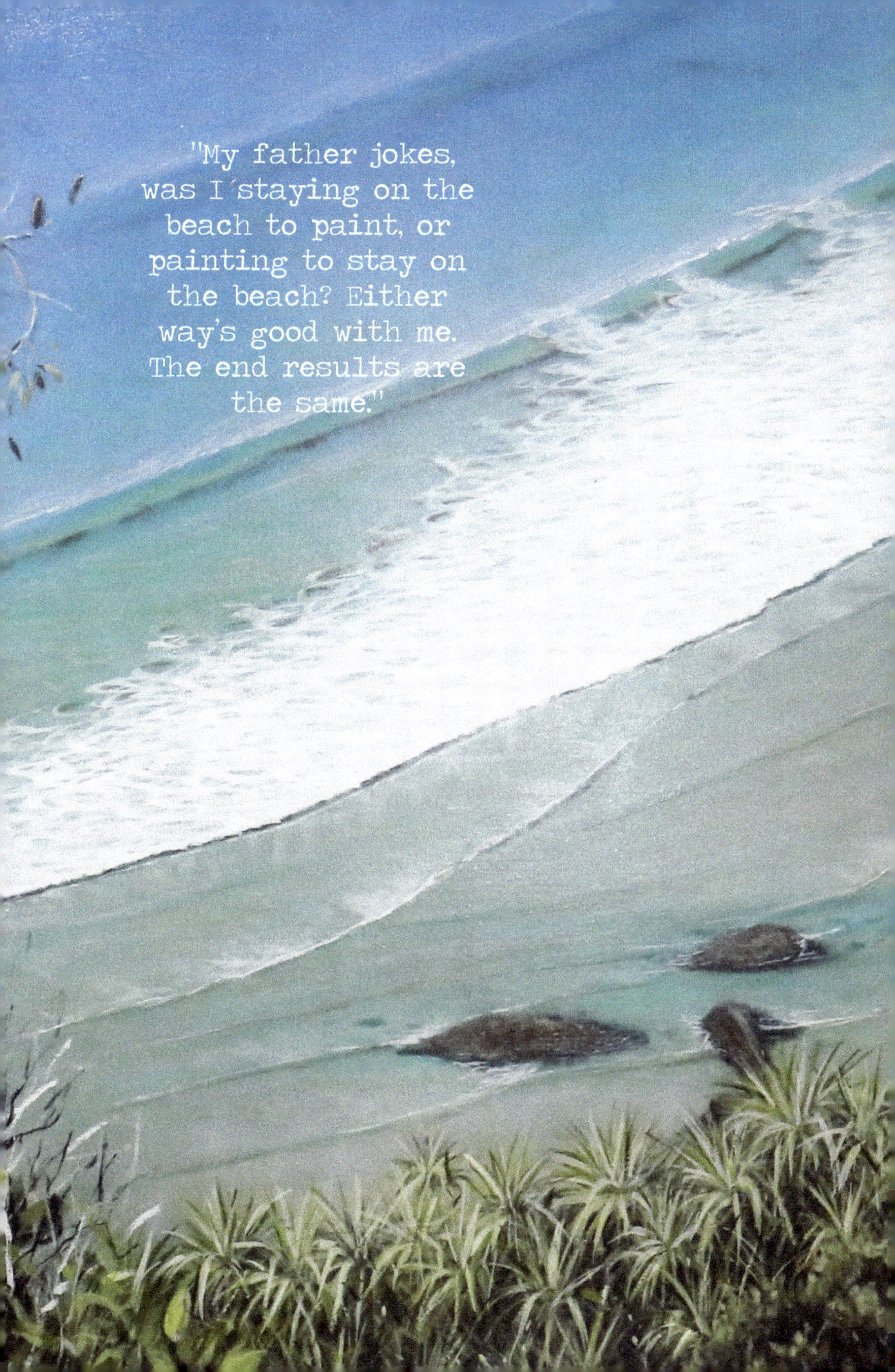
"My father jokes, was I staying on the beach to paint, or painting to stay on the beach? Either way's good with me. The end results are the same."